Sina A. Nitzsche
Poetic Resurrection

The series is edited by Rainer Winter.

Sina A. Nitzsche is the founder of the European Hiphop Studies Network and holds a PhD from the TU Dortmund. Her research interests include hip-hop, popular culture, urban, and media studies. She has also become one of the most renowned commenters on hip-hop culture in German media.

Sina A. Nitzsche

Poetic Resurrection

The Bronx in American Popular Culture

[transcript]

Für meine Eltern Annerose und Stephan Nitzsche.

This book is based on a dissertation submitted to the Faculty of Culture Studies at the TU Dortmund University (TU Dortmund). An earlier version of Chapter 4.1 was published as "Hip-Hop Culture as a Medial Contact Space: Local Encounters and Global Appropriations of *Wild Style*" in the volume *Contact Spaces of American Culture: Globalizing Local Phenomena*, edited by Petra Eckhard, Klaus Rieser, and Silvia Schultermandl.

Bibliographic information published by the Deutsche Nationalbibliothek
The Deutsche Nationalbibliothek lists this publication in the Deutsche National-bibliografie; detailed bibliographic data are available in the Internet at http://dnb.d-nb.de

Cover layout: Maria Arndt, Bielefeld
Cover illustration: *Bronx With a Ruin* by Scott Hyde (1970). Color photo-offset lithograph (10 1/4 x 8 3/8 in.), Smithsonian American Art Museum (1991.112.33). Copyright: Scott Hyde. Reprinted by friendly permission of the Scott Hyde Archive.
Proofread by Terence Kumpf
Printed by Majuskel Medienproduktion GmbH, Wetzlar
Print-ISBN 978-3-8376-5311-3
PDF-ISBN 978-3-8394-5311-7
https://doi.org/10.14361/9783839453117

Table of Contents

Preface

This is a study about how The Bronx overcame one of the biggest socio-economic crises in the late twentieth century through artistic creativity, community resilience, and cultural innovation. While finalizing the manuscript for publication in Spring 2020, my thoughts are with residents in The Bronx, in New York City, and beyond as they deal with the novel coronavirus pandemic. As this book shows how people in The Bronx have overcome crises of the past, I hope that it will inspire them in the present time and in the future.

Sina A. Nitzsche
Dortmund, March 2020

Acknowledgements

SPECIAL THANKS TO:

AMERICAN CONSULATE GENERAL, LEIPZIG

AMERICAN STUDIES AT TU CHEMNITZ

AMERICAN STUDIES AT TU DORTMUND

ANNE VOLKMANN

ANNEROSE NITZSCHE

BRONX COUNTY HISTORICAL SOCIETY

BRONX MUSEUM OF THE ARTS

CITY MUSEUM OF NEW YORK

BRONX DOCUMENTARY CENTER

BRONX COUNCIL OF THE ARTS

DAAD NY

ERIC G. ERBACHER

ERIKO OGIHARA-SCHUCK

EVANGELIA KINDINGER

FORDHAM UNIVERSITY

GEROYCHE

JULIA LEYDA

KENNETH T. JACKSON

MURRAY FORMAN

NEW YORK PUBLIC LIBRARY

PETER DERRICK

RANDI GUNZENHÄUSER

SCOTT HYDE ARCHIVE

SERGIO BESSA

SPACE COLLECTIVE

STEPHAN NITZSCHE

STUDENTS OF MY BRONX SEMINARS

TERENCE KUMPF

WALTER GRÜNZWEIG

TRANSCRIPT

Introduction
Welcome to The Bronx

Shrinking cities have long fascinated popular culture and its audiences. One of the most iconic shrinking urban spaces of the twentieth century is certainly The Bronx borough of New York City. Suffering from deindustrialization, abandonment, and population loss, The Bronx became the synonym for the so-called urban crisis which started after the end of World War II. At the same time, the declining borough inspired may writers, filmmakers, photographers, and artists to create a multitude of stories about its downfall and eventual resurrection. Some of them have grown into mythic narratives and iconic images which continue to shape the perception and imagination of the borough. In my study entitled *Poetic Resurrection: The Bronx in American Popular Culture* I examine how popular culture represented The Bronx in the late 1970s and early 1980s. I show how those representations function as complex and contested fields of meaning where larger issues in American culture, such as race, class, gender, and ideology are negotiated.

Specifically, I argue in this book that the shrinking of The Bronx – contrary to the conventional wisdom – was a productive phase in terms of cultural production and in re-thinking American (urban) identities and narratives. I propose here that while the urban space of The Bronx suffered from the consequences of shrinkage in the 1970s, popular culture created a powerful artistic counter discourse which promotes the borough's imaginary and spiritual rebirth. While The Bronx was disconnected from major American spatial and cultural narratives in the era of decline, popular culture reconnected The Bronx to such longstanding narratives as rags-to-riches, frontier, and the American Dream. I claim that these texts and narratives have functioned as a poetic resurrection, an artistic and imaginative rebirth of the borough, which preceded, promoted, and facilitated the spatial resurrection of The Bronx in the late twentieth century. The literary, and audio-/visual narratives therefore do important cultural work because they lay the groundwork for the spatial and spiritual rebirth of The Bronx in the 1990s and 2000s thus reinforcing the mantra of neoliberal capitalism.

My interest in the declining Bronx in popular culture is certainly of autobiographical nature. I grew up in Eastern Germany after the fall of the Berlin Wall in the midst of deindustrialization, population shrinkage, and an enormous wave of outmigration. The events of 1989 and the subsequent reunification resulted in large-scale factory closings because the former East German production plants could not compete of Western markets. As a consequence, the unemployment rate sharply increased, leaving some of my working-class family members jobless for years while others decided to emigrate to Western Germany in the search for better lives through steady, gainful employment. Although the abandoned industrial buildings in which my family and relatives used to work are sad symbols of this economic 'development,' they always fascinated my friends and me. We sneaked in and photographed what was left of the GDR textile production facilities. The bitter experience of post-reunification decline on the one hand and its liberating qualities on the other constitutes an important part of my adolescence.

Because of my experience of growing up in a shrinking region, my wish to explore The Bronx seemed only logical. When I decided to stay in the Kingsbridge Avenue area during my internship in New York City, I discovered a discrepancy between media representations and my own experiences. My white German friends imagined the borough to be a grim urban territory marked by decay and disaster based on what they had seen and read in the news, watched in movies, or heard in rap lyrics. When I arrived, I encountered a multifaceted and diverse place that resembled little of the dystopic film and news media imaginations. To me, then an (East) German graduate of American studies, The Bronx presented itself as a place with a rich cultural heritage and a vibrant street culture: for example, Spanish-speaking teenagers exchanged the latest neighborhood gossip on the sidewalk. My Irish American roommate introduced me to the history of my temporary lodging. The building's history started with the arrival of her Irish immigrant grandparents in the 1920s and has remained a family residence ever since. The Bronx was not only far from being a one-dimensional danger zone, but a place with a multitude of stories, memories, and contested meanings.

This discrepancy between The Bronx in news media and popular culture as well as my personal upbringing in shrinking post-unification Eastern Germany triggered a set of questions regarding the function of decline in cultural representations: How is this decline of the Bronx represented in popular culture? Which stories do cultural texts present and from which viewpoints? How do those representations reimagine long-standing cultural narratives? These questions of media representations, the public imagination, and my personal experience were the main sources of motivation for this research project.

My study scrutinizes different types of popular literary, audio-/visual, and musical texts. Literature is one of the oldest and most widely spread forms of expression in American culture. Hip-hop culture, a transnational Bronx-born youth musical and cultural movement, is the leading source of identity formation for young people, especially in the late twentieth century. Film is perhaps the most widespread audiovisual form throughout the twentieth century while photography is a very flexible medium which can be easily repurposed in different media forms. Other visual media such as flyers, posters, maps, and book covers are also discussed to show the cultural productivity in the era of decline in The Bronx. Cultural representations and pop cultural practices permanently write and re-write onto the urban space, thus, producing their own versions of the borough.

In this book, I understand The Bronx not only as a physical area, but as an imagined urban space which is expressed through various representations. Those spatial imaginations are connected to other formal features of media: Which genres dominate in which forms of expression and how do they influence spatial discourses and the American Dream narrative? Which narrative perspectives, types of characters, and modes of expression do we encounter across the texts and how do they comment on the idea of social upward mobility and the economic framework of (global) capitalism which is often blamed for the post-war downfall of American cities?

The objective of this study is to examine the representation of The Bronx in the late 1970s and early 1980s. As this time constitutes a period of larger shifts in American politics, economy, society, and culture, I investigate how those four areas are negotiated. The borough suffered from immense population and infrastructural decline as consequence of the larger post-World War II urban economic transformation processes, such as deindustrialization and (white) suburban flight. The news media reacted to this crisis by discounting The Bronx' rich cultural heritage and blamed the non-white urban poor for the downfall of the borough. The news organizations channeled the fear of the so-called inner city by reducing the entire borough to the imagined space of the South Bronx. This public perception has become a myth and iconic image which is subverted in popular culture. Therefore I will show that in the late

1970 and early 1980s a much more diverse and complex image of The Bronx existed in popular media forms which prove the one-dimensional representation of the borough in the public perception to be wrong.

This study aims to be the first book-length analysis on cultural representations of the shrinking Bronx. So far, research on the borough has mostly been conducted from an urban history perspective. Using population statistics, questionnaires, and other empirically-derived documents, historical research lacks an approach of texts as representations, that is, as constructions – not mirrors – of 'reality.' This kind of research tends to overlook the many books, films, songs, or photographs that artists have produced about The Bronx which equally contribute to the various issues at work at a given time. Writing from a cultural studies point of view, I assume that 'reality' and urban spaces are not something naturally given, but permanently produced and reproduced in those texts. Its meaning is culturally constructed and changes over time. It is necessary to investigate these popular cultural representations and practices in order to examine the different meanings of the shrinking Bronx. What I am doing might thus be called Bronx Studies, bringing together urban and regional studies from cultural, media, and communication studies angles which examine the different spatial and mediated discourses of The Bronx and how they affirm, comment on, or distort its public perception.

In examining the narrative, visual, and medial dimensions of urban shrinkage processes, my book contributes to the larger academic discourse on cultural imaginaries of shrinking cities. Researchers from the fields of urban studies, geography, urban history, and spatial planning have often analyzed shrinking American urban contexts, such as The Bronx, Detroit, Flint, and Newark. They understand shrinking processes primarily in terms of spatial, demographic, infrastructural, historic, and public policy change. Scholars from those fields investigate how and why cities are shrinking around the globe, which repercussions those shrinking processes entail for the local populations, economies, and infrastructures, and which policies can be undertaken to re-size them in a sustainable way.

This book is not so much about settlement patterns, infrastructural projects, and public policy-making in the era of decline. It rather shifts the focus to a wide range of cultural texts which were produced in a specific shrinking context. It interrogates how they reflect on the cultural, social, racial, ethnic, gender, and economic dimensions, which are the causes and consequences of deindustrialization. While my case study explores one particular urban territory, the spatial imaginaries analyzed here might help to build a larger framework of understanding of the cultural dimensions of contemporary shrinking processes in the United States and beyond.

My project raises an awareness of the complex connections between space, media, and popular culture. Spaces and places, as I will explain, cannot be viewed apart from the media constructing them. Media are produced and used by different social groups to present certain spaces and places and to attach a certain meaning to them at a given time. Media and pop cultural forms (including literature) provide a conceptual framework in which stories about spaces are told and make these stories accessible to different kinds of audiences. Finally, media can challenge the linear conceptualization of time by allowing a return to places of the past in the present time or by diachronically constructing spaces at various times. Space and media, as I will demonstrate, mutually influence each other. Accordingly, I understand the two concepts not as static categories, but as flexible phenomena which are culturally constructed and change over time. As such, they ultimately enable zones of cultural contact and contestation.

Assuming that "'culture' *is spatial*" (D. Mitchell, *Cultural Geography* 63, emphasis in original), my book is located at the intersection between American studies, cultural studies, media studies, and urban studies. It seeks to contribute to the spatial turn, a postmodern (Bachmann-Medick 284) and multidisciplinary (Döring and Thielmann 10) tendency concerned with space as a central object of theoretical and empirical investigation. It points to the influence of cultural representations, media, and popular forms in which spatial representations take place. It also connects representations of hip-hop culture which received a fairly large academic interest especially in hip-hop studies with other literary and cinematic representations which were also produced in the era of decline in The Bronx.

Literature, the focus of my second chapter, recalls neighborhoods that were destroyed during the era of decline from a first-person perspective. In analyzing *Bronx Primitive: Portraits in a Childhood* (Kate Simon, 1982), *The Old Neighborhood* (Avery Corman, 1980), and *Growing Up Bronx* (Gerald Rosen, 1984), this section will discuss the question of how autobiography is used as the dominant genre and mode of articulation in literature. I will ask how autobiography functions to re-create The Bronx of the past and what this literary recreation means for the re-imagination of the rags-to-riches narrative.

In my third chapter I will show how film critiques the news media notion of urban devastation by the use of horror, gangster, or crime genres, such as *Fort Apache: The Bronx* (dir. Daniel Petrie, 1981), *Gloria* (dir. John Cassavetes, 1980), and *Wolfen* (dir. Michael Wadleigh, 1981). I will discuss how the protagonists deal with the causes and consequences of decline and how these films subvert the public perception of the borough by revising the frontier narrative.

Chapter 4 will examine how hip-hop culture emerged as a creative response to the devastation and decline of the South Bronx. Hip-hop is a special genre because it is not only an Afro-diasporic musical form, but a lived practice and multimedia youth culture. This chapter therefore analyzes the song and music video "The Message" (1982) and the film *Wild Style* (dir. Charlie Ahearn, 1982). It also illustrates how the photo book *Born in The Bronx: A Visual Record of the Early Days of Hip-Hop* (2007) showcases a similar pattern in personalizing the urban experience compared to film and literature. What do the hip-hop texts tell us about the meaning of the American Dream for a new generation of artists and activists? I will discuss not only the sense of artistic community that hip-hop creates in those representations, but also how this cultural practice transcends the boundaries of music by including film, photography, and, eventually, literature in its aesthetic portfolio.

The concluding chapter will discuss how the poetic resurrection of The Bronx in the era of decline continued to evolve and change in the late twentieth and early twenty-first centuries across different media forms. Broadening the scope of my study, I will show how some of the mechanisms, discourses, debates of The Bronx of the 1970s and 1980s are reimagined and appropriated in contemporary shrinking city discourses in the United States. The final section therefore attempts to open up an arena in which the findings of my study might serve as a model to scrutinize the complexity and contestation of decline representations and its repercussions on spatial and cultural narratives in contemporary shrinking cities in the United States and on a global scale.

My next chapter will begin by investigating how The Bronx can be theorized as a heterotopia (Foucault), in how far decline and shrinkage are unique angles in urban studies and cultural studies, how the concept of representation ties in with urban decline and shrinkage, and how Henry Jenkins's idea of convergence culture can be used as a methodological framework to study them. But why are there so few scholarly publications on representations of The Bronx to begin with?

Chapter 1
Approaching the Boogie Down:
The Bronx, Popular Culture, and the Poetic
Resurrection

Compared to the abundance of academic literature on New York City, there are relatively few scholarly treatments of The Bronx. Searching for publications on The Bronx in library catalogues, digital databases, and online book stores, one will discover historic accounts (most notably by Lloyd Ultan) and many personal autobiographical narratives (Alda; Brady Hill and Butler Munch; Estrada; Hand; Jones; Manon; Mariani and Mariani; Naison, *White Boy*; Naison and Gumbs; Newell; Vásquez and Vaquedano; Vásquez and Vaquedano-Rose). In terms of academic studies, however, The Bronx has received surprisingly little attention in recent years. Why are there so few scholarly publications on The Bronx? What is the significance of the existing historical publications? How do they deal with The Bronx and what do they possibly overlook?

Before embarking on close analyses of representations of The Bronx in detail, this chapter will first provide a larger theoretical and methodological framework. It starts by taking a closer look at historical publications and examines their contribution to the understanding of The Bronx as an urban space (Ch. 1.1). Proposing that The Bronx has been a largely neglected subject matter in longer academic publications from a particular cultural studies point-of-view, this chapter builds on and expands existing historical research by theorizing The Bronx as a space of cultural difference, or Otherness, with the help of the concept of heterotopia formulated by French philosopher Michel Foucault. This notion of The Bronx as a space of cultural difference is necessary to understand not only the academic lack of interest but also the dynamics of the pop cultural representations in the 1970s and 1980s. Drawing on convergence culture as a lens to study the flow of media representations and signifying practices, Chapter 1.2 will explain how these shape people's perceptions of spaces and places. Henry Jenkins's notion of convergence culture helps readers to understand the interrelationships in the representation of The Bronx across a variety of (pop)cultural, media representations, and signifying practices.

The final parts of this chapter detail the specific urban, media, and cultural context of The Bronx in which this study is situated (Ch. 1.3). They propose a place-based approach to study Bronx representations and explain why the era of decline is the perfect time period to investigate how they open up unique spaces to subvert the dominant journalistic discourse and re-imagine spatial and cultural narratives (Ch. 1.4).

1.1 Mind the Gap: Historicizing The Bronx

Baseball. Highway. Hip-hop. Many outsiders reduce The Bronx to Yankee Stadium, home of the New York Yankees since the 1920s. Others associate the borough with the infamously gigantic Cross Bronx Expressway which was constructed in the 1950s as an urban renewal project (Bromley 217-20), which still cuts horizontally through the borough today. Music lovers think of 1520 Sedgewick Avenue, the mythical birthplace of global hip-hop culture in the early 1970s. In addition to hip-hop, students in my seminars often initially imagine The Bronx as a rather poor, largely non-white geographic entity north of Manhattan which underwent a rough phase especially in the late twentieth century. Aside from hip-hop culture, their assumptions about this space largely match that of the many historical approaches which view The Bronx as a fixed spatial entity.

This section explains how historians have dealt with The Bronx and how their approaches inspire my subsequent analysis of popular cultural texts from a cultural studies framework. I propose that The Bronx is a space of cultural difference with regard to its very etymological origin, its geography, topography, history, demography, and academic treatment. By introducing the borough as a space of cultural difference, or Otherness, which is a permanent site of struggle and contestation by different people, I hope to shed light on the dynamics between the popular cultural texts, their real and imagined spaces, and their narratives.

Besides urban studies, geography, and ethnography (Jakob; LeBlanc; Matuschewski; Tobier), history is the main field of research through which The Bronx has been examined so far. Urban historians use historical documents as a gateway to present a more or less chronological perspective on the borough's development from its colonial beginnings to the early twenty-first century. One key example in this field is Bronx historian Llyod Ultan, one of the borough's most dedicated chroniclers. He published several comprehensive books on its history, such as *The Bronx in the Frontier Era: From the Beginning to 1696* (1993), *The Birth of the Bronx: 1609-1900* (with Gary Hermalyn, 2000), *The Bronx in the Innocent Years: 1890-1925* (1985), and *The Bronx: It Was Only Yesterday: 1935-1965* (with Gary Hermalyn, 1992). These books are popular histories in which historic excerpts, documents, and photographs are presented alongside personal memories by former Bronxites. They are invaluable resources to learn about the dynamic history of The Bronx.

The strong historical perspective on The Bronx which enriches facts and figures with personal memories gained momentum especially during the decline of the borough in the 1970s. Ultan, for instance, started his Bronx history series with the publication of *The Beautiful Bronx: 1920-1950* in 1979, two years after it had been symbolically abandoned by the rest of America. Re-writing the borough's history as a people's history is certainly a powerful response against political neglect because such books record and preserve the many voices and local traditions threatened to be lost during urban decline. These books also comment on the older official histories *The Story of the Bronx from The Purchase Made by the Dutch from the Indians in 1639 to the Present Day* or *The Borough of the Bronx 1639-1913: Its Marvelous Development and Historical Surroundings*, published in 1912 and 1913, respectively.

Historical approaches of The Bronx enjoyed considerable attention on the book market in the 2000s. Ultan's 2009 monograph *The Northern Borough: A History of the Bronx* is the first 'official' historical book which "has been written since 1912" (Ultan i). In his comprehensive volume, he narrates the borough's history from the colonial era until today. Likewise, historian and journalist Jill Jonnes focuses on the recent history and politics of the South Bronx in her acclaimed study *South Bronx Rising: The Rise, Fall, and Resurrection of an American City* (2002).

While Jonnes' and Ultan's volumes are written in a more prosaic manner, Evelyn Gonzales' study entitled *The Bronx* (2005) uses a more academic writing style. An urban historian, Gonzales examines the borough's "long history of urban development, neighborhood change, and population movements, all key elements in the devastation and subsequent revival that occurred" (Gonzales 1). *The Bronx* offers a comprehensive survey of the population movements and demographic change in the borough from the mid-nineteenth to the early twenty-first centuries. Ultan, Jonnes, and Gonzales all pay special attention to the causes and consequences of the borough's downfall in the 1970s.

Likewise, Fordham University's Bronx African American History Project has compiled a comprehensive digital archive of local oral histories. The collaborative online project features black residents' narratives of growing up and living in The Bronx since the early twentieth century and makes those largely neglected voices accessible to wider national and global audiences. Mark Naison and Bob Gumbs published a selection of seventeen narratives in their book *Before the Fires: An Oral History of African American Life in The Bronx from the 1930s to the 1960s* (2016). Many of the newer historiographical accounts are supported, and some also published, by Fordham University Press and the Bronx County Historical Society, an institution founded in 1955 that aims at preserving the rich histories of the borough. Historicizing The Bronx means to collect people's oral histories, preserving them for a wide audience, and trying to make sense of the downfall in the 1970s.

Writing at the interface of literary, urban, and cultural history, Lloyd Ultan and poet/novelist Barbara Unger published the first literary history of the borough in 2000. *Bronx Accent: A Literary and Pictorial History of the Borough* "captures the *Zeitgeist* of The Bronx [and] its rich literary heritage" (vii, emphasis in original). The authors discuss a wide variety of texts including "fiction, nonfiction, drama, memoir, poetry, letters, journals, magazines, and newspapers" (Ultan and Unger viii). While this book provides an extensive overview of the literary production of the borough from its beginnings until today, Ultan and Unger again "maintain a [predominantly] historical perspective" (viii). As inevitable resources, the historical accounts are crucial for the understanding of its development from Native American settlements all the way to the twenty-first century. The books narrate historic, political, and social events, discuss their causes and consequences, and contextualize them with larger developments that take place at a certain time in American society. Presenting a wide array of materials, stories, and comments, these accounts constitute an indispensable gateway for further literary and cultural studies-related research on The Bronx.

Cultural studies assumes that spaces and places, however, are by no means unchanging and eternally stable as students, historians, politicians, and even urban planners would think (Bachmann-Medick; Barker and Jane

513-48; Longhurst et al. 107-39;). They are in a much broader sense a material space as well as a discourse, a way of talking about and making sense of spatial locations. Spaces and places such as The Bronx tell us about existing power relations in a society, which are determined by dominant social groups and are laden with certain hegemonic norms and values. At the same time, these power relations are also subverted and transgressed by other groups in subordinate social positions. Spaces and places are as much about boundaries as their constant re-/negotiation. Crossing those boundaries can be an offensive or subversive act which challenges norms or conventions connected to them. Hence, this broad definition of space acknowledges that they are not only a site of permanent struggle and negotiation between different societal groups and their world views. Rather it includes everything connected to identities, practices, narratives, and signifying systems, an important aspect which this book explores later in greater detail.

This broad definition of space as a contested and dynamic process has dominated most of the humanities scholarship in recent decades, attributable to the influence on French philosopher Henri Lefebvre. In his study *The Production of Space* (1974) Lefebvre argues that space consists not only of physical space but is actively produced as "social space" (73) and, thus, becomes embedded in uneven power relations. By extending the definition of space from a traditional history and urban planning perspective in which space is formed in the realm of practices and representations, Lefebvre set the stage for a much broader understanding. With this assumption he influenced poststructuralist and postmodern ideas of spaces and places commonly subsumed under the so-called spatial turn, which includes scholars such as Manuel Castells, David Harvey (*Postmodernity*), Doreen Massey, Edward Soja, Barney Wharf and Santa Arias, Jörg Döring and Tristan Thielmann.

According to this broad understanding of spaces and places as products of social interrelationships, The Bronx can be theorized as a space of cultural difference in many ways. For instance, cultural Otherness is already embedded in its very name. It is the only borough in New York City with the capitalized definite article "The." This pronoun refers to its history: around 1640 Jonas "Bronk, Bronck, or Brunk [who] was a Dane, or Swede" purchased parts of Keskeskeck land, as historian Stephen Jenkins writes in 1912 (26). The name eventually evolved from the new owner of the land, the "Bronk's," to "The Bronx" (St. Jenkins 26). While its name signifies estate, possession, and authority, it is more than just that. The definite article underlines the uniqueness of the borough as opposed to those without an article. It sounds more poetic as well:

"The Bronx" could easily refer to the title of an artwork or a family dynasty, such as the Morris's, the Van Cortland's, or the Pelham's. The article elevates the area above the average and suggests a place of century-old heritage and history.

The Bronx is literally 'above average' geographically because its territory and built environment takes up a special position on New York City's map. While the four boroughs Manhattan, Brooklyn, Queens, and Staten Island are all islands in the Atlantic Ocean, The Bronx is the only one located on the US American mainland. Due to this special geographic position the district developed into a major gateway and thoroughfare for the other parts of New York City with its many highways and bridges such as the Cross Bronx Expressway, the Bronx-River Parkway, the Bronx-Whitestone and Throggs-Neck Bridges.

The topography and architecture of The Bronx differs from Manhattan. While Manhattan is flat, The Bronx is hilly. While Manhattan consists of extensive skyscrapers with One World Trade Center as its currently highest incarnation (541 meters/1776 ft), the highest buildings in The Bronx are the twin apartment complexes Harlem River Park Towers I and II, which only measure a humble 123 meters/404 ft. These two buildings are symbolic of the landscape of the borough which is dominated by apartment buildings and high-rise housing projects. More than the corporate center of Manhattan, The Bronx has traditionally been a more residential area where people sleep and live.

The borough's cultural Otherness is further underlined in its history, which is exemplary of American history while at the same time deviates from what people have understood as 'American' in different periods. In the Colonial Era, for instance, the religious figure Anne Hutchinson opposed the rigid Puritan doctrine prevalent in New England and found a refuge in Pelham Neck in the 1640s (Cook 122; Ultan, *Northern Borough* 10-11). Neglecting Native American territories and their spatial traditions, her home was attacked and she died (Cook 122; Ultan, *Northern Borough* 11). For Hutchinson, the area's aura of cultural Otherness was a refuge and a trap at the same time.

The borough continued to be a space of Otherness in the nineteenth century. Until the mid-1800s, the landscape of what would eventually become The Bronx remained, in contrast to its southern neighbor Manhattan, "heavily forested" (Jonnes 14) and rural with occasional farms and manors (Ultan, *Northern Borough* 123; Jonnes 14). Urbanization north of the Harlem River occurred relatively late by New York standards and accelerated only in the late nineteenth century (Ultan, *Northern Borough* 173) when the borough was officially created in 1898. Writers such as Theodore Dreiser responded to the con-sequences of industrialization. Dreiser, a temporary resident in the Southern Mott Haven neighborhood (Ultan and Unger 55), critically reflected on the in-creasing "isolation and loneliness of heart" in his short essay "The Loneliness of the City" (474).

Because of its belated urbanization, The Bronx has far more parks and green spaces than other boroughs in New York City, such as Van Cortlandt Park, Pelham Bay Park, or the Bronx Zoo. This development is especially evi-dent in the South Bronx. A *New York Times* article dated 22 May 1896 highlights the area's amenities which "best combines the various requisites to be looked out for establishing a zoo" ("A Home for the Zoo"). Newspaper articles from this period build on the idea of The Bronx as a pastoral garden within the rapidly urbanizing New York City. The Bronx is imagined as a better public green than Manhattan's Central Park because it is "not as densely populated" ("Bronx Park for the Animals"). Bronx parks feature popular leisure time facil-ities for younger people and families, such as ice skating or picnicking, which are well documented in photographs (e.g. Byron Company's *Skating, Van Cort-landt Park*; Bracklow's *Bronx Park, On Rocking Stone*).

Until the mid-1930s, visitors could still find rural pockets in the rapidly ur-banizing borough. Photographer Berenice Abbott, for instance, documented the vanishing rural character in her pictures of the north-western neigh-borhood Spuyten Duyvil in her renowned photography project *Changing New York* while the Manhattan skyline reached for the stars with the Empire State Building, the Chrysler Building, and Rockefeller Center (Nitzsche, "Rural"). These examples affirm the position of The Bronx as a space of cultural Oth-erness in terms of its landscape and development, and especially the South Bronx, as a particular urban space in the twentieth century.

Throughout the twentieth century, The Bronx has been culturally different in terms of its demographic profile. It was home to many groups who were not part of the white Anglo Saxon Protestant middle class. The Bronx of the early twentieth century was an 'arrival borough' and destination for incoming immigration groups from Europe. The borough's population consisted mostly of a mixture of "Russian and Eastern European Jews, Christian and Jewish Germans, Irish Catholics, Italians, and a bit of everything" (Gonzales 98). Until the early 1950s, the area continued to be a rather quiet and unspectacular middle-class retreat for those recently arrived immigration groups (Tobier 78).

However, after World War II, the foundation for the later era of decline was laid when those, by that time middle-class, European immigrants left and a poorer generation of African Americans from the South and new immigration groups from the Latin American Global South arrived in the borough (Gonzales 113-18). As a result of economic instability, racial segregation, and political indifference, local decision makers, urban planners, and government officials increasingly isolated and marginalized The Bronx. The deterioration culminated in the image of the South Bronx as a place that was for most Americans outside the city: a nightmare of poverty, violence, and decay – in short, everything that America was not supposed to be.

As a result, the South Bronx has been the spatial reincarnation of cultural difference as it has evoked notions of the inner city and the periphery since the 1960s. At the turn of the twentieth century, the term South Bronx appeared first in the *New York Times* as "South Bronx Park" in an article on building efforts of a new park which would later become The Bronx Zoo. However, from as early as 1910 on, the "lower eastern Bronx" was demarcated as a space of immobility. The *New York Times* article "Bronx Dwellers Demand Subways" shows that the area's connection to the newly built subway system had been delayed by the authorities. By the 1960s, it was the departure point to suburbia and into an own 'American way of life' for many of the upwardly mobile first and second-generation European immigrants mentioned earlier. For the news media The Bronx became the scapegoat of the failure of urban renewal, "the nation's largest slum clearance program in the 1950s" led by New York's master builder Robert Moses (Ballon 94).

In the 1970s the imagined territory of the South Bronx constantly expanded northwards from a "one-mile-square neighborhood in the far southeast corner of Mott Haven [...] to include everything south of Fordham Road, or twenty square miles" (Jonnes 8). Observers and critics frequently compared the area's material condition to cities in the Old World that had suffered bombing damage in wars, such as Dresden, Hamburg, or Beirut. These observers and critics described the geographical expansion of decline by referring to the clinical metaphor of cancer (Jonnes 8). Between 1970 and 1980, the *New York Times* headlined 244 articles on the South Bronx, mostly reports on gang activity, rape, violence, killings, relief projects, and especially waves of arson. In 1974, parts of the worst hit area around Charlotte Street even disappeared from the city map for nearly a decade (Fernandez). The news media imagination of the South Bronx as an urban disaster zone reduced the cultural heterogeneity and historical complexity of The Bronx to the meaning of decline and decay. In comparison to Manhattan, which often serves as a point of reference from which the borough is imagined, the South Bronx has epitomized the negative sites of the inner city for some population groups until today.

At the beginning of the twenty-first century, The Bronx remains a borough of racial and class difference in the city of New York. According to the 2019 *US Census*, The Bronx is far less white ("White alone, not Hispanic or Latino," 8.93 to 47.0 per cent in Manhattan) ("Quick Facts: Bronx County;" "Quick Facts: New York County"). Almost twice as many African Americans (28.9) and Hispanics (56.4 per cent) live in the borough compared to Manhattan (17.9 and 25.9 per cent, respectively) ("Quick Facts: Bronx County;" "Quick Facts: New York County"). With an estimated per capita income of $20,850, local residents are much poorer than the inhabitants in Manhattan who earn $72,832 on average ("Quick Facts: Bronx County;" "Quick Facts: New York County"). While Manhattan signifies economic privilege, unlimited progress, and capitalist production, The Bronx remains one of the economically disadvantaged boroughs into the present. While New York City is perceived as an affluent, progressive, and cosmopolitan global or world city, the northern borough is poorer, racially, and ethnically more diverse, and less socially mobile.

Compared to Manhattan as the materialized version of the American Dream, The Bronx is hardly thought of this way by many observers and visitors. The southern island Manhattan constitutes not only the geographical, financial, and cultural center of New York City with Times Square, Wall Street, and Broadway, but also the imagined center of the world and global tourism's eternal mecca. While Manhattan is home to many nationally and internationally renowned museums, art galleries, media, political, and financial institutions, outside visitors rarely consider The Bronx as a place of similar financial and cultural significance. To many visitors it continues to embody the flipside of this version of the American Dream, namely (non-white) poverty, economic stagnation, and urban crisis.

Outsiders tend to forget that The Bronx was and continues to be a space where the Dream did come true for many. Jill Jonnes notes that "The Bronx of the 1920s, 1930s, and 1940s became a staging ground for the American Dream, the unremarkable home of 1.5 million first- and second-generation Americans" (4). With The Bronx as their home base, European immigration groups strove for integration into the greater American culture. The borough was a place of cultural, economic, and population growth similar to Manhattan, continuing its development from the early twentieth century (Ultan, *North-*

ern Borough 277). Today, the green picturesque Riverdale neighborhood, for instance, is home to Wall Street executives who have accomplished their version of upward mobility and decided to stay in its northwestern part. As this book will show, even during the socioeconomic crisis in the 1970s, The Bronx was the place where the narrative of the American Dream was imagined and re-imagined.

Othering processes such as that of The Bronx depend on specific media contexts as well. As a rather economically distressed and racially diverse borough, it competes with Manhattan for larger public attention where the collective interest in places and their histories is still largely shaped by an Anglo American white middle-class gaze. This gaze also explains the widespread indifference evident on the American Hollywood and TV screen, both of whom release far more feature films and broadcast shows set in Manhattan than in The Bronx. Well known titles include *Breakfast at Tiffany's* (dir. Blake Edwards, 1961), *Wall Street* (dir. Oliver Stone, 1987), or HBO's TV series *Sex and the City* (1998-2004). One advantage of The Bronx's marginal position, however, is that smaller independent productions and B-movies such as *Marty* (dir. Delbert Mann, 1955), *1990: Bronx Warriors* (dir. Enzo Castellari, 1982), *South Bronx Heroes* (dir. William Szarka, 1985), and *Mott Music* (dir. Jarred Alterman, 2005) chose The Bronx as the setting for their stories. This has allowed for experimentation with narrative, genre, and media conventions.

The notion of The Bronx as a marginalized urban space in American media is finally accompanied by a larger and ongoing disinterest in the boroughs' rich history, transnational heritage, and cultural diversity. As with many media productions, publications dealing with New York City oftentimes privilege Manhattan. This Manhattan-centered historical writing is also noted by Lloyd Ultan. He correctly observes that

> [t]here is an abundance of one volume histories of the city at large written by professional historians. Unfortunately, each one of them is in reality merely a history of the borough of Manhattan. [...] The story of The Bronx is not the same as the story of Manhattan. Nor is it the same as the story of Brooklyn, nor any of its other sister boroughs. (*Northern Borough* i)

Ultan emphasizes that many historians narrate the history of New York essentially as the history of Manhattan while other boroughs' narratives, historical movements, and local memories are largely sidelined.

One of the reasons The Bronx still lingers in the shades of Manhattan and Brooklyn as the northernmost borough is because it is mostly associated with working, lower class, and street cultures. While there are important postmodern literary texts set in the borough like E.L. Doctorow's *World's Fair* (1985), Tom Wolfe's *The Bonfire of the Vanities* (1987, later successfully adapted into a movie by director Brian de Palma), and Don DeLillo's *Underworld* (1997), they are often not approached as distinctively 'Bronx' by critics. Only hip-hop studies lead the way as this growing field unquestionably recognizes The Bronx as the mythical transnational birthplace of global hip-hop culture.

Because of its Otherness character, The Bronx can be conceptualized as a heterotopia, a term coined by French philosopher Michel Foucault which refers to the idea of spaces that deviate from the dominant societal order. In his lecture "On Other Spaces" (1967), Foucault argues that there are special places in a society that "are absolutely different from all the sites that they reflect and speak about" (24). Heterotopias are marked by several principles: multiplicity, temporality, their own set of rules, a system of inclusion and exclusion, as well as a special relation to the greater society. The Bronx can be understood as a heterotopia because of all the aforementioned characteristics: Its multiplicity is expressed in the simultaneous qualities of center and periphery, destination and departure point as well as the binary American Dream/American nightmare postulation. Its temporality refers to the 1970s and 1980s when American media viewed the downfall of The Bronx as an isolated incident. In terms of rules, The Bronx was attributed with its own (dystopic) social order when the borough became symbolically disconnected from larger socioeconomic problems, such as deindustrialization and shrinkage. Because the borough deviated from white American culture in terms of race, ethnicity, class, media, and academic reception, it faced mechanisms of inclusion and exclusion. The long history of The Bronx is finally marked by continuities within and ruptures from wider American history. Yet, despite these cultural differences The Bronx has always been a pivotal part of American politics, economy, society, and culture. Hence, the borough constitutes a heterotopia within the greater framework of the imagined space of America.

My conceptualization of The Bronx as a heterotopia ties in with the issue of space and place in American culture as complex and intertwined concepts. British geographer Doreen Massey, for instance, argues in her study *For Space* (2005) that the categories space/place, as well as local/global are interconnected in many reciprocal ways (184). A rather abstract space can develop into a concrete expression of local identity while a concrete place can become a space of possibilities at the same time. The heterotopic Bronx can therefore simultaneously be imagined as a space and a place. How this interconnected spatial imagination is bound to different media representations and signifying practices (Hall, *Representation*) will be explained in the next section.

1.2 Exploring Urban Spaces: Popular, Media, and Convergence Cultures

Few publications recognize popular, literary, and media representations of The Bronx. An early example of this research on The Bronx constitutes the 1982 study *All That Is Solid Melts into Air: The Experience of Modernity*. The author, American Marxist critic, philosopher, and political activist Marshall Berman, ends his study by connecting his main argument of modernity as a unifying and isolating development with his personal memories of growing up in The Bronx. For him, The Bronx of the 1970s epitomizes the ambivalent experience of modernity as its stable building structures and functioning communities are literally melted in the course of the downfall of the borough as a result of post-World War II urban renewal (290). In mourning the loss of his old neighborhood (295), Berman theorizes his former home as a powerful symbol of the fluidity of modernity marked by loss of structure and history. He envisions that this loss of structure eventually gives way for new artistic and democratic expressions one of which he calls the Bronx Mural (341). Berman believes in the regenerative potential of art and literature in times of socioeconomic and urban distress.

In the late 1990s, The Bronx Museum of the Arts acknowledged the importance of media and popular culture. The exhibition *Urban Mythologies: The Bronx Represented since the 1960s* "brings together a highly compelling and symbolically coded selection of images and objects assembled from the visual arts, vernacular and popular culture, and the mass media to investigate the many ways in which the Bronx has been constructed in the public imagination" (Nieves 6). This was the first time an exhibition centered on artistic, photographic, and youth cultural expressions of The Bronx in the late twentieth century. *Urban Mythologies* combined those art works with commentaries by renowned public and academic figures such as theorist Marshall Berman, art historian Rosalyn Deutsche, graffiti writer Phase 2, and Bronx Museum of the Arts curator Lydia Yee.

In the early 2000s, some scholars started recognizing the importance of representation for understanding The Bronx. American scholar Katherine Simpson, to give one example, combined a film studies and urban studies perspective in her 2002 article "Media Images of the Urban Landscape: The South Bronx in Film." She compared the changing representation of the South Bronx in *Fort Apache: The Bronx* and *Finding Forrester* (dir. Gus van Sant, 2000) to argue that "Hollywood now idealizes the same neighborhood it once condemned" (108). Simpson connected this changing image of the South Bronx not only to the transforming urban context, but also to the evolution of Hollywood's renditions of the borough since the 1980s. She thereby pinpointed the constructed character of one type of audio-visual representation with regard to urban space.

Simpson's research engaged in a wider strand of scholarship to examine urban contexts in primarily one media form. Most notable here are approaches to the city in literature or the city in film. Literary critic Richard Lehan, for example, examined "the ways the [Western] city has been conceptualized from its origin to the present time" (3) in *The City in Literature: An Intellectual and Cultural History* (1998). His comprehensive study discusses literary examples ranging from Enlightenment Europe to postmodern America. In another example, film scholars Mark Shiel and Tony Fitzmaurice combined Sociology and Film Studies in their anthology *Cinema and the City: Film and Urban Societies in a Global Context* (2001) to elaborate on the notion of the city in film in *Screening the City* (2003). Investigations within one media form reveal the cultural and aesthetic traditions to which more contemporary texts respond. However, they tend to overlook the complex spatial dynamics between different popular and media forms.

Newer approaches consider multiple media genres in the study of urban phenomena. *Urban Nightmares: The Media, the Right and the Moral Panic over the City* (2006) examines how the American news media, Hollywood film, and the advertising industry all contribute to the fear of the inner city in similar ways (Macek xvi). American communication scholar Steve Macek argues that "media representations of the postindustrial American city [in the 1980s and 1990s] for the most part reproduced and validated the right's discourse on the urban crisis while amplifying the suburban middle-class fears the discourse helped to generate" (xvi). He asserts a tendency across various media to dehumanize the urban space which works towards the ideology of fear perpetuated by predominantly white conservative groups in the American society. While the volumes by Lehan, Shiel, Fitzmaurice, and Macek are important for understanding the interrelationship between spaces and their respective cultural representations, these books work with diverse examples from different cities in one study. They lack a distinctly place-based approach on studying mediated urban spaces. I hope to extend their macro perspective by specializing on one particular place (The Bronx) to examine its manifold constructions across different forms of popular representation and signifying practices. The focus on The Bronx will allow me to reveal the unique dynamics between spatial discourses, media forms, and cultural narratives through the lens of convergence culture.

Henry Jenkins's concept of convergence culture provides a useful framework for the investigation of spatial imaginations and cultural narratives across various media and pop cultural forms. In *Convergence Culture: Where Old and New Media Collide* (2006), the American media scholar defines convergence culture as a realm "where old and new media collide, where grassroots and corporate media intersect, where the power of the media producer and the power of the media consumer interact in unpredictable ways" (2). Convergence culture assumes a "flow of content across multiple media platforms" (2). His definition maps convergence culture as a creative contact zone (Pratt) between different types of media, media producers, and media users embedded in different power relationships. Hence, characters, spaces, and narratives are not just bound to one specific medium or genre but are subject to a permanent re-contextualization and appropriation process on different levels of media production and consumption. Applied to the idea of spatial representations, The Bronx is constructed across a wide variety of media and its meaning is constantly transmitted, translated, and transformed into different media forms. Convergence culture thus enables a processual perspective on the construction of spaces and places across a wide range of media from an equally wide variety of power positions. These representations highlight the agency of the audience beyond cultural studies theorist Stuart Hall's idea of encoding/decoding ("Encoding") because recipients actively produce new texts and "interact with each other according to a new set of rules" (H. Jenkins 3). Media forms provide a platform to permanently articulate what The Bronx means to audiences in a given context.

The photo book *The New American Ghetto* (1997) by Chilean American photographer Camilo José Vergara serves as an example of how the converging spatial imaginations of The Bronx can be approached. The book cover displays various conditions of 178th Street and Vyse Avenue in The Bronx between June 1980 and October 1994. The eight photographs on the left and right-hand side of the cover map the transformation of the South Bronx over a period of 14 years. The first image on the upper left shows a tenement building which is first inhabited by African American and Puerto Rican boys and girls playing in front of the house. The architecture of the apartment building points to the early twentieth century when many of those large buildings were erected in order to accommodate incoming immigration groups from Central and Eastern Europe. The children in the first picture are representatives of a newer generation of African American and Latinx residents who called the buildings their home in the early 1980s. The picture towards the bottom left shows the increasing deterioration of the building and its surroundings. This infrastructural decline is expressed in the locked or broken windows and the wall built in front of the entrance to prevent unauthorized people from entering the abandoned building. The photograph from 1988 on the top right of the cover shows the nearly total destruction of the building. It is indicated by a pile of rubble as the only evidence of the former housing stock. The destruction opens up a new view to previously blocked apartment buildings. The absence of the house is an analogy to the absence of residents who once called this building home. Finally, the last picture on the bottom right, taken in 1994, shows how the former empty lot was rebuilt with multi-unit townhouse architecture. Those small attached apartment houses constitute a post-devastation way of living which is marked by a suburban car-oriented culture to serve the needs of lower middle-class Puerto Ricans and African Americans.

The medium of photography plays a central role in the re-/construction of the South Bronx on the book cover of *The New American Ghetto*. Photographs, as Susan Sontag noted in her 1977 study *On Photography*, are a "privileged moment, turned into a slim object that one can keep and look at again" (18). Echoing Sontag, Vergara returned to the same street corner and building over a longer period of time and took pictures from the same camera angle. The eight photographs arranged on the book cover therefore visually map the transformation of 178th Street and Vyse Avenue between 1980 and 1994. One can compare the individual photographs with each other and analyze how the transformation of the area took place. The viewer establishes a connection between eight photographs which record the permanently changing urban landscape over a period of time affirming that space is by no means a fixed category.

The photographs on the cover of *The New American Ghetto* do not only document the condition of the apartment building at different moments in time, they also converge into different media and cultural contexts. The original slides of Vergara's project are archived at the Bronx County Historical Society for future research. As color images, they are displayed on the cover of the photo book and reappear inside as black and white photographs. Inside

the book, the author-photographer added a critical commentary to the photographs: "Two Bronxes are visible in these photographs: one that died too
soon and one too flimsy to last" (Vergara 69). Here, the photographs and the
accompanying image descriptions serve to underline the photo book's disap-
proval of the senseless destruction of the old housing stock and the displacement of the community. Vergara's photographs are rearranged, repurposed,
and remediated (Bolter and Grusin) from slides into books into (new) media
and public contexts.

Vergara's pictures were further displayed at art exhibits such as at the Urban Center and Storefront for Art and Architecture show in the SoHo district
of Manhattan in 1991, or at the National Building Museum in Washington,
D.C., in 2009. Exhibitions provide a new angle to the photographs because
they are treated as documentary evidence of urban change in America, or as
an artistic expression of the neglect of a marginalized urban population. As
photographic art, they constitute collectors' items and commodities on the art
market. Finally, the photographs appear online in various weblogs and social
media sites about 1980s New York or about street photography and, more recently ruin porn, where bloggers admire Vergara's cycle of devastation and
resurrection. Web platforms and social networks, such as Instagram, Pin-
terest, and Flickr, establish new links to other declining cities in the US and
around the world. Thus, by re-contextualizing, re-presenting, and converging
with other media forms, these photographs of the South Bronx are not only
accessible to different audiences at different locations, but they also constitute
diverse forms of meaning in different media contexts. They are also powerful
examples which foreshadow the coming convergence that takes place across
literature, the moving image, and audio texts.

The cycle of photographs discussed here are only a first step in appreciat-
ing the multi-facetted nature of The Bronx in media representations, signifying practices, and popular culture. I am convinced that cultural representations present specific spaces and places in The Bronx, connect them to specific
cultural narratives, and introduce specific statements about what it means to
be American. The next chapter will elaborate on the urban and cultural contexts of this study which are necessary to understand the poetic resurrection
of The Bronx.

1.3 Spectacular Ruins: Mapping the Era of Decline in The Bronx

The 1970s and the early 1980s were an era of decline in American culture. Beginning with the 1973 oil crisis and the 1975 New York fiscal crisis (both of which contributed to a mid-1970s stagflation), several economic crises followed one another, including the 1979 energy crisis and the subsequent 1981-82 economic recession. As a result of these crises, scholars increasingly became aware of the impact of economic downturns. They began conceptualizing decline as a critical category which evolved from the scholarly occupation with the consequences of deindustrialization, which mainly took place in the former industrial centers of the North East. Scholars such as American economists Barry Bluestone and Bennett Harrison defined deindustrialization in their ground-breaking study *The Deindustrialization of America* (1982) as "a widespread, systematic disinvestment in the nation's basic productive capacity" (6). They understood it as a process largely limited to the ways in which working-class blue-collar production is replaced by white-collar corporate, financial, and investment activities. At that time, deindustrialization primarily meant economic shrinkage.

The concept of decline broadened in the 1990s in urban studies circles with the rise of cultural studies theories in the United States. In his study *Voices of Decline: The Postwar Fate of US Cities* (1993), Robert A. Beauregard defined the term decline as a contested discourse which is culturally constructed, historically flexible, and shaped by a variety of voices from many different societal positions and ideological backgrounds (35). Borrowing from poststructuralist theories, he aimed to "convey, in all its intricacy and inconsistencies, what was said and written about urban decline" (5). Beauregard emphasized the importance of representational practices in analyzing urban transformation processes. He stated that the realities of urban decline are mediated by a wide variety of channels and outlets (36). In extending the study of urban spaces to the realm of representation, power, and meaning-making processes, Beauregard thus works with assumptions prevalent in cultural studies.

Beauregard, however, is aware that he analyzes mainly official media discourses such as newspapers and journalistic texts. They were produced by "white, male, middle-class America" (46) which are oftentimes in line with the official ideology which feared the inner city and demonized the so-called 'urban crisis,' a euphemism for the racial tensions underlining this urban shrinkage process (see Macek). Thus Beauregard leaves out representations of and from traditionally disenfranchised groups of society in terms of race, ethnicity, gender, sexuality, and age, some of which are addressed in this study.

Borrowing from urban studies research on shrinking cities (Doucet; Hollander; Oswalt; Pallagst et al.), this book asserts that the era of decline encompasses first and foremost a period in which the socioeconomic, cultural, transnational, and ideological restructurings in The Bronx are articulated, negotiated, and navigated. My analysis will be guided by approaches which situate local urban shrinkage processes within larger global developments (Cunningham-Sabot et al. 23). Assuming that the borough is a heterotopic space within American culture, the various race, class, gender, and ideological reconfigurations are therefore exemplary for wider shifts in late twentieth-century American culture and beyond.

In The Bronx, the era of decline refers to a time period between the late 1970s and the early 1980s (ca. 1978-1984) in which the borough experienced massive population loss, widespread urban shrinkage, and decreasing overall socioeconomic growth. Compared to 1970, the 1980 *US Census* recorded a population loss of 20.6 per cent for the entire borough and a shocking 46.7 per cent for the South Bronx alone (Ultan, *Northern Borough* 302). The main reason for the stark population decline was the strategic use of arson to decimate the borough's housing stock. This, in turn, accelerated the physical deterioration of the area which had begun the 1960s (Ultan, *Northern Borough* 302).

During that time, The Bronx received far more media attention than ever before. As The Bronx is part of New York City, the capital of the Western world and a (post-)modern metropolis, The Bronx became the visual focal point during the sociopolitical and financial turmoil. As a "global city" (Sassen) where the production and flow of information, news, and technologies originate, culminate, and emanate, New York City received the most attention during the era of decline compared to other parts of the United States. Because of its close proximity to Manhattan, events in The Bronx were amplified in various national and international media channels. The high density of media corporations and institutions of (inter-)national importance in Manhattan, such as CBS, NBC, and ABC, allowed news teams to immediately broadcast from the devastated sites just north of the Harlem River, especially at the height of the wave of arson in the mid- to late 1970s. One of the most iconic and most cited moments was created when ABC host Howard Cosell opened the broadcast of the World Series at Yankee Stadium on 12 October 1977 with the exclamation "Ladies and Gentlemen, the Bronx is burning" (Ultan, *Northern Borough* 300-01).

A second iconic moment was created when President Carter visited the South Bronx on 5 October 1977. Carter, and also his successor Ronald Reagan in 1980, toured the severely damaged Charlotte Street area in the South Bronx only a few days after a massive blackout had hit the entire city. A panoramic shot of Charlotte Street, which appeared on the front cover of *The New York Times*, epitomizes the area as an American nightmare. Jimmy Carter and his entourage of journalists and activists are the only people who walk determinedly across the area assessing the demolition of what looks like an urban disaster zone. Instead of buildings, the area in the foreground is taken up by garbage and waste. Remnants of urban architecture can be seen in the background to the left and the landscape evokes visual metaphors of war. Despite the sunny and bright day, the area appears as a dystopic and dehumanized landscape void of any local traditions and rich histories.

The picture along with Howard Cosell's comment to open the World Series shaped the dominant perception of The Bronx as a place of civic devastation and the incarnation of the American nightmare for years to come. The iconography of decay mediated in the news media instantly destroyed "[t]he old nationwide image of the upwardly mobile middle class Bronx" (Ultan, *Northern Borough* 300). Due to the journalistic coverage of national TV stations, newspapers, and magazines about fires, arson, and crime, the borough has gained an iconic status as a hostile urban space in the public perception since the 1970s. The photograph affirmed Carter's inability to deal with the socioeconomic problems of American society: "Americans could look at Carter and feel that the American Dream was either destined to break apart, a casualty of malaise, or that the American Dream was itself a participant in the malaise" (Klimmage 31).

The era of decline is of special importance as the 1970s and early 1980s constituted a period of recurring crisis and immense transformation in American culture. As mentioned earlier, during the 1970s American society experienced several political, socioeconomic, urban, transnational, and cultural crisis moments which triggered massive processes of reorganization, relocation, and repositioning. The first crisis took place in the political sphere. The catastrophic ending of the Vietnam War and the Watergate scandal in the first half of the 1970s questioned the fundamental values of the country. Second, the mid-1970s experienced several economic and fiscal crises which resulted in stagflation, stagnating economic activity paired with increasing inflation, and accelerated the deindustrialization of the North East. The third crisis resulted in the increasing geographical, social, and racial disparity between urban and

suburban, rich and poor, liberal and conservative groups of society. As affluent white population groups settled in the suburbs, lower class areas such
as The Bronx continued to deteriorate. At the same time, white male Anglo
American supremacy began to be scrutinized. Previously marginalized population groups in terms of race, gender, and sexuality achieved wider public
and social recognition with their powerful grassroots movements such as the
Civil Rights, the women's rights, and the gay liberation movements. Those associations increasingly voiced their members' experiences of discrimination
and marginalization in a still predominantly white heterosexual and male-
dominated culture.

The media crisis was the final main tendency in the era of decline. In the
1970s, Hollywood struggled with the aftermath of the collapse of the old studio
system, resulting in the disparate, transitional phase of New Hollywood with
experimental and controversial movies, but also with popular blockbusters
such as *Jaws* (dir. Steven Spielberg, 1975) and *Star Wars* (dir. George Lucas,
1977). Especially *Star Wars* set new standards in media, economic, and technological convergence as the film's release was supported by nation-wide marketing and merchandizing campaigns. New media forms and genres such as
desktop computers, computer games, VCRs, the launch of HBO (1972) and
CNN and MTV (1980 and 1981, respectively) profoundly changed media production and consumption habits. The rapidly shifting media landscape along
with postmodern attitudes of anything goes and the breakdown the boundaries of high and popular culture presaged the representation of The Bronx
across various media precisely because many of these outlets had fixated on
the decline of The Bronx.

1.4 Beyond Ruins: The Poetic Resurrection

Literature, film, photography, and music are long-standing and widely popular forms of expression in American culture, and the decline of The Bronx
has been explored in all of them. Literature has a long tradition as a medium
that negotiates cultural identities. Film is a more recent media form which,
similarly to photography and TV, unfolded its cultural potential in the twentieth century. Because of the strong visual iconography of the declining Bronx,
film companies released a relatively large number of movies, such as *Gloria*,
Fort Apache: The Bronx, 1990: *The Bronx Warriors*, *The Wanderers* (dir. Philipp Kaufmann, 1979), and *Wolfen*. Audiences enjoyed these films in large numbers, and

these movies inspired a few publications mostly by film scholars (see Ch. 3). Viewers continue to watch these films even today as they are available as DVD, Blue Ray releases, streaming services such as Netflix and even on illegal pirated streaming websites.

The third popular form of expression, music, includes hip-hop culture, which started in The Bronx in the 1970s. Popular music in general and a converging cultural practice such as hip-hop in particular have been a primary means of identification for many younger Americans in times of political, social, or economic crisis. All of the literary and filmic representations and pop cultural practices from and about The Bronx are in dialogue with each other across their media boundaries about the causes and consequences of shrinkage.

These cultural representations (Hall, *Representation*) will be investigated in three steps. First, spatial and medial considerations help me to analyze cultural narratives and ideologies. The first aspect refers to the question of which and how shrinking spaces and places are represented. The Bronx as a heterotopic space consists of a multiplicity of different inhabitants, individuals, neighborhoods, and communities. Which buildings, streets, and neighborhoods are introduced? What kinds of connections are established and/or boundaries are drawn between them? Which meanings do they unfold in the course of narration and for which respective protagonists?

Secondly, I will scrutinize how spatial imaginaries are connected to very specific genres and modes of expression. Genres are socially constructed classification systems of literary, filmic, musical, and artistic texts (Tudor 7; Zarzosa 10). A western movie, for instance, has specific settings (the frontier), characters (cowboys, Natives), and plot elements (shootouts). While genres are "specified through properties, modes are specified through modifications" (Zarzosa 13). Modes, by contrast, are means of articulation that are not necessarily genre- or media- specific. For example, a western movie can be shot in different kinds of modes, such as the documentary, melodramatic, gothic or the autobiographic modes. A western shot in the melodramatic mode, for example, centers on the characters' destiny, their gender identities, and uses cinematic means of excess and exaggeration. Genres and modes underline Jenkins's convergence aspect as they can appear across many different media forms.

Both spatial and medial considerations lead to the third step of cultural narratives. As in any locality, decline temporarily destabilizes cultural narratives in The Bronx. When The Bronx was shrinking in the 1970s, its settlement patterns, socioeconomic functions, and its larger spatial order started to change. For instance, factories, which once constituted the heart of economic progress and the spearhead of industrial growth, lost their economic and cultural significance. Places once occupied by the workforce and, by extension, their surrounding communities and municipalities with employment, upward mobility, and the facilitating of one's personal American Dream turned into spatialized economic nightmares in the public imagination. They became metaphors for the failure of economic productivity in a globalized capitalist world.

Popular cultural texts counter this destabilization process by creating artistic, aesthetic, and imaginary spaces which offer extrapolations, alternatives, revisions, reflections, contemplations, memories, critiques, subversions, and renewals of existing themes and narratives. As such, they provide a much-needed cultural catharsis to the experience of shrinkage. Oftentimes, such narratives are highly individualized as they elevate individual subject positions over that of a larger community and reinforce individualism, one of America's central virtues. Those narratives are voiced by a wide variety of people in terms of their racial, gender, class, and age backgrounds. Thus, the popular and media representations of The Bronx in the era of decline anticipate revised spatial and cultural narratives which are marked by post-modern, post-colonial, and post-growth characteristics.

Although popular culture reconnects decaying cities with American narratives and critiques the causes and consequences of decline, it strangely stabilizes deindustrialization by rarely uttering a more radical systemic critique of neoliberal capitalism, racial, class, and sexual oppression in the 1970s and 1980s. This is somewhat surprising because in the early twentieth century, The Bronx was a hotbed of communist resistance to capitalism. In the 1930s, for instance, many local communist groups and activists rallied against capitalist exploitation during the Great Rent Strike War (Naison, "Eviction Resistance"). Perhaps those radical movements and cultural texts also existed in the 1970s, but the entertainment market and culture industries functioned as gatekeepers to prevent more critical texts from being widely circulated.

The Bronx as a declining space opens up a unique opportunity to reconfigure individual as well as collective American cultural narratives, such as the rags-to-riches story, the frontier narrative, and the American Dream. The American Dream narrative will serve here as exemplary in this regard. It is one of the most pervasive and recurring stories in American history which has shaped and continues to shape the identity of many Americans at home and people's perception of the United States all over the world (Rank, Hirschl, and Forster). American cultural historian Jim Cullen explains in his study *The American Dream: A Short History of an Idea That Shaped a Nation* (2003) that elements of this cultural narrative are as old as the first settlers to Virginia and New England in the seventeenth century (11-34). Most famously, the Founding Fathers included the phrase "pursuit of happiness" in the "Declaration of Independence" (Cullen 38). This phrase embodies the central beliefs of the narrative to achieve individual freedom through happiness. In the nineteenth century, many immigrants followed the Dream's mythical calling to the Unites States leaving their old homes in Europe. An abundance of artists and activists dealt with, reflected on, and were inspired by the American Dream/nightmare binary in the twentieth century, such as playwright Edward Albee, Civil Rights activist Dr. Martin Luther King Jr. and documentary filmmaker Barbara Kopple to name but a very few. Until today, the Dream is a stable theme in secondary and higher education where students all over the world learn about it in English as a Foreign/Second Language in high school classes and in introductory courses to American Studies at universities. "[D]eeply embedded in American mythology and in the consciousness of its citizens" (White and Hanson, "Introduction" 7), the American Dream continues to be one of the longest running and recurring narratives, myths, and ideologies in American cultural history inside and outside the United States.

The American Dream is a particularly relevant cultural narrative in times of socioeconomic and urban crisis (Cullen; Hanson and White; Samuel). A narrative of growth, advancement, optimism, and hope, the Dream moves to the center of the national imagination and constitutes a metaphorical lingua franca and an engine of cultural, spiritual, and national renewal especially in times of social and economic change (Cullen 6). Whenever America experienced a time of crisis, the Dream narrative proved to be resilient and adjustable (Samuel 4). It was flexible and dynamic because Americans from all cultural backgrounds could imagine and realize their own individual versions of it (Samuel 3-4).

The debate about the Dream intensified during the financial crises of the 1970s when America's socioeconomic confidence was severely shaken (Kuhre 33). In his article "The American Dream in Crisis" (1992), sociologist Bruce Kuhre examined its consequences at a time when the gap between rich and poor in the face of de-industrialization and neoliberal globalization widened (45). Examining predominantly socioeconomic factors such as income distributions, family income, and weekly earnings, Kuhre explains that the age of prosperity lasting from post-World War II to the mid-1970s had ended (36). In the 1970s, for instance, the US suffered from a declining median family income as a result of the economic distress (39). The ending of this prosperity phase resulted in the widening gap between income and wealth and the increasing disbelief in the ideology of the American Dream (33). The economic restructuring processes in the 1970s destabilized the conventional narrative of the American Dream (39). Kuhre observes that

> [a]n increasing segment of the population sees their chances of upward mobility vanish and actually experiences downward mobility, as the prospects of home ownership become much more remote, as the economic security of old age and retirement intensify, the belief in the American Dream will lose its significance for the majority of the population. (47)

The sociologist contends that the socioeconomic crises of the 1970s threaten the foundations of the norms, ideologies, and belief systems of the American Dream and render its cultural significance increasingly irrelevant.

But the American Dream does not lose its significance in times of crisis. In conversations, Bronxites tend to pride themselves that their borough is a place which has largely resisted a generalized or assimilationist notion of the Dream. To them, it has been a place where people could follow their own dreams, either by leaving The Bronx behind or by finding other ways to pursue their individual journeys. Scholars such as Sarah L. Hanson and John K. White correctly affirm in their essay collection *The American Dream in the Twenty-First Century* (2011) that one of the strengths of this myth is its "endurance," its ability to adapt, and to be resilient even during the Great Recession of the 2000s ("Introduction" 7). In his cultural history published in 2012, Lawrence Samuel acknowledged the fact that "the Dream has always managed to bounce back to life" (4). The American Dream might have come under scrutiny in the light of recent economic, social, and urban transformation processes, but it is still one of the most important myths, ideologies, and narratives in American culture.

Its resiliency, adaptability, and flexibility makes this narrative one of the core ideas of American culture which embodies central American values such as freedom and equality, individualism, optimism, and strength (White and Hanson, "Introduction" 8). Because of its openness and belief in "perpetual progress" (Samuel 6), the Dream alongside the frontier and success narratives remains an important analytic lens of investigation of contemporary American culture whereby its conflicts, struggles, and dynamics can be excavated and, hopefully, better understood. Because all of these are prevalent across racial, class, gender, sexual, and age lines, they are the perfect prisms through which urban transformation processes and their media convergence can be studied.

This study will expand existing urban studies and historical accounts of The Bronx by exploring how popular culture revises cultural narratives in and of The Bronx during the era of decline. I claim that the 1970s economic, social, and urban changes open up a unique window to redefine American norms, values, and belief systems. Specifically, I argue that the cultural representations of the shrinking Bronx are the site where the reconfiguration, re-imagination, and revision of the American experiment takes place. Thus, the texts anticipate the spatial rebirth of The Bronx across a wide variety of genre and media boundaries at a time when especially the southern parts of the borough were declining, decaying, and abandoning. As a kind of 'spiritual renaissance,' this turn or shift is expressed, studied, and compared by analyzing how those cultural narratives are represented across genre and media boundaries and how they specifically contribute to the imaginary renewal of The Bronx.

As I will show in the chapters to come, the texts value the legacy of the borough, its critical spirit, and its artistic potential. I will demonstrate how cultural and media representations of the declining Bronx introduce a variety of new anti-essentialist identity formations, establish historical and cultural continuities by aesthetically converging earlier art forms, and by re-thinking the capitalist mantra of progress and growth. I argue that those converging narratives are ahead of their time as they constitute an imaginary, artistic, and cultural renewal of the borough and anticipate and envision its spatial resurrection in the 1990s and 2000s. As a result, the representations contribute immensely to the urban transformation of The Bronx because they symbolically reconnect the place to central American cultural narratives. Even though some of the texts are rather critical of the causes and consequences of shrinkage, their symbolic reconnection to longstanding American cultural narratives reaffirms neoliberal capitalist mechanisms of the 1970s and 1980s.

I call this symbolic rebound the poetic resurrection of The Bronx. By poetic I refer to specific artistic, aesthetic, and fictional qualities of popular media texts which go beyond pragmatic everyday communicative use of language precisely because these formulations have a certain beauty attached to them. I borrow the term resurrection from an interdisciplinary and multimedia exhibition *Devastation/Resurrection: The South Bronx* hosted at the Bronx Museum of the Arts from November 1979 to January 1980. This exhibition provided an important, balanced, and much needed local counter discourse on The Bronx's urban transformation processes in the 1970s. Compared to synonyms such as re-birth, regeneration, and the more negatively connoted term of (urban) re-newal, resurrection highlights spatial, historical, and cultural continuities in the process of regeneration. It also accentuates a more dramatic, mythical, and spiritual recovery of The Bronx.

Poetic Resurrection: The Bronx in American Popular Culture has three objectives. First, it seeks to show that these representations affirm The Bronx as a productive space in the era of decline. This book will demonstrate how cultural representations, signifying practices, and popular media not only criticized, distorted, contested, and subverted the common dystopic de-humanized perception of The Bronx in journalism and news media, but also how they reimagine one of the most central cultural narratives, the American Dream. This case study introduces a new aspect in the treatment of urban shrinkage processes in The Bronx by highlighting the potential of representations to re-examine existing spatial and cultural narratives. Thus, this study shows how the mediated Bronx is an exciting, complex, and multifaceted heterotopia which allows for the discussion of larger urban, cultural, and "glocal" (Robertson) transformation processes in late twentieth-century American society.

Second, this is the first book-length study of The Bronx which expands upon existing historic research and brings different literary, media, and (pop) cultural representations into dialogue with each other. Ranging from literature to film and hip-hop culture, all of the converging representations need to be taken seriously because they facilitate the spatial rebirth of the borough by re-imagining The Bronx as a place of strength, history, and innovation. Therefore, this volume continues and expands earlier historical studies by taking up a comparative media perspective and analyzing how literary, audio-visual, and performative cultures constructed The Bronx in the 1970s and 1980s. My study thus aims at bringing in a new angle in the popular, historical, and academic treatment of The Bronx by investigating this space from a cultural and media studies perspective.

Third, this book confirms that the real and imagined Bronx continues to be an exciting area of research. Its aim is to counter the current academic blind spot of The Bronx to create an awareness of this place as a legitimate and important subject of study in New York and American culture. Ideally, a field such as Bronx Studies focuses on the multiplicity of spaces, places, people, voices, narratives, practices, and texts that are produced of, about, for, and from The Bronx. These various inputs culminate in a constructionist analytical approach from disciplines as diverse as (urban) history, urban studies, cultural studies, literary studies, media studies, African American studies, Latinx studies, gender studies, performance studies, and cultural theory. This interdisciplinary approach is necessary to bring The Bronx into focus when talking about New York City and urban America.

My book fills this gap by showing the great diversity of the borough, acknowledging its contribution to American culture and its narratives, and by elevating The Bronx as a subject of study in the humanities and social sciences. It seeks to reconfigure the existing canon on New York City by highlighting the artistic complexity as well as the rich cultural and literary heritage of The Bronx.

The next chapter begins by examining literature. When studying literature of the early 1980s, my first realization was that most of the books published during that time were autobiographical narratives. This observation corresponds strongly to my research experiences outlined in the beginning of this chapter. This leads to questions of why there are so many autobiographical narratives written about the borough, but also who writes them and from which perspectives. By analyzing *Bronx Primitive: Portraits in a Childhood*, *Growing Up Bronx*, *The Old Neighborhood*, the following chapter will show how autobiographical narratives reimagine The Bronx as a place of personal success in the era of decline.

Chapter 2
The Bronx is Not Lost:
Remembering the Success Story in Literature

Literature is a very flexible medium when it comes to the construction of spaces. This medium creates spaces and places in one dimension, the written language. British writer and literary critic David Lodge explains that authors can create all sorts of spaces when they craft stories that transport readers into outer space, inside the bodies and minds of fictional human beings, or in stories that are set in prisons (Lodge 70). Literature, Lodge points out, can create those spaces and places without taking into consideration practical issues arising in other media, such as production costs of film sets or a photographer's efforts to travel to places in order to do an on-location photo shooting (70-71). As fiction triggers the reader's imagination, the question arises how those spaces and places are imagined specifically through the use of language, narrative perspective, plot, and setting.

Urban decline, as it occurs over time, lends itself particularly well to the literary imagination. Authors can choose to write about transforming cityscapes without the need to be physically present. They verbally or metaphorically recreate disappearing architecture or changing communities. Writers have the freedom to combine personal memories and spatial imaginaries in their works of fiction or autobiography. Genres such as autobiography or the coming-of-age novel add an important dimension to the imagination of a declining space. Most importantly, they employ a variety of stylistic or rhetoric devices such as the use of metaphor, narrative perspective and narrative time, or humor in order to make the decline accessible to their readership. Fiction and autobiography introduce a subjective and everyday dimension to the experience of decline.

Most fictional texts on The Bronx published during the age of decline came out in the early 1980s. The autobiography *Bronx Primitive: Portraits in a Childhood* (Kate Simon) was published in 1982, *Growing Up Bronx* (Gerald Rosen) in 1984, and *The Old Neighborhood* (Avery Corman) already in 1980. It seems that writers more so than filmmakers need more time to respond to deindustrialization as writers take more time to process, reflect, and articulate the borough's spatial transformation. All three books are located in different neighborhoods East Tremont, Highbridge, and Kingsbridge/Grand Concourse which were part of the South Bronx at the time of publication. The specific setting opens up a series of questions: Why are these novels and the autobiography set in the South Bronx and what attitude towards the place is showcased? Who are the main characters and what relationships do they have to the various neighborhoods? What do the various genres and stylistic devices tell us about the perception of The Bronx in the era of decline?

I argue that the texts deconstruct the public imagination of The Bronx as a burned-out and hostile urban area by re-writing it as a place where the protagonists' personal success stories take place. The success story is a major cultural narrative which writer Horatio Alger Jr. popularized in his novel *Ragged Dick; or Street Life in New York with the Boot Blacks* (1867) (Klepper 123). Alger's dime novel is about a boy in New York City who rises to fame. The origins of this narrative, also referred to as self-made man and rags-to-riches story, go back to at least the Early Republic with texts such as Benjamin Franklin's *Autobiography* (1791) which chronicles the Founding Father's road to success as a politician, inventor, husband, and public figure, has many similar sentiments. The success/rags-to-riches story is based on the idea that hard work results in economic success. As such it feeds into the notion of the American Dream (see Ch. 1.4), but it is personalized through fictional characters and is, as Klepper argues, "inherently narrative" (129).

Popular literature in the era of decline centers on Bronxites coming of age and reminds readers of the borough's legacy of the success story in times of crisis. The semi-autobiographic novel *Growing Up Bronx* centers on a Jewish American protagonists' childhood and adolescence in the Highbridge neighborhood in the 1940s and 1950s. In *The Old Neighborhood* a male Jewish American hero who also grew up in The Bronx returns to the place of his youth in later life. This chapter will start, however, with *Bronx Primitive: Portraits in a Childhood*. Writer Kate Simon's autobiography presents a heroine who recollects her childhood memories in the East Tremont neighborhood in the early twentieth century.

2.1 "I was the queen of my block": Polish Immigration, Tremont Challenges, and Jewish American Female Empowerment in *Bronx Primitive: Portraits in a Childhood* (1982)

A strong sense of place is one of the more intriguing aspects of *Bronx Primitive: Portraits in a Childhood* (*BP*). Published in 1982 by Viking Press when The Bronx was suffering from the loss of several neighborhoods, the autobiography recollects the vivid childhood memories of Jewish American author Kate Simon, who spent her early years between the ages of four and 13 in East Tremont. The neighborhood is located in the center of The Bronx roughly between north of Crotona Park and south of Fordham University, west of the Bronx Zoo, and east of the Grand Concourse. Her visualization of neighborhood and community in *Bronx Primitive* raises important questions about the meaning of decline in literature of The Bronx. What is the significance of this highly localized sense of place? What does it tell us about neighborhood, community, and sense of belonging as she is growing up? How does the story of her childhood revise the success story in the era of decline?

I argue that by framing the main character's localized experiences in the Tremont neighborhood as a story of struggle, empowerment, and success, *Bronx Primitive: Portraits in a Childhood* (Penguin edition) demonstrates how comparable crises and challenges can be overcome in the era of decline. Recent scholarship on *Bronx Primitive*, which has interpreted the memoir from predominantly feminist literary perspectives (Gagnier; Rishoi), will help to answer the question of how the experience of loss and decline can be the basis of a female success narrative in The Bronx by way of self-reliance, self-empowerment, and self-education.

The strong sense of neighborhood is already reinforced in the exposition of the book. The first chapter, entitled "Lafontaine Near Tremont," opens with a very detailed portrait of Tremont. The chapter title and the first sentence literally map the home turf of the female protagonist: "We lived at 2029 Lafontaine, the last house on the west side of the street from 178th to 179th, a row of five-story tenements that ended at a hat factory" (*BP* 1). The neighborhood is characterized as a mixture of residential and industrial buildings. By providing the exact spatial coordinates of the story, "2029 Lafontaine" Avenue, the opening showcases the importance of the local neighborhood for the narrator's identity.

With great precision, the female first-person narrator visualizes the richness of the place by including different types of buildings, modes of transportation, and groups of people in the first chapter. She describes the various types of architecture, such as "five-story tenements" (1), "Italian frame houses" (1), and "Irish houses" (8) where residents live. The neighborhood further offers various commercial buildings like "Mrs. Katz' candy store" (1), the "hat factory" (1), a "movie house" (2), "the barber shop where I went for my Buster Brown haircut" (3) as well as the retail area along nearby Bathgate Avenue which "was the market street where mothers bought yard goods early in the week" (3). The area also offers a variety of public buildings, such as the "public library" (3) and the school "P.S. 58 on Washington Avenue at 176th Street" (7), which provided Simon with different kinds of education. Simon points out how the "El" (2), an elevated train, connects the Tremont neighborhood with Manhattan and enables its residents to use the shopping and entertainment facilities downtown. Finally, Simon also includes the recreation area in nearby Crotona Park in her personal mapping which offers different opportunities for the residents, such as spaces for sports and recreation (3).

The detailed mapping constructs the surrounding in such a way that the reader is able to imagine it as a closely-knit urban community and share the narrator's enthusiasm. The qualifier "Mrs. Katz'" in the name of the candy store (1) suggests a personal connection between the owner of the store and Simon. In describing residential architecture with adjectives such as "Italian" (1) and "Irish" (8), the writer provides an insight into the cultural diversity of the district. She suggests early that Tremont was a functioning (lower) middle-class immigrant urban community which has a stable infrastructure and provides for everything that its residents need within a small perimeter. She re-constructs the neighborhood in such detail that it can be imagined even by an audience who is not familiar with this area.

In order to establish a close connection between the place of her childhood and the reader, Simon also uses indirect speech and a first-person narrative perspective in her autobiography. These literary strategies establish Simon's experiences as the sole source of her memories and make them appear as a very personal testimony which tightly links her individual memories to the urban environment. The focalization of the narrative through the eyes of a young girl underlines the function of The Bronx as a place of growing up and coming of age. As a result, the main figure that readers encounter is a young girl who reimagines the neighborhood as her own space. It is through Simon's experiences that readers are able to identify with her and this particular neighborhood in The Bronx.

Simon continues to zoom in on her family's apartment on Lafontaine Avenue in the opening chapter of *Bronx Primitive*. The family's "top-floor railroad flat" (3) is created as a personalized zone of memory by assigning each room a different character and meaning. The kitchen is not only the spatial center of the apartment, it is also the family center "where we chattered, ate, [and] fought" (4). In contrast to the much-used kitchen, the living room is "almost always unused" (5) and functions as "mother's art museum" (5) where the children are not supposed to touch anything. This humorous metaphor, for instance, suggests that the living room is an elegant and, because of the different objects, also a very valuable space that is dominated by the mother. Narrator Kate's warmest memory is the parents' bedroom where "my brother and I played most peaceably, most happily" (6). The family's bathroom is described as an ambivalent private space. On the one hand it is "a luxurious thing" (3) because it features the latest amenities of the era such as "a tub, a sink, and a toilet that didn't have to be shared with neighbors" (3-4). On the other hand, it is the "torture chamber" (4) where her father would beat her, exerting his violent masculine dominance over the young girl. The fire escape, "our viewing balcony down on the eventful lot we shared with Monterey Avenue" (7), also served as a "minute bedroom on hot nights" (7).

As each room is filled with different kinds of family memories, the narrator highlights the strong connection between the people and the place. It is in her home, the private space, where Simon's most intense memories are situated. The detailed personal and visual account of the home is an important aspect which helps the reader to identify with and connect to the narrator's experience already at the beginning of the autobiography. Literary scholar Christy Rishoi attributes this specific local perspective to the coming-of-age narrative which "is profoundly affected by a complex web of factors and experiences – geographic and historic location, gender, ethnicity, sexuality, class – that are far from universal" (138).

Tremont is by no means presented as a smooth, harmonic, or even nostalgic urban space. *Bronx Primitive* constructs a fabric of different conflicting cultural and ethnic identities in The Bronx. East Tremont consists of a heterogeneous neighborhood of (Eastern) European inhabitants, such as "Rumanian ladies" (8), "Hungarian men" (8), or the "daughters of Polish janitors" (8). Narrator Kate, for instance, distinguishes between her "Jewish-German-Polish-Greek-Hungarian-Rumanian side" (1) and the other side of the street dominated by "Italian frame houses" (1). She soon learns about the various territories: "As the street, the shops, the people became more familiar, there were also rules to learn" (8). Those rules include specific borders, boundaries, and geographical territories which are claimed by different groups in the neighborhood.

While ethnic groups fight over different areas, they are united in their dislike of the dominating social group, the white English-speaking Americans:

> The Jews stuck together, the Neapolitans and Sicilians stuck together, altogether apart from the northern Italians. Yet, in spite of momentary flareups, a mutter of anti-Semitism, "savage" thrown at a Sicilian, they clung to one another, arranging and re-arranging the symbiotic couplings of the poor and uncomprehending in confrontations with the enemy, the outsider who spoke English without an accent. (8)

The boundary is not drawn along the different ethnic lines, but along the competency in the English language. It is spoken by Anglo Americans, "[t]his confident, inimical enclave that spoke fast English and ate peanut butter sandwiches on white bread [and] sat at our edge of Crotona Park" (9). However, this Anglo American "enclave" is in a superior power position whereas the speakers of the accented English (native speakers of Yiddish, Hungarian, Romanian, Italian) find themselves in subordinate positions: Simon states how the Anglo Americans dominate the official authorities in The Bronx in their professions as "truant officers, visiting nurses, people from the naturalization offices" (9) and are therefore treated with distrust and suspicion by the various immigrant groups. Hence, in creating a boundary between the various nonnative English groups and Anglo American culture, *Bronx Primitive* establishes an interethnic relationship of migrant solidarity.

Similar to her Polish Jewish ethnic identity, the first-person narrator initially finds herself in a subordinate power position in the private sphere. She experiences several instances of domestic violence and sexual abuse. Her father beats her in the bathroom where "the swish of the strap becoming a burning scream through my whole body" (76). Her cousin Yankel "would appear in his underwear at our bedroom door" (123). Her father's niece Bessie was "as greedy for pleasure as for learning English" (125), abusing Simon's body for her own sexual desires. A friend of the family, Mr. Silverberg, molests her when they watch a Nita Naldi movie at Loew's Paradise Theatre (161-62). The first-person narrator is painfully reminded of her marginalized femininity as she is living in a space of permanent crisis, abuse, and rupture. Yet, in contrast to earlier writers of autobiographical narratives, she openly addresses those previously silenced issues of suppression and violence which have already been central to the feminist movement in the 1960s and 1970s (Rishoi 139).

Bronx Primitive presents different strategies of overcoming the various challenges situated in The Bronx. A first strategy is subversion, that is, to invert the existing ethnic, gender, and linguistic hierarchies. Simon subverts asymmetrical power and spatial relationships by marginalizing not the immigrants, but the native English speakers. The phrase *"Them* of the bewildering powers" (*BP* 9, emphasis in original) is such an example. The italicized personal pronoun *"Them"* refers to the English-native speakers. The pronoun homogenizes the entire population group as an entity and suggests that white Anglo Americans are the cultural Other and not the immigrant inhabitants. The adjective "bewildering," in addition, denotes the group as strange and distorted creatures. As a result, the author's own Polish Jewish background as that of a marginal immigrant identity is elevated. The writer Simon recreates The Bronx as a place of power and its people in charge of their own space.

In subverting this hegemonic perspective, Kate's subjectivity can be interpreted as being in what postcolonial scholar Gayatri Chakravorty Spivak calls a subaltern position in her essay "Can the Subaltern Speak?" (1988). Spivak defines the subaltern as marginalized groups, such as women or ethnic minorities (285). Those subaltern subjects speak up against hegemonic and colonial forces in a society. They are marginalized individuals who express their disagreement with a group's dominant power position and resulting colonial or hegemonic attitude. The character Kate, a Polish Jewish immigrant to the United States, constitutes such a subaltern voice. She expresses her dislike of the white Anglo dominance in The Bronx through her description of spatial relations and symbolically exerts control over the native-English speakers. She does not simply imagine different power hierarchies, but gains momentum through the symbolic appropriation of the urban space by subverting spatial relations. The East Tremont neighborhood therefore functions as a specific territory where recently arrived migrants win poetic battles over power positions and eventually gain self-confidence.

A second strategy of overcoming the challenges of the place in *Bronx Primitive* is female empowerment. The Bronx functions as a space where personal emancipation is possible. As narrator Kate "studied every landmark, every turning of our new surroundings" (7), she exercises power, order, and control over her situation:

> I was the queen of my block. No one but I knew it and I knew it well, each morning making a royal progress on my empty street, among my big garbage cans, my limp window curtains, my sheet of newspaper slowly turning and sliding in the gutter, my morning glory on Mrs. Roberti's porch vine, my waiting stoops fronting my sleeping houses; my hat factory on the corner of 179th Street, resting from its hours of blowing pink and blue and purple dye smoke; my Kleins, my Rizzos, my Petrides, my Clancys safely in bed, guarded by my strength and will. (58)

Although the East Tremont neighborhood appears as a little charming urban area which consists of an "empty street," "big garbage cans," and "limp window curtains," the quote clearly illustrates that Kate imagines herself as the "queen of the block" by appropriating the urban landscape with the pronoun "my." Assigning herself the title "queen" means putting herself in a superior, even aristocratic female power position while simultaneously elevating her immediate environment from a busy industrial urban area to a kingdom of royal possessions.

This strategy indicates a strong sense of ownership of the streets, buildings, and its people, and is reinforced by the fact that the narrative perspective is that of a child. By establishing a close connection to the neighborhood Simon grew up in, Kate's book appeals to a local audience in The Bronx of the 1980s for whom it offers ways out of dealing with crisis. On a larger scale, *Bronx Primitive* offers readers outside of The Bronx a narrative of inspiration and empowerment who experience similar conflict situations such as domestic violence, ethnic discrimination, or sexual abuse. The spaces and places of the Tremont neighborhood therefore do not just function as a setting, but they also provide the very foundations for Kate's and the readers' narratives of empowerment.

A third strategy of overcoming ethnic, gender, and class challenges in Tremont is everyday culture. Simon learns from what she sees in school, but she also finds much inspiration in the streets of her neighborhood, and, most importantly, by way of films (Rishoi 144):

> The brightest, most informative school was the movies. We learned how tennis was played and golf, what a swimming pool was and what to wear if you ever got to drive a car. We learned how tables were set, "How do you do? Pleased to meet you," how primped and starched little girls should be, how neat and straight boys should be, even when they were temporarily ragamuffins. (BP 44-45)

In the nickelodeons, inexpensive entertainment spaces where especially poorer migrants could turn to narrative respite from their daily surroundings, she learns about white Anglo American middle-class social and gender conventions such as "what a swimming pool was" or "how neat and straight boys should be." The narrator affirms Hollywood movies as educational media outside of established institutions such as schools which offer its young audiences valuable lessons on social and cultural norms, conventions, and values. At the same time, such movies reinforce the narrative of socioeconomic uplift for recently arrived migrants, such as the narrator Kate.

The writer Simon acknowledges the importance of movie theaters for Bronx residents and their local communities and economies. In the early twentieth century, The Bronx was home to many nickelodeons, movie theaters, and vaudeville houses, most importantly Loew's Paradise Theatre mentioned earlier, but also RKO Fordham or Keith's Royal Theatre (Ultan, *Beautiful Bronx* 34-35). Some of them were abandoned and torn down as a consequence of post-World War II urban renewal processes, but also due to the changing tastes and media consumption habits of audiences. Literary scholar Regenia Gagnier highlights the importance of early Hollywood cinema and especially of female starlets for Simon's personal development in that she "is explicit in her acknowledgment of 'the movies' as urgently needed cultural, and especially gender, training" (Gagnier 143). Simon's inspiration of early silent Hollywood cinema is further significant as it is a form of popular and converging culture which remains a central medium in American society throughout the twentieth century. As a relatively new medium in the early twentieth century, film allows the cinematic construction and appropriation of new ethnic, class, gender identities and communities.

Bronx Primitive suggests that the narrator gains confidence and knowledge of herself not necessarily by established institutions such as "P.S. 59" (*BP* 44). Rather the popular and everyday cultures and locations, such as movies, literature, neighborhood nickelodeons, theaters, and libraries, move support her identity formation. This also resonates with the genre of autobiography which provides the narrative framework for the story. While autobiography has been one of the longest-running forms of written prose in American history, female autobiography was not taken seriously by literary critics before 1970s postmodernism (Smith and Watson 4). Character Kate's autobiographic self-discovery echoes the increasing appreciation of female autobiography and popular and vernacular forms of literature.

The emphasis of popular and everyday cultures as an important means of learning outside official public institutions is also reinforced in the last sentence of her memoir: The narrator Kate ends her story as a more confident self in the third person by crediting and comparing herself to three immensely popular silent film actresses of the 1920s: "As desirable as Gloria Swanson, as steely as Nita Naldi, and winsome as Marion Davies, she was, like them, invincible and immortal" (BP 179). Swanson, Naldi, and Davies function as role models for the creation of Kate's individual femininity. By choosing the third person narrative perspective in the final part of the autobiography, the writer Simon symbolically elevates her literary self to the same level as these female American icons who embody success and empowerment in the early twentieth century. The writer's personal success story ends on a hopeful, optimistic, strong, and confident outlook on the future, an outlook which values the contribution of women in the history of popular media and resembles deeply American virtues such as success and upward mobility.

In addressing themes of violence, abuse, and power inequalities, *Bronx Primitive* differs from early twentieth century autobiographies that "sanctioned" such issues (Rishoi 147). Hence, Simon's education outside the school classroom differs from that of "earlier women, since tradition would have bound them to their mothers' sides to learn domestic arts" (137). As a result, the writer belongs to a new generation of female Jewish autobiographical writers who "provided a spectrum of positions on the self and its diverse claims as woman, writer, member of ethnic or gay community, and politically committed social actor" (Gagnier 146).

Bronx Primitive resonates with other autobiographical accounts of Tremont of that time. In the popular history book *The Bronx in the Innocent Years: 1890-1925* published by Lloyd Ultan and Gary Hermalyn, former Tremont resident George Diamond, for instance, sadly recollects the vibrant community and rich infrastructure such as bars and stores that used to be in the neighborhood – "[m]ost of them are now memories of Tremont" (Diamond 54). Both the characters of Diamond and Simon echo cultural critic Marshall Berman's mourning of the loss of neighborhood and community (295), but contrary to Simon's outspoken articulation of her hardships as a young immigrant woman, Diamond's romanticized account of the old days hardly addresses ethnic, class, or gender struggles. Unlike Diamond, Simon as an author firmly connects her past pains and memories with her present success as a young woman and writer.

Growing up in The Bronx of the 1920s enables the female protagonist to strive for a subject position which is marked by a transnational, transcultural (Welsch), and postmodern identity in the 1980s. The author's family's escape from the "Warsaw ghetto" (*BP* 12) to New York City results in the formation of her own "hybrid subject position" (Rishoi 134). Originally named Kaila after her mother's grandmother (*BP* 23), Ellis Island immigration officials changed the narrator's name to Caroline when she arrives in the United States:

> Because my Polish birth certificate said "Jew-child Carolina" I was dubbed and registered as "Caroline," a barbed-wire fence that divided me from myself throughout my school years. I hated it [...]. How we got to Kate I don't know. My mother must have sought it out to keep as clear as possible the link to her grandmother Kaila, not realizing how intensely Catholic a name it then was. Being serenaded as "K-K-K-Katy, my beautiful Katy" was a flattering bewilderment until I realized it was not written for me [...]. (23)

Once she arrived in New York City in 1916 as a four-year old girl, she is given a new name and identity by the authorities. While her new name Kate complicates her subject position by highlighting the tensions between her personal Jewish upbringing and her public identity, it also shows that it lacks a sense of definite, ultimate, and essentialist origin at the same time. Such seemingly stable and essentialist identity constructions are given up in *Bronx Primitive* in favor of "creat[ing Kate's] own identities" (Rishoi 147) While she describes the sometimes difficult navigation between the various names and identities as a "bewilderment," they open up a range of possibilities by allowing her to navigate between different societal ethnic, class, and gender expectations. As a result, the East Tremont neighborhood depicted in *Bronx Primitive* gains special importance as it serves Kate as a means to create and literally construct a new anti-essentialist identity because her old self has become under scrutiny due to the persecution and subsequent "exodus" (12) of her Jewish family from Europe. Her transnational and transcultural experiences then resonate with new (im)migration groups from the American South or from the Caribbean who faced similar difficulties in integrating into The Bronx life after World War II in particular and into larger American culture in general.

The narrator's stories of eventually overcoming the various gender, class, and ethnic challenges as a result of living in the Tremont neighborhood are closely connected to the generic frameworks of autobiography and the coming-of-age novel. Literary scholar Linda Anderson defines the literary genre as a "developmental narrative which orders both time and the personality according to a purpose or goal" (Anderson 8). Similarly, American literary scholar Gerri Reaves explains in her study *Mapping the Private Geography: Autobiography, Identity, and America* (2001) the connection of autobiography, space, and a personal identity: "[t]he birth of a spatial identity is concurrent with the birth of a psychological identity" (Reaves 15). Both quotes demonstrate that as a genre autobiography is closely related with space and place.

Christy Rishoi argues with regard to *Bronx Primitive* that this generic framework constitutes "an interpretation of memories, a construction of meanings that make sense of the individual herself in the historical, political, ideological, and discursive context of her life" (138). This autobiographic framework highlights the experience of the Jewish female writing subject as she faces different kinds of challenges in order to eventually succeed them in her life. It frames them as manageable incidents which can eventually be overcome by self-education, self-articulation, and self-empowerment. Hence, *Bronx Primitive* affirms that, first, they present not only a threat, but an opportunity for the protagonist to grow and learn, and second, the character's story then functions as a tale of survival which uses the first-person narrator's experiences in the Tremont neighborhood of the 1920s exemplary to symbolically empower the displaced and disenfranchised readers in The Bronx of the 1970s and 1980s. It then resonates with the contemporary age of decline as a manageable challenge that can be overcome and, most importantly, as an opportunity to learn, speak up, and grow.

Bronx Primitive affirms that Tremont in particular and The Bronx in a larger context was a site of major social and cultural transformations already in the early twentieth century. In the first half of the twentieth century, East Tremont consisted of predominantly Jewish inhabitants who could afford to move up from Manhattan's Lower East Side (Jonnes 4). In the wake of urban renewal, Tremont's southern part was razed and replaced by the Cross Bronx Expressway in the 1950s, which cut across the neighborhood destroying many homes, displacing many people, and fundamentally transforming the area in the subsequent years (Jonnes 122). Before the Jewish middle class left The Bronx after World War II, the borough was a hub of Jewish Eastern European culture in New York City and "*the* place for people who saw themselves and their children taking a step up the socio-economic ladder" (Ultan and Unger 78, emphasis in original). The Bronx was therefore a starting point for their version of the American Dream. The borough was not only the home to a grand cinema, Loew's Paradise Theatre, the Biograph film studio called The Bronx also called The Bronx its home. The importance of The Bronx as an incremental site in New York Jewish culture was further reinforced in a variety of shows and films such as the avant-garde film "A Bronx Morning" directed by Jay Leyda (1931).

Other novels and films and their protagonists that deal with The Bronx shed similar light onto the experience of Jewish migrants to the area in the first part of the twentieth century. In the first talkie, *The Jazz Singer* (dir. Alan Crosland, 1927), the main protagonist Jakie Rabinowitz shouts euphorically: "Mama, I'm rich! We're moving to the Bronx!" (Jonnes 37). Katie Gold, the mother of a lower-class immigrant family from the densely populated Lower East Side, is fascinated by the green Bronx Park when she exclaims in Michael Gold's novel *Jews Without Money* (1931): "[I]t's like Hungary! There is so much room, and the sky is so big and blue! One can breathe here!" (151). Bronx Park represents Katie's personal heterotopia which reminds her of her former home Hungary. The picaresque first-person narrator Harry Bogen in Jerome Weidman's novel *I Can Get it for You Wholesale* (1937), for instance, hopes for his personal Bronx-based success story as a worker in Manhattan's garment district. Molly Goldberg, the matriarchic heroine of the long-standing and highly popular radio program *The Rise of the Goldbergs* – on air from 1929 to 1945 and broadcasted as *The Goldbergs* on CBS television from 1949 to 1954 – undoubtedly shaped the national imagination of The Bronx as a predominantly middle-class Jewish borough in mid-twentieth century America. The TV show ended with "the family's move from a Bronx apartment to the suburbs [thus culminating their] integration into the American mainstream" (Hoberman and Shandler). *Bronx Primitive* recollects this theme of social upward mobility, the pursuit of individual happiness, and The Bronx as a mythic site for the formation of the American Dream of the early twentieth century.

The detailed mapping of Tremont mentioned earlier fulfils an important function with regard to the writer's success story. The writer Simon poetically rebuilds the neighborhood and addresses the challenges that were connected to the area during her childhood while the Tremont infrastructure was lost, communities were destroyed, and residents were displaced. In recreating a seemingly socio-economically stable urban area which is nevertheless dangerous for young immigrant girls, *Bronx Primitive* mourns and criticizes the loss of community, identity, and infrastructure against the backdrop of the contemporary destruction in the early 1980s. Kate's first-person narration through Simon affirms how those challenges of battles against abuse, violence, and discrimination can be a basis for self-empowerment in The Bronx. The autobiography therefore exemplarily discusses the challenges and opportunities of the inhabitants in neighborhoods affected by contemporary decline and social inequality by re-imagining the area's challenges and opportunities of the past. As a result, the two specific spatial imaginations of Tremont of the 1920s in the narrated time of the autobiography and the 1980s as the publication time converge with each other across space and time: the narrated Tremont neighborhood of the 1920s serves as a spatial signifier for the urban decline of the late 1970s. As the protagonist of the 1920s managed to overcome the challenges in the area, Bronxites in the 1980s will also succeed in overcoming urban, racial, and socio-economic challenges.

Yet, the challenges presented in *Bronx Primitive* are of a slightly different nature than the ones caused by urban renewal and so-called white flight. While the narrator's crisis in *Bronx Primitive* consisted of domestic violence and sexual abuse in an urbanizing neighborhood, the shrinking processes of the 1970s have larger socioeconomic causes such as structural racism resulting into poverty and crime. While Simon's challenges are presented as from within the neighborhood, the crisis caused by deindustrialization can rather be attributed to larger structural factors, that is, mistakes in urban planning or the neglect of authorities. While the problems are situated differently, the challenge to overcome them is very similar to Simon's success story. *Bronx Primitive* therefore speaks to the current age of decline in The Bronx as well and suggests ways of how to deal with it: by American virtues, such as self-reliance, self-help, as well as trust and optimism towards the future despite the hardships of the present.

The cover art of the 1982 Viking Press edition converges those two spatial imaginaries as well. In the foreground, the sepia color dominates as main filler in the author's name, as outlines of the title segment "Bronx Primitive," and in the photograph on the lower left-hand side of the cover. Sepia as a main color in lettering besides white connotes pastness, nostalgia, and reference to an earlier time. This idea is also reinforced in the ornamental typeface which echoes art nouveau, one of the dominant visual art and design movements in the early twentieth century when the narrative of *Bronx Primitive* takes place. The upper left corner of the photograph is decorated with an ornament which can often be seen in colorful artwork, lithographs, glass and graphic designs of the time. Hence, the visual design in the foreground of the cover relates back to a time in American and Bronx history marked by urbanization, industrialization, and growth. The simple black background starkly deviates from the bright colors and ornamental design as it symbolizes the present urban condition of decline. Taken together, the visual composition of the bright title, author name, family portrait, and playful white and beige font suggests a nostalgic look back to the beginning of the twentieth century and simultaneously disrupts the decline signified by the black background color which is quite unusual for original art nouveau designs.

While spaces and places are referenced in the 1982 Viking Press edition on the back cover only in a blurb on Simon's strengths as a writer, the 1997 Penguin edition superimposes a sepia portrait photograph of the author in front of the elevated train in the background. She is looking off to the right which suggests that she is looking for a way out of her old Tremont neighborhood, the space of her childhood memories. The title *Bronx Primitive: Portraits in a Childhood*, positioned prominently in the upper part of the cover, refers to the experiences of the author and the portrait photograph. The title "portraits" indicates that her experiences are not part of one coherent and unifying story line, but they are sketches and glimpses from her neighborhood which helped shaped her identity as a female Jewish immigrant child. "Portraits" also alludes to the visual account of the neighborhood as one of the main ways to deal with loss discussed earlier. The title further is reminiscent of other books, such as Joyce's autobiographical novel "Portrait of the Artist as a Young Man" (1917), or Henry James' *Portrait of a Lady* (1881) which also center on coming-of-age narratives. As the narrator sees herself as a cultural outsider who nevertheless belongs to this neighborhood, she declares herself "primitive." This metaphor highlights the narrator's subjectivity and her strong sense of belonging. It is also somewhat problematic because in claiming to be primitive or indigenous to the area, the immigrant writer symbolically eliminates the existence of Algonquians and other Native American tribes who had long left The Bronx before Simon arrived as an immigrant in the early 1900s.

Like many other Jewish American writers and artists, Simon had moved out of The Bronx by the time the book was published in 1982. During her career, Simon's oeuvre continued to highlight her strong interest in people, places, and the stories connected to them. She was "a writer of popular, literate and vivid travel guides" (Flint) on England, Mexico, Italy, and her home city of New York. Simon's experiences of reinventing her own identity growing up in The Bronx also have an important influence on her work as a writer. Critic J. H. Plumb argued that she revises the genre of travel writing by transforming "one of the dullest forms of literature [into] a brilliant work of art" (qtd. in Yglesias). She also published a sequel to her memoir *Bronx Primitive* entitled *A Wider World* in 1986 in which she recollects her teenage years in The Bronx and in New York City.

The writer's extradiegetic career proves the fulfilment of her own personal success story described in *Bronx Primitive*. To Simon, growing up in The Bronx was an important prerequisite for her future career as a writer and public figure. Overcoming the challenges of the neighborhood through virtues such as strength, resilience, and creative ways of learning renders her as an exceptional female character. The autobiography suggests that it was because, not despite, growing up in The Bronx that she was able to become who she wanted to be, which also enabled her to pursue her own take on writing and telling stories. Simon's autobiographic success story and her successful writing career symbolize the borough's potential to envision, narrate, and materialize its residents' personal success stories. In writing about the Jewish Bronx of the 1920s, *Bronx Primitive* re-interprets modernism's urbanization, immigration, and industrialization as important elements in the borough's postmodern resurrection.

The analysis of the first literary example, *Bronx Primitive: Portraits in a Childhood*, has shown that The Bronx is immensely important for the main character's personal success story. The visual language recreates and immediately personalizes the writer's home for the reader. The detailed mapping of the place is the specific feature of autobiography and coming-of-age genres both function not only as ways to rewrite and reconfigure the narrator's life, but also closely connect her experiences to this place that helped form her identity. As such, the narrative voice is that of a younger Kate who does not have an omniscient position but is on her subjective way of gaining knowledge about herself, her home, and the power inequalities in her immediate surroundings. Readers are able to relate to and empathize with Simon's experiences in the Tremont section of The Bronx, which includes different kinds of challenges and opportunities of ethnic discrimination, domestic violence, and sexual abuse in terms of her ethnic, class, and gender identity. Her open treatment of those challenges is striking as those negative incidents which come largely from within the neighborhood community have been silenced by earlier writers of autobiographies and autobiographical narratives. In functioning as an imagined literary space to discuss Simon's hardships, the Tremont neighborhood also offers the potential for the renegotiation of her own identity by means of subversion, empowerment, and education. Above all, The Bronx as a heterotopia presents challenges, provides a sense of ownership, and allows personal development. As a result, Kate imagines her Bronx as a space of personal empowerment and growth because of the various conflicts that occur there.

In remembering Simon's childhood years in the immigrant Bronx of the 1920s as a success story, *Bronx Primitive* symbolically restores the rags-to-riches story in The Bronx. It highlights the importance of places, personal interrelationships, and popular culture from the female protagonist's adolescence. The autobiography demonstrates that the narrator's tragic and traumatic experiences of growing up in The Bronx in the early twentieth century form the very basis of her female identity. Simon's autobiography centers on female subjectivity because her specific experience of growing up as a young girl gives her enough agency to pursue her career and take the freedom to do what she wants. Her identity formation is guided by virtues such as resilience, self-reliance, creative learning, and self-empowerment. Expanding Benjamin Franklin's iconic success story which affirms formal and informal education as key ingredients for success, *Bronx Primitive* celebrates early twentieth-century popular culture as important media of learning and inspiration for the protagonist's own success story. *Bronx Primitive*'s biggest contribution is certainly that it brings back the community and vibrancy that ceased to exist in the era of decline and is missing in the public imagination on the South Bronx in the late 1970s.

As the protagonist recollects how she overcame the challenges of the 1920s, the book simultaneously speaks to the era of decline in the early 1980s. It points to the fact that post-World War II deindustrialization and shrinkage, like early twentieth-century urbanization and industrialization, are manageable challenges if American narratives and virtues such as self-reliance, optimism, hope, and belief in a better future (Samuel 5) continue to be guiding principles. Simon's coming-of-age narrative in *Bronx Primitive* can be read as an allegory of the spatial resurrection in the era of decline of the 1970s and early 1980s.

Bronx Primitive strongly affirms that the Tremont neighborhood serves as a basis for the success story of the writer's later life as a feminist and popular writer of guidebooks and autobiographies. The literary work claims that living in The Bronx provides its residents and readers outside of it with the necessary skills to survive and eventually succeed. In other words, if you can make it there as a young girl, you can make it anywhere. Simon's book also speaks to a younger generation of readers, telling them that the struggle for survival has been around for a long time, but that conflicts are manageable and can be overcome eventually. She asserts also that one can be successful in overcoming white Anglo American male dominance – incidentally the people who are in hierarchical positions responsible for the decline of The Bronx after World

War II. The challenges Simon is confronted with help her to develop her own identity as a young Jewish woman who performs an anti-essential identity away from conventional gender expectations. In a sense, her personal story is an American success story by way of seeing decline as a challenge and opportunity for a new cycle of social upward mobility. To her, success means not so much hard work, economic success, and becoming rich, but growing intellectually as a person, becoming stronger, and pursuing one's individual goals.

This success story is striking because the declining Bronx was often excluded from the American Dream narrative and rags-to-riches ideology in the late 1970s (see Ch. 1.3). *Bronx Primitive* asserts that challenges are manageable by highlighting the individual as an agent of change. In elevating the individual as an agent to overcome crisis, the autobiography appeals to the notion of individualism, which is a long-standing value in American culture. It is therefore an American text narrated from an immigrant experience which engages in an American literary tradition and values even though it was published at a time when white suburban middle class did not consider The Bronx a part of an imagined American nation. Here, The Bronx is the setting for a female rags-to-riches story which means to manage, adapt, and respond to the challenges and threats that occur especially to women in the neighborhood, to survive, and to eventually succeed. Simon's autobiography questions the responsibility and the senselessness of the destruction in the 1970s while at the same time it is an inspiration for (local) readers to not give up. *Bronx Primitive* therefore affirms the belief in American virtues and myths such as the success story instead of critically interrogating the causes and consequences of decline, neoliberal capitalism, racial, ethnic, and sexual oppression.

The success of this post-industrial narrative can also be seen in the fact that *Bronx Primitive* has been published in the series Penguin Classics since 1997. In contrast to the novel *Growing Up Bronx* which will be discussed in the next section, *Bronx Primitive* has stayed in print affirming its topical empowerment narrative. Eventually, Simon's success story tells us about the multilayered meanings of this part of New York City, which is even more clearly illustrated in the next two literary examples, which emphasize that one 'had it made' once he or she 'got out.'

2.2 "I hoped we would not let happen to the entire world what we had let happen to The Bronx": Highbridge Masculinity, Jewish Humor, and the Global Dimensions of Devastation in *Growing Up Bronx* (1984)

Gerald Rosen's semi-autobiographic novel *Growing Up Bronx* (*GUP*) is concerned with The Bronx of the era of decline as part of a wider global network of personal interrelationships and transnational geopolitical events. Rosen, author of the anti-war novel *Blues for a Dying Nation* (1972) and the road novel *Carmen Miranda Memorial Flagpole* (1977), presents the coming of age of Danny Schwartz in the Highbridge neighborhood in the south western Bronx during the Cold War.

Although Rosen's fiction presents the borough as an adventurous urban territory roamed by juvenile gangs, critics frequently observe the novel's humor: Lloyd Ultan and Barbara Unger characterize it as a "humorous memoir" (Ultan and Unger 153), literary scholar Jerome Klinkowitz notes its "California comic style" (104), and *Library Journal* reviewer Rochelle Ratner critically comments on the writer "who is too self-conscious about being funny" (89). What is the significance of humor in connection to the borough's deindustrialization? I argue that *Growing Up Bronx* reconnects The Bronx to the American experience by foregrounding the borough's importance for the male protagonist's personal success story, by highlighting the global character of destruction, and by using humor to reinforce the critical tone of the novel towards decline and devastation.

The first chapter of *Growing Up Bronx* situates Danny in the center of the narration by introducing him and his birth date by way of a first-person perspective: "I was born on January 6, 1939. [...] I was born in the Royal Hospital on the Grand Concourse" (*GUP* 9). In preceding his own subject position when he states his birthplace "I call it The Bronx" (9), the narrator firmly anchors himself, his success story, and his life in his home of The Bronx. The narrative perspective establishes a close connection between the narrator, the place, and the reader through the use of the first-person pronoun and by localizing the subject in a closely demarcated space. This strong sense of belonging is therefore very similar to the narrative voice in *Bronx Primitive*.

However, the exposition slightly differs from Simon's memoir. While *Bronx Primitive* starts off by firmly grounding her narrative to the people and places of the Tremont section of The Bronx, *Growing Up Bronx* immediately establishes The Bronx as a deeply transnational space:

> The place into which I was born had been called by many names: The Jewish
> people call it the Diaspora, the land of exile and alienation. The Hindus call
> it maya, the veil of illusion. The Christians call it a vale of tears or a testing
> ground for the human soul. The Buddhists call it samsara, the ocean of birth
> and death. (9)

The Bronx here functions as a complex and multidimensional place marked
by global migration and part of wider networks of people, places, languages,
religions, and histories which all come together in the borough. References to
different world religions ("Jewish people," "Hindus," "Christians," "Buddhists")
and their respective meanings of The Bronx as a "land of exile and alienation"
or a "veil of illusion" establish the borough as a spiritual and mythical space,
yet at the same time, everyday place. The narrator Danny introduces his home
as a polysemic, transnational, and relational space.

Danny's vision of The Bronx as a transnational and relational space is a
result of his Jewish cultural background. He describes the borough's significance to the Jewish diaspora: "The Bronx was the third stop [after Harlem
and the Lower East Side] on the Jewish Oregon Trail which continued on to
a fourth stop in Yonkers and Mt. Vernon. The fifth and the final stop on this
trail was Jewish nirvana, also known as the Greater Miami area" (9-10). Referring to the Oregon Trail, a famous nineteenth century trajectory that enabled westward expansion, Danny humorously equates Jewish American immigrants with nineteenth century settlers and pioneers. Unlike the explorers
of the West, however, Jewish American elders end up in retirement homes in
the South. The narrator situates himself between those transcultural, interre-
ligious, and intergenerational networks of people and spaces ("the Diaspora,"
9) and the concrete local building where he was born ("Royal Hospital on the
Grand Concourse," 9).

The narrator continues to describe the Schwartz family residence in The
Bronx in relation to the larger family network as well. Their home base is
a "ground floor walk-in apartment of the building my grandfather owned on
Nelson Avenue" (11) situated on top of Blum's restaurant (11). Both of his grandparents escaped Jewish persecution and anti-Semitic pogroms in Austria and
Russia before coming to The Bronx from the Lower East Side (11). His maternal grandparents and aunt live next door to the Schwartz's. Similarly, uncle
Bernie and aunt Bessie "lived two blocks away in the grandest building in our
part of The Bronx – the Noonan Plaza" which is located nearby on 168th Street

(11). Other relatives live in Brooklyn, a borough which Danny ironically exaggerates as "the other side of the world" (10-11).

Growing Up Bronx constructs Highbridge as a tightly knit network of family and relatives spanned over the various local neighborhoods who are tied to different places in New York City and Europe. Literary scholar Jerome Klinkowitz highlights Rosen's emphasis on networks and relationships as "any subject matter, any object in the world, is not so much a thing in itself as it is a factor which generates a relationship – and that while the object itself may not be seized, the relationship can" (Klinkowitz 104). Danny's experience of growing up in Highbridge is therefore as defined by his relationship to the material urban space as it is by his relationship to his family and relatives.

The novel's relational approach to spaces and people extends to the level of the family's class identity. Danny's mother Ceil who invites comparisons to the Jewish mother figure self-identifies as a member of a higher social class: "According to my mother, she was not like the other mothers on the block – she didn't serve us stale food. Only fresh food. Fresher than any other mother on the block" (*GUP* 72). His grandfather and later his father Sid who was stingy and "knew the value of the dollar" (11) both own real estate that earn their loved ones a regular income and establish the family as middle class. While the female narrator Kate is walking or riding the subway in *Bronx Primitive*, Danny's parents own a car, which underscores their Jewish middle-class background.

The Schwartz family is as exceptional as Highbridge. Danny introduces their neighborhood by joking about its working-class character from his family's middle-class perspective: "Dostoevsky, in our neighborhood, was a name that evoked suggestions of Einstein. Of the super-human mind" (144). Highbridge, probably named after the landmark High Bridge aqueduct spanning the Harlem River, used to be an "old Irish neighborhood" (Jonnes 4, 344; Ultan, *Beautiful Bronx* 15). Situated further west than Kate Simon's East Tremont neighborhood and predominantly south of the Cross Bronx Expressway, Highbridge borders to the east on Jerome Avenue and to the south on the Yankee Stadium. It is a geologically interesting area as it slopes down the Harlem River to the west creating a relatively steep bluff. Highbridge was home to Bronx Borough President James J. Lyons (Ultan, *Northern Borough* 253) and playwright William Gibson (Ultan, *Northern Borough* 275). While it was a destination for lower class Irish immigrants from Manhattan in the early twentieth century, it became part of the South Bronx during the era of decline (Jonnes 8). The novel constructs his family as exceptional from the rest of the predominantly lower working-class (Irish) neighborhood the south western Bronx of the 1940s and 1950s as they are economically better off and geographically more connected across space.

In that sense, *Bronx Primitive* and *Growing Up Bronx* conceptualize the urban space in a quite different way: Even more than in *Bronx Primitive*, the opening chapters of *Growing Up Bronx* situate The Bronx within a greater fabric of family networks as well as personal and diasporic journeys. This difference has two reasons: the book's genre and the narrator's gender. First, as an autobiography, *Bronx Primitive* aims at an authentic re-collection of the neighborhood community by reconstructing the urban fabric. By authentic I mean that the narrator reframes her life story in the autobiography as a truthful account of what happened. However, such autobiographical works are (wo)man-made stories who emphasize one aspect of a life story while silencing other aspects (see Anderson). The novel *Growing Up Bronx* presents a much less localized and more transnational perspective of the urban space as it allows the author to focus more on the people and relationships.

A second reason why Danny of *Growing Up Bronx* and Kate of *Bronx Primitive* have such different spatial experiences of the borough is their gender. As a girl, Kate is raised in the tradition of domesticity although she eventually escapes from this traditional Jewish immigrant context. Danny roams the public space already as a boy, which makes gangs and territories more important in his process of growing up. *Growing Up Bronx* affirms the area as a highly gender-separated space where boys/men control the public and girls/women control the private spheres: "Boys and girls had been raised pretty much separately in our neighborhood. We were like two universes, matter and antimatter, which existed in the same space but were largely invisible to each other" (123). This separation is also reinforced by the family structure. Danny's mother Ceil and his grandmother Yettie are "dedicated to the hearth and family" (10), while the men in the family involved in public business activities. As a result, Danny spends much time in the various public spaces of The Bronx and engages in more territorial conflicts in contrast to the female narrator of *Bronx Primitive*, where danger and violence is mostly, if not exclusively, presented in the private sphere.

Although *Growing Up Bronx* constructs The Bronx as a relational and diasporic space, it nevertheless manages to establish a strong connection between the writer/narrator, his neighborhood, and, ultimately, the reader. This strategy of localizing manifests in several ways. First, *Growing Up Bronx* bears autobiographic features of the life of the author. Gerald Rosen was born around the same time as its fictional hero Danny Schwartz, in December 1938. Both author and fictional narrator grew up in The Bronx and left it to study engineering (Fagan). The fathers of both, author and narrator, owned a liquor store in Harlem, and both figures have a criminal uncle with the name of Lenny who also lived close by (Fagan). Danny's specific whereabouts are unclear at the end of the narrative whereas Rosen obtained his PhD in American literature and moved to California to become an English professor at Sonoma State University (Fagan). This is also where he published *Growing Up Bronx* with the independent publisher North Atlantic Books based in Berkeley. The book therefore is inspired by Rosen's own experiences and memories of his family in The Bronx. His localizing strategy is insofar unique as he contributes to the discourse of the declining Bronx from the far away West Coast.

The second, stylistic, reason for the localization of The Bronx can be found in the fiction's language and narrative perspective. The book is written from a first-person perspective predominantly in the past tense, a tense which is widely used in autobiography and popular fiction. This narrative perspective stresses the author's own experience and personalizes it through his voice, gaze, and language. The past tense suggests that the narrator looks back on his life from a later point in time. The tense shifts to the present in the "Epilogue" chapter when the narrative flashes forward to how Danny's family moved out of The Bronx in the subsequent years. It highlights the importance of the past and affirms the retrospective character of Rosen's prose text in order to establish a close connection to a place that does not exist any longer. At the same time, this shift to the present tense creates a 'lived experience' on the recipient's side as it suggests an immediate connection between the novel, the reader, and the spatial imagination of The Bronx. Bookending past recollections of events with 'real-time' storytelling helps to affirm the non-fictional feel and texture of the previous narrative. Those narrative features provide a subjective point of view to Danny's coming-of-age narrative in the mid-twentieth century Highbridge neighborhood and help novel's audience to identify with his experiences.

Thirdly, the coming-of-age narrative focuses on the main character's childhood, teenage, and maturing years in that particular place. The narrated time of 38 chapters ranges from Danny's birth to his departure for college. The chapters concentrate on his childhood and youth years of the 1940s and 1950s in The Bronx. A central aspect of this coming-of-age story is how the boy copes with the various challenges in the neighborhood and how they help form his identity. Very similarly to Simon's East Tremont neighborhood, the place takes up a central position in the protagonist's coming-of-age tale. Rosen recreates the Highbridge neighborhood as a space of territories and gang violence. Growing up on Nelson Avenue means for Danny learning about the existence and demarcation of boundaries, as well as about the consequences when violating their rules:

> I slowly expanded my territory, no longer wary of going into the territory of Ronoso on the next block, or frightened of the Shakespeare Tong.
> On the other hand we still had our territorial limits. If your new range was slightly larger, the people on its fringes were older and more dangerous. And even in our own neighborhood, there were still pockets of forbidden territory. (100)

The neighborhood is composed of Jewish, Irish or Catholic "gang[s] of kids [each] led by a lunatic" (53). The Latino Ronoso (Spanish for "dirty") gang foreshadows the ethnic change about to come when Puerto Rican and Dominican immigrants move into The Bronx after World War II. Those gangs claim the urban space as their own and fight for it if someone violates their territorial limits. Going to school or to the movies, for instance, is a dangerous activity for Danny because he needs to navigate through this – at least for him – adventurous urban space. Moving successfully across this environment consisting of many different kinds of borders and boundaries requires a detailed knowledge of the permitted and 'forbidden' territories.

Danny reacts similarly to the violence that occurs in the neighborhood than Kate in *Bronx Primitive*. While Kate compensates the domestic abuse by shifting her focus on her own individual success story, Danny views the violence as an athletic challenge that its inhabitants need to overcome in the process of growing up:

> One thing we learned in The Bronx was the sheer power of naked, unadulterated, irrational force. You learned early that if you were going to get through life, you were going to have to pay certain tolls. There was a point beyond which you had to let go of ideas of justice and notions of dignity and individual rights and give up a lunch or a jacket if you wanted to keep your teeth. (95)

Danny's childhood and teenage years in The Bronx are a means of learning to cope with violence and repression. Speaking in the first-person plural pronoun "we" in this quote, he acknowledges the young people's experiences in the streets of The Bronx as an essential testing ground for the formation of their masculine identities as well as an important means of education for the challenges in their future lives. The boys gain crucial knowledge about how to survive territorial and/or power struggles as well as how to acquire the necessary survival skills such as mindfulness, assertiveness, and eventually self-confidence. Overcoming those challenges distinguishes the neighborhood boys from other young male Americans: "We could come to feel that The Bronx might not be everything one could desire, but we took pride in our belief that '[a] Nebraska guy wouldn't last here a week'" (81). For both Danny Schwartz and Kate Simon growing up in The Bronx is a highly specific and place-based learning process that prepares the Jewish kids for their struggle for a successful adulthood in the larger white American culture.

Despite the fact that The Bronx is presented as a mostly rough, gang-infiltrated, and adventurous territory in *Growing Up Bronx*, the urban space appears generally safe. This is mainly due to the widespread use of humor as a coping mechanism. Scenes that contain violence are counteracted with a humorous catharsis that diminishes their seriousness or gravity and gives them an ironic twist. For example, the narrator compares Danny's choleric, violent, and chaotic father Sid to a "crazed lobster" (157). When the patriarch tries to beat up his son after he returns from secretly attending a party at 3 a.m., Danny manages to keep him out of his own bedroom (156). After this incident, Danny ironically comments on how his parents deal with violence: "They were quite a Tin Pan Alley team in the old soft shoe of domestic abuse" (157). Tin Pan Alley refers to a form of early twentieth-century Anglo American popular music. By calling his parents a "Tin Pan Alley team," the narrator ridicules their uses of force to gain respect as less threatening. This wide use of a humorous literary style was also noticed by *New York Times* reviewer Martha B. Tack in 1985 who observed that "[t]he scenes of violence [are] the novel's funniest." The violence in the novel is therefore neither seriously threatening nor does it come across as hostile due to the use of humorous comments, slapstick elements, and one-liner jokes. Humor thus serves as a strategy of survival and empowerment.

Teenager Danny eventually comes to terms with the violence in the area. As the novel was published in 1984, its comedic elements can also be read as a literary coping mechanism in the era of decline of the 1980s. Klinkowitz argues that humor serves as the main device to structure the "void" of subject matter in Rosen's work (91). He defines the void as topics which are difficult to describe and which can be accessed mainly by way of relationality, as for instance, through love (1-2). Klinkowitz observes that this phenomenon is especially evident in postmodern literature: "As structurings of the void progress into the 1980s, comedy becomes only more important, beginning with a rhythmic joy of inflected language and triumphing with pure comedic effect, unsupported by autobiography, ritual, or other fabrications bridging the void of subject matter" (91). Loss presents an empty space which is equally difficult to describe and to access as love. It encompasses Danny's Jewish heritage which is marked by the loss of family, relationships, and community during and after the atrocities of the Shoah. It also speaks to the loss caused by deindustrialization and shrinkage which resulted in the decline of the neighborhood and the displacement of people. On an abstract level, Rosen's widespread use of humor can then be seen as a way of dealing with decline and loss in the 1970s and 1980s (see Berman), a way of making the unspeakable tangible, by generating a catharsis to those destructive and traumatic events. Danny then bears similarities to a self-made man who manages to succeed his various challenges in the neighborhood. Together with his quirky family, his humor works to present Highbridge of the 1940s and 1950s as a space of manageable challenges and eventually, it paves the way for the narrator's individual success.

Similarly to *Bronx Primitive*, *Growing Up Bronx* establishes The Bronx of the 1940s and 1950s as a place of many established and creative educational opportunities. Danny attends the famous De Witt High School, where many Modernist writers and artists had gone to school, such as the Harlem Renaissance poet Countee Cullen or the TV producer Paddy Chaefsky who directed the award-winning film *Marty* in 1954. Although going to the movies presents dangers because of the various gang rivalries, cultural/art activities and philosophical movements provide an important intellectual stimulus and informal education for Danny. He discovers modernist literature (Virginia Woolf's *The Waves*, 144) and music (Béla Bartók, 144), theater, ballet (108, 142-44) as well as existentialist philosophy (142): "This opened up a new world to me" (108). American novelists form "a new family" (108) and listening to popular rhythm and blues music (153) constitutes the "beginning of my connection with an underground of people in America who were reaching out for something electric and vibrant" (153). Learning about a broad range of arts, culture, and philosophy eventually helps forming his masculine Jewish American identity and for his life outside of The Bronx. Like Kate Simon, Danny Schwartz learns as much through official school education as through his own self-education, self-reliance, and by pursuing his individual interests. Both texts emphasize the importance of the arts and popular culture for their protagonists to learn about gender, race, and class issues in American culture. Both texts also affirm that good education was possible in The Bronx and that learning about the transatlantic and transnational intellectual heritage was the key for an individual rags-to-riches story as it helped form the characters' and especially Danny's identity as a critical observer of socioeconomic processes.

At the end of the fictional narrative, Danny leaves The Bronx in order to pursue his career in the American business world. His reason for leaving Highbridge at the end of the novel, however, is not necessarily connected to the gang violence as readers might expect. His mother Ceil embodies this fearful attitude towards The Bronx as she is most concerned with how the violence in the streets affects the adolescence of her son. When Danny is beaten up by Ikes' gang, she hysterically shouts at father Sid: "'Look at this boy! Look at what they did to him! He's a brilliant boy. He doesn't need this. We gotta get him out of here. Do you hear me? We gotta get him out of here!'" (175). Ceil's hysteric reaction to Danny's beating up reveals his unique perspective on the neighborhood. Compared to his humorous narrative, she is extremely serious and fearful about the space. Her reaction also exposes the hypocritical double standard of the family which blames the outside for the disintegration of the family rather than failed communication processes within it.

In fact, Danny decides to leave The Bronx because of the death of his beloved and admired aunt Rose in the final chapter 38 (183). Initially an outgoing feminist and open-minded character admired for her Eleanor Roosevelt impersonations (28), Rose becomes an increasingly tragic figure whose health condition slowly yet steadily and severely deteriorates as the novel progresses. She suffers from several illnesses, such as depression (88) after an abortion to which she was forced by her family. She is also diagnosed with multiple sclerosis (179) and, finally, suffers from insanity (182). This diagnosis is quite common for women who did not 'fit' into the narrow roles ascribed to them by patriarchal society. She eventually passes away because she does not fit into the traditional Jewish family structure and the conformist climate of 1950s American society. Danny even compares her to Henry James' tragic sister Alice (152). After Rose's death, Danny realizes: "My Aunt Rose was gone, and it was time for me to leave as well. It was time to leave The Bronx and to go off on my own, seeking a wider world, a world of larger scope and greater possibilities" (183). Aunt Rose's health issues can be read as a metaphor for the neighborhood's rigid and reactionary moral value system which prevents her from forming her own female empowerment narrative in the spirit of Kate Simon from *Bronx Primitive*. As Rose does not fit in this conformist climate, her death affirms that Danny's most important reason for leaving The Bronx are the failure of close relationships within the family rather than the dangerous territories outside.

The conformist heteronormative attitude of the neighborhood is also reinforced in the tragic figure of 'Pop' Goldman, a single man and trainer of Danny's basketball team "The Philadelphians S.A.C. of The Bronx, New York" (84). Goldman is from the East Bronx. It is an older geographical term which refers to the poorer section in the south eastern part of the borough before it was merged into the 'South Bronx' in the 1970s (Gonzales 7). Coach Goldman is a substitute father figure for Danny, but the Highbridge fathers treat him with suspicion because he allegedly molested boys (*GUP* 168-74). Without an official legal representative present ("The trial was a farce," 169), the fathers exercise self-justice and find 'Pop' Goldman guilty of alleged child harassment (170): "Perversity in Greenwich Village was one thing, but this was The Bronx!" (169). They eventually ban Goldman from Highbridge (169-70) affirming it as a typically conformist hetero-normative neighborhood in the 1950s where traditional sexual identities are lived. While the narrator reinforces the idea of Highbridge as a heteronormative middle-class neighborhood, he imagines the East Bronx as a poorer and tougher part of The Bronx. The poorer East/South Bronx is established as the sexual Other which foreshadows its image as a problematic space before its downfall in the 1960s and 1970s.

Paradoxically, Danny's rags-to-riches story outside of The Bronx as a result of the loss of relationships is made possible by his family. His abusive father, the flat character Sid, initially resents his son going to college, but he is delighted when he hears that his son wants to become an engineer even if it means the father has "to go into debt and struggle" (177):

> And my father, who not only never traveled, but who didn't even own a goddamn imitation-leather toilet kit, my father who would walk ten blocks before he would pay a penny to park in the street, my father would beg and borrow thousands of dollars, and, for whatever reason, would in fact get me out of The Bronx, and would give me the opportunities an education afforded, the education that he had never been able to obtain. Yes, my mother and my father would sacrifice whatever it took to see that I got a fair chance to make something of myself in my life.
> As my Uncle Lenny used to say before he was arrested and died in prison, "Go figure baseball!" (184)

Danny's professional achievement is possible primarily because of the restless efforts of his stingy and frugal father, which he repeatedly addresses in the above quote and, to a lesser extent, because of his mother. Sid hopes that his son's career will shine back on him and his social status in the neighborhood (177). He even works so hard at his Harlem liquor store to finance his son's college education that he eventually drops dead at the age of 56 (185). Contrary to Kate Simon's individual female success story, this narrative affirms the entire family's unlimited support for the next generation to pursue their version of the American Dream. The final chapter ends therefore on a high note which affirms that the Highbridge neighborhood is a place where the dream of social upward mobility comes with a price. Living there prepares Danny for his future life as an engineer. The novel suggests that The Bronx is the borough where a success story is possible because there is a network of people who rely on each other and help. This positive climax of the novel is finally completed with uncle Lenny's funny running gag and one-liner joke "Go figure baseball!" (184).

The end of *Growing Up Bronx* differs from that of the autobiography by an epilogue which re-establishes a transnational and inter-relational perspective as it emphasizes the senselessness of destruction. The "Epilogue" which is separated from the 38 previous chapters flashes forward in time. Danny looks back at the place and people from an unspecified point in time and space alluding to Rosen's new life in California. The last segment of the novel highlights the stark difference between Danny's adventurous adolescence in Highbridge and his current situation after he left The Bronx. He narrates how the Schwartz and Farber families left The Bronx: his father died, his mother moved to Miami, and his uncle Bernie and aunt Bessie to Southern California (185-86). Returning to the theme of transnational interconnections established in the first chapter, the narration comes full circle as the "Epilogue" marks the completion of the family's journey out of The Bronx.

Most importantly, the "Epilogue" as a separate chapter functions to connect Danny's coming of age of the past with the decline in The Bronx. While the main part of the novel focusing on the 1940s and 1950s is predominantly written in a past tense, the "Epilogue" comments on the arbitrary nature of the wave of arson in the 1970s using the present tense: "As for myself, I don't go back to The Bronx often. No one I know lives there anymore, and much of The Bronx is in ruins: a violated, bombed-out, enrubbled sad hulk of a city" (187). Here, Danny's two imagined spaces collide: the functioning Bronx of Danny's fond memories and the devastated Bronx of the present. Particularly devastating is the loss of family relationships and personal networks when Danny notes that "[n]o one I know lives here anymore." Equally devastating is the destruction of the urban fabric which he describes by way of visual language and naturalistic adjectives such as "violated, bombed-out, enrubbled [, and] sad." Humor or irony are completely absent in this passage which underscores the seriousness of the situation. The comparison of the destruction caused by urban decline and the loss Jewish people experienced in the Shoah help establish a relationship between those who survived.

While the last chapter ended on a high note, Danny's observations on the declining Bronx appear even more shocking: They address the absurdity of the destruction which does not only involve the downfall of an urban fabric, the disintegration of a community, but, first and foremost, the idea of The Bronx as a starting point for a male Jewish American rags-to-riches narrative. *Growing Up Bronx* takes the success theme further than *Bronx Primitive* because the readers learn about what has happened after the narrator leaves The Bronx. It thus addresses The Bronx in the era of decline more directly as the protagonist's return triggers questions about the arbitrariness of destruction and capitalism's responsibility for it.

The final moments of the "Epilogue" contain the most important message of the entire novel. The decline of The Bronx is not an isolated case as often heard in public discourse, but it is part of a larger movement of abandonment across the globe:

> When I realized this [that he "descended from pioneers" (187)], I was forced to recognize that I too was engaged in a long and dangerous voyage from which there was no turning back. I was signed on for a life and death journey into the nuclear age.
>
> My generation did not have to go to sea. On August 6, 1945, the sea came to us.
>
> It was going to be a dangerous trip, but somehow I continued to hope that we could make it through. I hoped we would not let happen to the entire world what we had let happen to The Bronx.
>
> Somehow I knew, if we were brave enough, we could make it through to a land we had not yet been able to imagine. (187-88)

Danny comes back to the transnational perspective by allegorizing the devastation of The Bronx with that of the nuclear age during the Cold War in the Japanese city of Hiroshima. He criticizes both events as arbitrary and senseless actions which leave people displaced, lost, and in great trauma which is passed on to the next generations. This transnational dimension is further re-inforced in his statement that "the sea came to us." It alludes to famous Civil Rights activist Malcolm X's expression, "We didn't land on Plymouth Rock, my brothers and sisters – Plymouth Rock landed on *us!*" (Haley 201, emphasis in original). The narrator contextualizes the fate of The Bronx with a global his-tory of oppression (and resistance) of people of color by white supremacists.

In his final sentences, Danny takes up the idea of the voyage and mobility from the book's opening. He envisions a utopian space where people would not be displaced and urban landscapes destroyed, "a land we had not yet been able to imagine." The epilogue, thus, functions as the novel's main concern which connects Jewish persecution, the nuclear age during the Cold War, and the destruction of The Bronx in the age of decline as senseless and unneces-sary human actions destroying places, leaving people displaced and trauma-tized. The stylistic change from a humorous to a serious narrative voice in the epilogue makes this matter even more urgent.

The book's focus on the loss of neighborhood, home, and community in the era of decline is also reinforced by its cover illustration as it only features a young man in front of a pale white background. His gaze, clear and firm with his mouth closed, is directed to the reader and suggests a thoughtful and melancholic attitude because the former home of his family has been destroyed. The white background can be interpreted as the void, the loss of the young man's former neighborhood caused by the wave of arson in the late 1970s leaving him only with memories. This attitude is further reinforced by the brownish coloring reminiscent of the nostalgic color sepia which is also the dominant color theme in the cover of *Bronx Primitive*. The cover lacks any reference to the novel's humorous literary style, but the young man's body language stresses that growing up in The Bronx results in a self-confident attitude. The novel's title *Growing Up Bronx* therefore suggests that The Bronx as a place takes on a central role in his coming-of-age narrative as it presents those particular challenges and the familial and communal support systems the self-made man Danny eventually overcomes, which prepare him for his professional career as an engineer outside of the borough.

Growing Up Bronx converges *Bronx Primitive*'s memory discourse on The Bronx in a similar way. Both texts can be categorized as 'stories of survival,' empowerment, and success which reimagine The Bronx in the era of decline by a first-person Jewish American narrative perspective, including the auto-biographical feature of the respective authors. These narrative perspectives al-ready demonstrate that The Bronx was a starting point for social upward mobility in the early- and mid-twentieth century in spite of the fact that it was a place of various individual and social challenges. Both texts highlight the fact that growing up in The Bronx is an important building block of their characters' rags-to-riches narratives as they depict self-made heroes and heroines who succeed in overcoming various challenges in public and private spaces such as gang violence, discrimination, domestic abuse, and molestation. Their experiences of growing up and learning from school, popular culture, and art prepares them for their individual pursuit of happiness outside of the borough. Both texts therefore strongly elevate the function of The Bronx in the era of decline as a space where individual identity is formed and where important 'survival' skills, characteristics, and virtues are acquired to eventually succeed as immigrant children in American society. *Growing Up Bronx* and *Bronx Primitive* constitute powerful literary counter discourses to the public perception of the early 1980s when The Bronx was neither imagined as a place of home nor as a place of opportunity for many Americans.

Yet, there are also differences between the two books with regard to the use of humor and the scope of decline. Humor eases the violent sequences in *Growing Up Bronx* and paves the way for the protagonist's coming-of-age narrative. First, it enables the identification between him, his neighborhood, and the reader. Second, it underlines the boy's adventurous character. As a result, Danny comes across as a youthful and picaresque hero who manages the various challenges he is faced with in his immediate surroundings. American historian Joseph Boskin argues in that regard that while American culture has suffered from many kinds of crises that question the American project, "in each instance an incongruous humor informs the circumstance and reaffirms the Dream's magic. A national comic vigil has constantly highlighted the optimistic" (23). Even though the novel is much more critical of the political, social, transnational, and economic forces of destruction and decay, humor affirms the novel's optimism, stabilizes the narrator's situation, and enables his success story.

Growing Up Bronx criticizes the causes and consequences of the era of decline in the 1970s by integrating urban shrinkage processes into larger societal and geopolitical contexts. It stresses the importance of various personal relationships, such as family networks, sports teams, or street gangs, and mourns the loss of those communities in the wake of de-industrialization. Therefore, the loss of a close family member, and not the territorial violation of street gangs, is the reason the protagonist decides to leave. The novel's re-imagination of The Bronx as a system of interrelated familial and personal networks has repercussions on the story's message: Growing up in The Bronx is an exceptional experience where a specific Jewish masculine identity is formed, but the fate of the neighborhood during the era of decline in the 1970s is not. *Growing Up Bronx* links the destruction of The Bronx with global geopolitical, transnational, and diasporic events in the twentieth century such as consequences of slavery and the Jim Crow era, the Shoah, and the bombing of Hiroshima, where millions of people were innocently victimized, traumatized, and killed. As all of those events were informed by white supremacist thinking, Rosen therefore criticizes political, economic and other social elites for arbitrarily taking into account death, murder, and trauma for their highly questionable local and global power plays.

Linking the destruction of The Bronx with the Shoah in Europe, the oppression of people of color in the US, and the atomic bomb drop in Hiroshima, Rosen's novel critiques the capitalist logic of efficiency which lead to destruction and displacement of people and communities in other parts of the globe. The book's link to historic world events is somewhat hyperbolic as residents and communities have not faced similar systematic destruction in The Bronx, but they suffered destruction as a result of a capitalist logic of post-war urban renewal which aimed to create more efficient urban mobility and make New York City more competitive on a national and a global stage. Because The Bronx' destiny is interlinked with other events of destruction in the world, Danny's success story in *Growing Up Bronx* becomes even more dramatic, urgent, and exceptional.

All in all, Gerald Rosen and Kate Simon 'write back' to their Bronx of the past from a different time and from different places and spaces. They respond to the era of decline in the 1970s and early 1980s by highlighting the importance of those spaces for their personal success stories thus assigning them new functions. At the same time, Rosen and Simon both wrote their narratives when they established their lives outside of the borough: Rosen as an English professor in California and Simon as a travel writer in other parts of New York and the world. Writers and their fictional main characters have often joined the white middle class in leaving The Bronx after World War II when so-called white flight and suburbanization fundamentally changed socioeconomic circumstances and demographic composition of the area. As a consequence, they and their characters display a distanced attitude towards The Bronx. The next example, *The Old Neighborhood*, presents a third literary approach to the declining space as the protagonist not just grows up there and leaves but returns to The Bronx in his later life.

2.3 "I was trading in my dreams of the fifties for a new beginning": Kingsbridge Memories, Jewish American Masculinity, and Post-Industrial Well-Being in *The Old Neighborhood* (1980)

At first glance, *The Old Neighborhood* (*TON*, Linden Press edition) shares similarities with the two works discussed earlier. The semi-autobiographical novel *The Old Neighborhood* was written by Jewish American writer Avery Corman. Corman is probably best known for his divorce drama *Kramer vs. Kramer* (1977) which was famously adapted for the big screen with Dustin Hoffman and Meryl Streep, receiving five Academy Awards in 1980 ("52nd Academy Awards"). Like *Bronx Primitive* and *Growing Up Bronx*, it remembers the hero's Steven/Stevie Robbins childhood and early teenage years in The Bronx from a Jewish American perspective.

However, Corman's fiction differs from the earlier literary texts examined especially with regard to narrated time. While Kate left The Bronx for good at the end of her autobiography and Danny comes back only briefly at the end of the novel, Steven physically returns to the declining Bronx at a later stage of his life. This extended temporal frame in which the novel follows the protagonist's return to The Bronx results in its different meaning in the age of decline. It opens up questions about the place's significance for the narrator when he lived in the neighborhood as a young boy and what it means to him when he returns as a middle-aged man. Moreover, the importance of the past and present in dealing with the main character's identity crises affect the story's success narrative. *The Old Neighborhood* reconnects The Bronx to the cultural narrative of success by highlighting that the borough is a place of perpetual spiritual renewal as it not only helps the male protagonist to grow up but also to grow old. As his personal destiny can be interpreted as a metaphor for The Bronx' spatial destiny, the novel demonstrates how spiritual regeneration involves the reconsideration of existing ideas of growth and economic dimensions of the success story.

At the beginning of the novel, the first-person narrator Steven describes his home on Morris Avenue in the west Bronx as a middle-class retreat:

> We lived in the Kingsbridge Road-Grand Concourse section of the Bronx in a red brick building on Morris Avenue. Flamingoes caroused on the wallpaper in the lobby and art deco nymphs were painted on the elevator door of "Beatrice Arms," named for the landlord's wife, Beatrice. The building's most

distinguished citizen was The Dentist, who had an office on the ground floor, [and] the smell of ether lingered in the lobby. (11)

The building evokes the feel of a rather wealthy multi-family residence with an elevator as a sign of modernist technology, decorative paintings in the lobby, and its name "Beatrice Arms" bears royalist connotations. The property name "Beatrice Arms" evokes associations of coats of arms typical for wealthy medieval English and Irish family clans. The verb "to carouse" in the personification "flamingoes caroused" (11) is a poetic expression for drinking and suggests a similar majesty of the lobby's interior. Steven elevates his family's social status to the middle class because they "were the only people in the building to read *The New York Times*, not held in high regard in the neighborhood, as it did not have horse-racing tips or the comics" (14). The Robbins are an educated family who live in rather well-off circumstances as the apartment's interior "was decorated modestly, bare wood floors, mahogany pieces, wing chairs and a greenish tweed couch in the living room" (14). Although the narrator describes the character of their apartment as "modest," the family owns valuable objects and high-quality materials in the living room ("mahogany pieces"). The opening of the novel establishes a close relationship between the material space and immediate surroundings of Steven's home and the people, their community spirit, and the larger geopolitical context of the 1940s.

Steven introduces the Morris Avenue/Grand Concourse area as a cohesive community that stands united during World War II:

In the neighborhood, the sense of participation, of being part of a nation at war was palpable. [...] It was a working-class neighborhood divided between Jews and Irish Catholics. [...] But the religious issue generally was set aside during those years, Jews and Catholics were in the Big Fight together and on the killing of Christ it was acknowledged that, at the very least, the event was pre-war. (16)

The protagonist describes his home as a multi-ethnic area where the war context serves as a uniting force across the different ethnic and religious identities. Cultural differences are set aside in favor of the idea of the American nation at war that everyone belongs to: "There was a feeling that the people in the neighborhood had been through something together" (19). Thus, the prose postulates that the war had a homogenizing effect on the different population groups in The Bronx. As the narrator remarks, this strong sense of community "was special and profound and I have never forgotten it" (19). It shapes

Steven's childhood memories of the 1940s and is also the most decisive appeal that brings him back to The Bronx in the decline era at a later point in the text. Similarly to *Bronx Primitive* and *Growing Up Bronx*, *The Old Neighborhood* weaves The Bronx together with greater global, transnational, and geopolitical tendencies.

The Old Neighborhood strongly mediates the protagonist's experience in The Bronx by way of the autobiographical mode. First, the novel is semi-autobiographical as inspiration for it came after Corman had visited nearby St. James Park in 1977 (Sullivan BR6). The story is relayed by the male narrator Steven Robbins who grew up in The Bronx like Avery Corman. Corman, a Jewish American writer, was born in The Bronx one year after Steven, in 1935. Both Corman and Robbins started out in the field of advertising in their youth (Sullivan BR6). *New York Times* journalist Dinitia Smith concludes that he "depicts something of the lost world of his Bronx childhood" ("Following Up"). Like Gerald Rosen before him, Corman's personal connection to the borough shapes his imagination of the space.

Secondly, the two novels are similar with regard to the use of the past tense, characterizing it as a testimonial of the narrator's experiences. *The Old Neighborhood* narrates Steven's memories from childhood to his mid-1940s. Only the last section of the final chapter changes to the present tense when Steven provides an overview of his current situation after he opens an antiques store in Manhattan following the divorce of his wife Beverly. This late change to the present tense confirms the importance of Steven's past memories and experiences in The Bronx for his current identity.

Thirdly, *The Old Neighborhood* combines autobiography with coming-of-age strategies. It captures Steven's struggle of growing up in his environment which is a dominant theme in many autobiographies and coming-of-age stories (see Ch. 2.1 and 2.2). He remembers his difficulties in getting out of The Bronx and in integrating into 1950s and 1960s professional life. After graduating from college, Steven unsuccessfully sends "letters to thirty-six New York advertising agencies" (35). When applying for jobs, Steven encounters that the predominantly working-class class perception of The Bronx presents a disadvantage in the Manhattan advertising world he wants to get into: "I was ashamed of the place where I lived. Was there anybody at the McCann-Erickson agency, or any Madison Avenue agency, who lived in a neighborhood like mine? I hated the fact that I had to put a Bronx address on my resume. I was convinced my address alone disqualified me" (37). The lower-class stigma of a Bronx zip code constitutes an entrance barrier to the elitist white American-dominated advertising industry. Steven is marked as an outsider: "I may have wanted to get away from my background, but I could not escape my background" (35-36). This statement resonates with similar ideas of The Bronx as a working-class district in *Bronx Primitive* and *Growing Up Bronx*. All of these protagonists, Kate, Danny, and Steven see their Bronx home as a rough testing ground in the formation of their personal identity and their coming of age. Comparing himself to the advertising agents on Manhattan's Madison Avenue, Steven concludes that he "had never felt so low-class and poor" (31). According to the coming-of-age genre conventions, The Bronx background is first a challenge, but eventually provides an opportunity in his career and professional success story.

The biggest difference with regard to the coming-of-age theme within the framework of decline consists of *The Old Neighborhood*'s extension of temporal relations. While *Bronx Primitive* and *Growing Up Bronx* end their stories in their protagonists' arrival to adulthood, *The Old Neighborhood* narrates Steven's development from the 1940s to the 1970s after he left The Bronx. The text condenses 35 years of narrated time into the first eight chapters which resemble his personal coming-of-age and his professional career as an advertising specialist. They feature Steven's childhood and teenage years in The Bronx, his bumpy search for a job in the advertising business in Manhattan as well as his eventual success as a renowned copywriter in California where his Jewish working-class background is an advantage. He gets a job as a copy writer because of the fact that he is a witty and smart "street kid" (40) from New York City: "I had a job. I was getting out of the neighborhood. I had wanted so desperately to find a job in advertising and could not – because of my background. Now I was being hired because of my background" (40). His successful departure from The Bronx is possible because the West Coast stands for a more open-minded and democratic work attitude than the hierarchical Manhattan marketing world. The Bronx upbringing which results in a street-smart attitude and witty sense of humor prepares him for his career in the California advertising business. Steven's professional success story also shows that the meaning of The Bronx varies according to geographical context, but also that it has different meanings for different people. This approach resonates with the idea of The Bronx as a relational space discussed earlier in *Growing Up Bronx*.

Steven's career is accompanied by his personal success story. He meets his future wife, Beverly, who is upper-class "California Jewish" (48), and they evolve into a family of four, with their two daughters Sara and Amy. The West

Coast thus allows Steven to pursue his individual rags-to-riches story which consists of a professional career in advertising and starting a family. Steven achieves economic and personal success according to what is generally envisioned as the pursuit of happiness after World War II. His California dream which includes a heterosexual marriage, a nuclear family, a house in the suburbs, and a white-collar job nevertheless resembles a common, picture-perfect, and utterly conformist post-war idea of the American Dream. The relocation of the novel's plot to California has therefore important repercussions on the hero's identity and the representation of The Bronx in the age of decline. It allows readers to follow Steven's escape from New York as an upwardly mobile young man, his achievement of this social position in California, and his return to The Bronx when the foundations of this sociocultural status are shaken.

The first eight chapters provide a prelude to the protagonist's midlife crisis which leads him back to the declining Bronx later in the novel. The narrator even makes a self-referential comment on his success narrative by saying "the story should end right here" (74). Steven's crisis consists of professional as well as personal transformation processes as they return to the tristate area in 1969 (70) and buy a house in suburban Long Island (68):

> I was in the house, reading the report, when Amy bounded past me wearing her latest button, "Save the Whales."
> "Fuck the whales!" I said to myself, under my breath.
> She stopped in her tracks.
> "What did you say, Daddy?"
> "I said, Fuck the whales. You're saving whales and I'm sinking into the sea."
> "Oh, Daddy – don't be so ethnocentric."
> They grow up to call you names that don't even make sense. I sat with "The Homosexual Market in America" and she went off to save whales. (105-06)

In his private life, he witnesses a generational change which is expressed by the growing environmental awareness of his teenage daughter Amy who becomes an environmental activist and mocks her father by calling him "ethnocentric." Steven is also increasingly alienated in his role as husband by his wife Beverly's increasing professional success which accelerates her emancipation from the traditional gender role as a domesticated wife and dedicated mother.

In his professional career, Steven has to cope with the change of the advertising business "from the old line white Anglo-Saxon Protestant character of the agencies" (70) to a new focus on "ethnics" (70), "young people" (70), and, as indicated in the quote before, to an increasingly important sexually diverse consumer base. Steven, member of an ethnic group himself, has become an authority in his job as an advertising executive. The changing advertising market constitutes a challenge for his old power position as a heterosexual white male. He deals with those personal and professional changes through humor, which functions as a temporary stabilizer for his masculine identity crisis.

Steven's crisis is informed by the socio-cultural changes of American society between 1960 and 1970, such as environmental awareness, counterculture, second-wave feminism, Civil Rights, and the gay liberation movements. These changes leave him disoriented as he metaphorically refers to himself as "sinking into the sea." Dissatisfied as head of his own Manhattan-based Robbins and Tolchin Advertising Agency, his wife Beverly having her own career, and his daughters growing into a new counter-cultural teenager generation, Steve undergoes a crisis of his masculinity which is embodied in his "middle-aged paunch" (80). He projects his professional and personal crisis onto his former home of The Bronx which he remembers as less troubled, more communal, and more stable than the present. The extension of the novel's time frame beyond Steven's supposed fulfillment of his professional and personal success story allows the reader to witness his return and the subsequent transformation of The Bronx.

The second part of *The Old Neighborhood* suggests that Steven *can* work through his identity crisis by returning to his former home. Chapters ten to 16 extend the narrated time to the summer of 1979 when he returns to the declining Bronx. Here, his personal and professional and professional troubles coincide with the borough's ongoing urban crisis. Walking in his old neighborhood which has been transformed into the north end of the South Bronx, Steven observes different stages of decline:

> I continued along the Grand Concourse, walking slowly, trying to absorb the sensations, worried that I was about to come upon a row of condemned buildings, burnt mattresses in the street, cars abandoned and stripped – my childhood neighborhood desecrated. But this section of the Bronx, north of Fordham Road near Kingsbridge Road, was not blighted. I reached Poe Park, it seemed the neighborhood was still predominantly Irish Catholic and Jewish. (137)

He expects different degrees of devastation but notices that there are still some pockets of integrity, stability, and continuity. The Bronx presents itself as "shabbier, somewhat dirtier" (135), but it is "still a functioning urban neighborhood" (137) which is generally safe and has a working economic infrastructure. Perhaps surprisingly, it bears little of the "sensations" and "the photos I had seen of the South Bronx" (137), by which he alludes to the dominant discourse of the era of decline discussed earlier (Ch. 1.3).

Stevie even compares the area in The Bronx with his new residential home in the affluent community of Great Neck on Long Island and comes to the conclusion that "[e]ven on a warm summer day the pulse was more active than anything I had known in the suburbs" (140). He experiences a worn-down place which still bears a vibrant street life. Compared to dystopic news media reports of the 1970s which imagined The Bronx as burned-out and dehumanized urban territory, Steven's narration suggests that there are still places which are less affected by shrinkage and devastation. Steven's destiny personifies the destiny of The Bronx because his personal crisis as a middle-aged man epitomizes the spatial crisis as a result of socioeconomic restructuring processes. As urban development happens in waves, life also consists of ups and downs. Since some Bronx neighborhoods are intact, there is still hope for the area and room for urban development. Likewise, Steven's crisis of masculinity can be overcome by rethinking his goals in life, his take on growth, and his understanding of success.

As the devastation of the area is a metaphor for Steven's psychological state of being in a midlife crisis, the search for his memories leads him to revisiting his old apartment building, the Beatrice Arms. Here his past and the neighborhood's current situation conflate. The change in the neighborhood can be seen in his description of the entrance hall, which was already mentioned to in the first chapter:

> I stopped in front of Beatrice Arms and I shuddered from the impact of seeing the building again. [...] I stood in the vestibule checking the names on the bells. I did not know anyone. The entrance door was locked and I waited for someone to come along. A little boy walked out and I went inside, the flamingo wallpaper was gone, the walls were green, the elevator door with the art deco nymphs was now painted with black enamel. (138)

In the present time, the building resembles a fortress with the closed entrance door. Its former elegance indicated earlier by the personification of carousing flamingoes is gone. The rich art nouveau details are pragmatically and plainly painted over with the monochrome colors black and green. The former residents have moved away, signifying the larger post-war population shift from

European-born working and middle classes to Southern-born African Americans and Puerto Rican-born working classes (Gonzales 109).

In comparing the place of his past with the present condition, Steven projects his own warm childhood memories from the 1940s and 1950s Bronx onto the urban space. He takes his memories even further when he rings the doorbell of his old apartment. He encounters the current tenant, a "sturdy-looking" (*TON* 138) police officer who lives there with his family. Treated with suspicion by the new tenant who greets him with the question "Are you a burglar?" (138), Steven is eventually allowed to enter and rediscovers a drawing he had hidden in his bedroom when he was a boy (139). His encounter with the new tenant affirms that his old neighborhood is unsafe and its current residents are suspicious towards strangers. As he is initially mistaken as a criminal, he has to invest more effort in order to reestablish connection to his former home. In having Steven rediscover his old drawing, Corman strikingly highlights the continuity of his former area which is often associated with the destruction of continuity, the loss of history, and the absence of any place which some people could call home.

In *The Old Neighborhood* the past gains a more significant role for the narrator than in the previously analyzed *Growing Up Bronx*. The former temporarily reintegrates Steven Robbins back into the area whereas in the latter Danny Schwartz has moved on with his life and is disconnected from his former home. In *The Old Neighborhood*, Steven's return to The Bronx is a means to come to terms with his present identity: "When I stepped out onto the street I became dizzy with the flood of memories" (135). The re-visiting and re-imagination of his childhood and the memories of his youth located in this neighborhood provide him with strength and stability even though he is initially viewed as an outsider and treated with suspicion.

Steve's return to The Bronx has a stabilizing function for the middle-aged protagonist's identity formation as well as for his declining neighborhood. He actively helps rebuilding it when he starts to work at Fisher's candy store (157), a store he used to go to when he was a child. Owned by a Greek American owner (141), Chris Anton, Steven helps to transform and renovate the store according to his childhood memories:

"Chris, excuse me for meddling." I finally said to him. "But this store – it lacks detail."

"Detail?"

"Things. Items. Nickel-and-dime items, quarter items, dollar items. Things in cases and hanging from cards. Penlight batteries, rubber bands, ballpoint pens. Things that people don't know they need until they see them." (150)

Stevie's suggestion of how to re-create the candy store as a place of his past symbolizes his back-to-the-roots mentality. Going back to The Bronx helps him come to terms with his class background and the meaning of the borough, which initially was an obstacle when applying for jobs in the downtown advertising world. He accepts that his wife wants to get divorced as well as that his daughters are growing up, and he understands the value of memories for his own identity development. Reintegrating into the declining Bronx therefore helps him to come to terms with his own past and his new masculine identity. Eventually, Steven creates a new sense of belonging in The Bronx. Engaging with the past includes not only his return to his former home but also his re-engagement with and a re-creation of the working-class culture of The Bronx. As *New York Times* journalist Christopher Lehmann-Haupt remarks in his review of the book, for "most urban Americans there is no old neighborhood to go back to" (C30). Given that Steven is able to work through his crises by returning to his old, albeit changed, neighborhood, this is particularly salient.

Returning to the old Bronx, even though the area suffers from downfall, nevertheless has a healing effect for Steven's shattered identity and perhaps also for the urban community. This is probably one of the most important functions of The Bronx in this work of fiction. It is therefore not just a point of departure for the people who grew up there as seen in *Growing Up Bronx* or *Bronx Primitive*. In *The Old Neighborhood* the place is first and foremost a destination for a spiritual regeneration: Steven comes back to his former home in order to move forward.

The Bronx of the decline era is also the place where Steven finds out what he wants to do with the rest of his life. Fisher's candy store provides Steven with a concrete example of how to re-configure his professional identity. It signifies a different stage in the American economic system, namely a small-town, pre-Fordist, and the retail-oriented economy of the 1940s and 1950s. Fisher's re-establishes The Bronx as a place of small-scale, locally-owned economy before the arrival of global capitalism. Working at the privately-owned store contrasts the increasingly mushrooming fast-food chains which pose an entrepreneurial threat. Owner Chris criticizes his disloyal costumers: "They come in here for newspapers with their Big Mac containers in their hands. It's insulting" (149). The privately-owned store faces stark competition by globally-run (but nevertheless American) fast food restaurants, but selling products at the candy store is a 'hands-on' activity for Steven in contrast to selling slogans and creating ads in his advertising agency. He even invents his own sundae called "'Stevie's Special'" (160) which shows that he has power over the production process and creates something physical and immediately consumable. Returning to The Bronx gives Steven an important inspiration for his post-crisis life and for his re-integration into the economic system.

The Bronx as a space of reconfiguration has fulfilled its function when Steven's personal regeneration also leads to a professional rehabilitation. In the second-to-last chapter of the book, Steven leaves the neighborhood a second time after experiencing "cabin fever" (206-07): "My link with the neighborhood as I had once known it was broken with Sam's passing. The new people I had met were leaving [...]. I needed to move on, to leave the neighborhood – just as I had done twenty years before. Only this time I was not ashamed of who I was, and where I came from" (209). Similar to *Growing Up Bronx*, the hero's reason for leaving The Bronx is once again the death of a close person, his long-term friend Sam. His passing symbolizes the loss of all people who left The Bronx for good as well as the loss of community which marked the neighborhood's initial appeal and uniqueness. Yet this time Steven leaves his former home proudly and spiritually renewed because he accepts who he is and where he comes from.

In the novel's final moments, Steven puts his renewed personal and professional spirit gained in The Bronx into practice. He opens an antiquity shop on 75th Street/1st and 2nd Avenues in Manhattan's Upper East Side which he calls "The Old Neighborhood" (213). The shop is a continuation of the candy shop as both engage in the same mode of production, distribution, and the same way of dealing with the past and heritage of a place. This time, however, Steven is in charge. In buying and selling objects which he calls "nostalgia pieces" (211), the connection to the memories of his neighborhood is expressed in a variety of antiques from the 1940s (212-14), which have a certain price attached to them and can thus be cashed in on. Hence, Steven reintegrates himself into the capitalist production and consumption cycle by incorporating the past in his very own business even though he earns less money than before. He reveals, now in the present tense, that "I am learning to live on less income" (219) and explains his new identity as "a kind of custodian of people's memories" (219). Steven displays American qualities such as inventiveness, optimism, and pragmatism and recognizes that many people along with him rediscover the importance of their past. He eventually creates a business which allows him to pursue a job similar to that of his father in the 1940s and 1950s. Buying and selling antiquities allows Steven to see how other people attach emotions to old objects while cherishing his own attitude towards his life through such objects.

In cherishing the past and framing Steven's old neighborhood as a source of identity re-configuration, Corman's novel resonates with a particular *zeitgeist* described by Marshall Berman in *All that is Solid Melts into Air* (see Ch. 1.2). This post-modern sensibility emphasizes the reinforcement of the past for one's own identity formation in the present and constitutes an important shift in contemporary American culture in the 1960s and 1970s. Berman explains the distinction to the previous period: "At a moment when modern society seemed to lose the capacity to create a brave new future, modernism was under intense pressure to discover new sources of life through imaginative encounters with the past" (332). While modernists believed in the present and the future as a source of cultural inspiration and innovation, the so-called 'new modernists' had to learn to come to terms with what they have and how they were required to remember the past modes of their life (Berman 332). This rediscovery of the past is therefore connected to the rediscovery of spaces and places that played a decisive role in this past. The post-modern attitude then also means to reconsider one's own take on growth and success. The modernist belief in urban progress was increasingly criticized and came under scrutiny, especially in the context of The Bronx. In re-imagining his past in terms of his own identity and his sense of spatial belonging, Steven undermines the dominant ideas of progress which privilege the present and the future.

This re-appreciation of the past also translates to the book cover of the Linden Press hardcover edition. The central object is a beverage container on a marble-colored counter in the bottom part of the cover illustration beneath the book's author and title. The illustration indicates an indoor space, probably the candy store. The traditional milk shake container might contain his own Stevie's Special, or perhaps an egg cream, which he prepared for his wife after their separation (186). It captures the time and space of Stevie's identity reconstruction. It references his job at the candy store, which is concerned with producing materially consumable goods such as milk shakes instead of immaterial products such as advertising. This 1950s style glass indicates a shift back from capitalist corporatist postindustrial production of slogans and ads to an earlier, smaller-scale production. The marble counter conveys the illusion of financial success as marble signifies wealth and status. Steven gains ownership of the product again which signifies the small-town appeal and his longing for the past in his old neighborhood. The fact that there is a product on the marble counter leads to the conclusion that the book cover celebrates a traditional idea of The Bronx, affirms small-scale employment, and idealizes material industrial production.

The cover illustration reinforces the quasi-universal character of the story. The fading light orange background without any clearly recognizable sense of place suggests that *The Old Neighborhood* could be set anywhere and that readers could connect their own memories to the book (see Fluck, "Funktionsgeschichte"). This attitude already mentioned in the beginning of this chapter is also reinforced by the blurb on the jacket: "This is a novel for everyone who has ever left a place to be someone else, to do something else" (front flap, back flap).

Both fictional texts, *Growing Up Bronx* and *The Old Neighborhood*, feature such a single-color background in their cover art. Both take up a rather universal perspective on The Bronx in contrast to the autobiography *Bronx Primitive*. This universal appeal is kept up in subsequent editions. Instead of referencing a particular urban space, early 1980s Bantam and Double Day paperback editions feature a family portrait on the front cover and the slogan "go back to where the dreams began." The design of the Linden Press hardcover can therefore be interpreted as the symbolic void of meaning which is created by decline and as an allegory of the vanishing of communities which simultaneously affirms the importance of home in the wake deindustrialization everywhere in the United States.

The Old Neighborhood reevaluates this void by claiming that the success story does not necessarily consist of material growth but of spiritual growth. Steven's reconfigured pursuit of happiness no longer results from material wealth or a perfect marriage, but from the achievement of personal inner satisfaction. His reexamination of his own masculine identity foreshadows the narrative of well-being which became a dominant cultural narrative in the 1980s in which "people seek to be faithful to the true inner self, and success is imagined in terms of developing a sense of well-being" (Betsworth 81). One can of course criticize this strategy of idealizing the decreasing living-standards of the main character and the book of being too nostalgic or pathetic. However, this strategy is a worthwhile thought-experiment which *New York Times* journalist Christopher Lehmann-Haupt called an "extremely appealing fantasy" (C30). The novel suggests that a revised rags-to-riches narrative consists of accepting one's situation even if individual well-being leads to less material wealth and living with what one has for people who have already realized their personal success stories.

To conclude, in *The Old Neighborhood* The Bronx of the decline era therefore functions as an urban space where an individual regeneration process can happen. Corman's novel suggests that the hero's identity crisis can be overcome by returning to his old neighborhood. Reintegrating into The Bronx helps him to come to terms with his memories where he creates a new sense of home, belonging, and meaning. Steven's life story thus personifies the spatial destiny of The Bronx. As Steven manages to overcome his personal crisis by accepting his past and his aging masculinity, The Bronx also manages to overcome its spatial crisis. The self-made man's return to The Bronx allows him to gain strength again for a new phase in his life where he eventually returns to become an empowered entrepreneur. Because The Bronx helped the protagonist to grow up as a teenager and grow old as a middle-aged man, the borough adapts qualities of perpetual spiritual renewal. Thus, the story challenges common assumptions that declining urban contexts are no longer places of home, history, and heritage.

The Old Neighborhood achieves the revision of the success narrative stylistically by extending the timeframe of the novel. In contrast to the other works examined in this chapter, *The Old Neighborhood* follows the protagonist out of the borough and back in. Thus, the transforming urban landscape in The Bronx is tied to the transformation of the hero's personal identity which happens both elsewhere and in The Bronx. Compared to Simon's autobiography *Bronx Primitive*, Corman's novel develops a sense of place especially in the latter part of the book when the protagonist's personal reconfiguration takes place. In the earlier two stories, the modernist Bronx prepares the protagonists for the world lying ahead.

The Bronx in *The Old Neighborhood* is therefore a space where the rags-to-riches story is revised. Corman's text suggests that one possible strategy of dealing with decline is to adjust the individual meaning of the rags-to-riches story from purely material and economic parameters to individual ones of personal happiness and well-being. The novel thus questions the neoliberal capitalist ideology of global unlimited growth and large-scale material achievements which guarantees ever more wealth. Pointing to its grim consequences especially for local communities, the novel envisions, perhaps too optimistically, a return to a privately owned locally-grown businesses as a strategy of coping. This revised, highly individual, and euphemistic success narrative propagates an idea of relational growth and personal pursuit of happiness where less can mean more. Decline in the novel forces people and ideas to change while leaving larger social structures untouched.

Indeed, the strategy seemed to resonate with reviewers in the early 1980s. *New York Times* journalist Jack Sullivan notes that the book made it to the "The Times Bestseller List" in December 1980 selling over 60,000 copies in its first three months, from September to December 1980 (Sullivan BR6). Some reviewers are intrigued by its 'back to the roots' mentality (Lehmann-Haupt C30; Miner 15). Taking *The Old Neighborhood* as an example of midlife-crisis literature, theologian Jim Conway identifies several challenges in his Christian self-help book *Men in Midlife Crisis* (1997) that men in the midst of midlife crisis have to deal with, such as work, family, and the body (71-74). Although Corman's novel has not been republished since the 1980s, its main themes resonate with the decline of the Great Recession. It comes therefore as no surprise that the online store *Amazon* republished the manuscript as an e-book in 2013 and Avery Corman published a similar memoir entitled *My Old Neighborhood Remembered: A Memoir* in the following year.

Finally, *The Old Neighborhood* engages in a tendency similarly to *Bronx Primitive* and *Growing Up Bronx*, where popular Jewish American immigrant authors utilize literature as a medium to re-frame The Bronx as an American space and re-examine the success story as a personal and flexible cultural narrative.

2.4 Conclusion

Literature reconnects The Bronx with the cultural narrative of the success story in the era of decline. The autobiography *Bronx Primitive: Portraits in a Childhood* and the two novels *Growing Up Bronx* and *The Old Neighborhood* recollect the borough's immense contribution for their characters' individual success stories. *Bronx Primitive*, for instance, localizes the female protagonist Kate's experience by closely weaving it to certain streets, buildings, and her own private space. As Kate gains control over her neighborhood and its sociocultural challenges in her coming-of-age narrative, she gains control of her female identity. The novel *Growing Up Bronx* establishes a sense of place by way of a first-person narrative perspective that draw on the writer's experiences during the Cold War. The Bronx even functions twice as a space of overcoming individual and collective challenges in the semi-autobiographic novel *The Old Neighborhood*. Steven returns to his former home of The Bronx at a later age in his life. Kate Simon, Gerald Rosen, and Avery Corman all recreate the 'lost' Bronx of their past from a localized and highly personalized narrative perspective. They honor The Bronx as a home where their personal success stories began.

The localized memory discourse of The Bronx expresses the writers' search for home, roots, and one's own past in the wake of various socioeconomic crises of the 1970s (Berman 333). All of the writers revisit The Bronx of their childhood and emphasize personal spaces, such as their homes, streets, and communities. They are "obsessed with the homes, the families and neighborhoods they left in order to be modern in the modes of the 1950s and '60s" (Berman 332). In revisiting the past communities and spatialized memories, Simon, Corman, and Rosen create a symbolic continuity and envision possible coping strategies for their own, their communities', and their borough's future.

All three of these literary narratives highlight the ongoing appeal of the success story. For example, in *The Old Neighborhood* Steven's return to The Bronx affirms the boroughs' function as a space of individual regeneration and identity reconfiguration. The books affirm that The Bronx has been a place of successfully overcoming various crises in the past to suggest that it will continue to do so in the future. On the one hand, these books empower their protagonists and readers by showing that crises are frequent and multidimensional. On the other, Bronxites manage to overcome challenges by learning from the past and by growing into stronger human beings in the future.

The autobiography and the novels indicate that there are alternatives to conventional understandings of the success story. While the main characters highlight the role of formal and institutionalized education, such as schools, apprenticeships, and libraries, informal education teaches them equally valuable if not more important lessons on how to become successful in American society and culture. By watching, reading, and listening, reflecting, and appropriating, the protagonists learn from their role models and encounter and rehearse new ways to participate in American society.

While material wealth is certainly important to the characters' success stories, the books also suggest immaterial and personal parameters. *Bronx Primitive* highlights the narrator's female empowerment as an important component for achieving success. *The Old Neighborhood* affirms that success does not necessarily mean commercial, professional, or material success, but that it has spiritual dimensions where less can mean more, i.e. personal well-being. *Growing Up Bronx* suggests humor as a strategy of coping and conflict resolution. Becoming who you are or who you want to be is more important to the writers than pursuing purely socioeconomic measures of post-World War II success.

But the books are by no means romanticized, naïve, and overtly nostalgic accounts of the 'old days.' More than the Jamesonian sensibility of postmodern nostalgia which expresses a longing for a seemingly better past (Jameson 19), the characters are successful because they voice, reflect on, and manage to overcome the struggles presented to them. This also strongly corresponds to Berman's observation of a post-modern sensibility in which the artists are not nostalgic, but "bring to bear on their past the selves they have become in the present, to bring into those old homes visons and values that may clash radically with them – and maybe re-enact the very tragic struggles that drove them from their homes in the first place" (Berman 333). The novels and autobiography affirm that the characters become successful because they managed to overcome the struggles, challenges, and problems in their neighborhoods and communities. Growing up in The Bronx allowed them to practice necessary survival skills and allowed them to obtain American virtues, such as self-reliance, self-determination, resilience, humor, and optimism. Thus, the elderly Jewish American writers subvert the dominant decline discourse often found in news media and journalism which dehumanizes The Bronx at the expense of residents of color who had to endure the era of decline.

The writers' remembering of their individual success stories corresponds strongly with a larger tendency in Jewish American culture since the 1970s in which members of this ethnic group achieve their own American Dream. Editors Jules Chametzky, John Felstiner, Helene Flanzbaum, and Kathryn Hellerstein explain in their anthology of Jewish American literature that

> Jewish Americans in this period have found themselves into the cloth of national identity. As the last vessels of institutionalized anti-Semitism disappear and isolated incidents of anti-Semitism decline, American Jews continue to rise to high levels in politics and culture. As secretaries of state, senators, presidential advisers, producers and directors, Nobel prizewinners and owners of championship sports teams, American Jews have participated in all aspects of mainstream American culture. (979)

The authors emphasize that Jewish Americans have increasingly taken center stage in American culture and society since the 1970s. Jewish American writers, some of whom were born and raised in The Bronx such as Irving Howe and Cynthia Ozick, have dominated the American literary market. The Nobel

Prize for Literature was awarded in 1976 to Saul Bellow and in 1978 to Isaac Ba-shevis Singer, whose novel *Enemies: A Love Story* (1972) included an encounter at the Bronx Zoo (Ultan and Unger 155-57). Jewish American filmmakers based in New York City such as Woody Allen produced critically acclaimed come-dies such as *Annie Hall* (1977) and *Manhattan* (1979). As many Jewish American artists became successful in American society, they were also the first gener-ation who started reflecting on their position in American society as well as on American values, norms, and cultural narratives.

Bronx Primitive, Growing Up Bronx, and *The Old Neighborhood* also engage in a new challenge which surfaced as many Jewish American writers, artists, and public figures moved to the center of American society (Chametzky et al. 979, 981): What does it mean to be Jewish? The autobiographical narratives ana-lyzed here joined one tendency described by Chametzky et al. in which some artists and writers turned their gaze around and started looking back in time in their search for a new Jewish American identity (981). The literary repre-sentations explicate that urban shrinkage stimulates a process where Jewish American identity is reimagined and the decaying Bronx is the symbolic place where this identity search is accomplished. They confirm that shrinkage al-lows probing new ethnic, class, and gender identity formations as well as new variations of the American Dream, success, and progress narratives.

Although these literary works problematize the capitalist efficiency and display post-growth characteristics, they refrain from uttering a systemic cri-tique of capitalism. By highlighting popular and consumer culture as an im-portant inspiration for individual coming-of-age stories, the books affirm the logic of market-oriented production, distribution, and consumption. They celebrate popular culture and media as American consumer culture and high-light its function in the renewal of people, communities, and neighborhoods. They also affirm the neoliberal logic of individualism in order to overcome the era of decline: rebuilding the borough is the responsibility of the indi-vidual bodies, not the political or bureaucratic apparatus. The texts therefore assist in jumpstarting the spatial resurrection of The Bronx by assigning the individual with the greatest agency possible.

By adding such complex layers of meaning to the literary Bronx of the era of decline, the novels rewrite The Bronx back into the American experience. They critique the public discourse of the devastated Bronx as an unfortunate and singular event in American urban history. While the greater public imag-ines a dehumanized and dystopic place, Simon, Rosen, and Corman shift the attention to the people who have lived there in the past and re-imagine individual success stories of the former immigrant working-class area that has been mostly devastated and lost since the 1970s. They critique the past and present destruction of The Bronx communities and neighborhoods and view its destruction as a transnational process which affects people primarily in the northern hemisphere. At the same time, they are pragmatic and optimistic as they suggest ways of coping with destruction by postulating a poetic resurrection.

That Simon, Rosen, and, to a lesser extent, Corman recreate their neighborhoods without having been to the borough points to the specific benefit of literature. Conversely, filmmakers engage in the decline of The Bronx differently as they are required to take their technical equipment to the borough if they want to tell their stories. The next chapter will therefore examine filmic representations in order to find out how audio-visual texts anticipate and envision a spatial resurrection of The Bronx in the era of decline.

Chapter 3
Zooming in on the Devastation:
The Bronx as an Urban Frontier in Film

We have seen how autobiographic and fictional literary texts facilitate the poetic resurrection of The Bronx by reconnecting it to the cultural narrative of growth and success. If literature revisits the modern Bronx, in what ways do filmic productions facilitate its poetic resurrection in the age of decline? Film as a medium to imagine cultural narratives differs from literature in three regards. First, it has different medial features than literary texts which result in different representations of space. Having been around for more than 100 years, film has developed different conventions and medial features than literature. While literature functions mainly on the linguistic level, film incorporates at least three types of media: the verbal, the visual, and the aural. Cinema as a medium frames a physical space dynamically through camera movement and through shots, camera angles, and mis-en-scène strategies as well as diegetic or non-diegetic verbal language and the visual overlay of text. Film also has an important sound dimension, that is, "speech, music, and noise (also called *sound effects*)" as film scholars David Bordwell and Kristin Thompson state (268, emphasis in original). This soundscape, that is, the sounds that create a sonic dimension of an urban space, can accentuate or undermine what is shown in the frame.

Secondly, film presents different individual subject positions in space. The previous chapter has shown that the autobiography genre, for instance, is used in literature to present an inside perspective of the protagonists and their memories through the use of first-person narration. Film has difficulties in providing this inside perspective simply because it operates with a camera that focuses on the figure in a given environment from the outside. How, then, does film provide an inside perspective to the characters and their experiences in the shrinking borough?

Thirdly, film creates a special sense of spatial realism. Viewers often tend to mistake the fictitious characters and places for real as films capture 'real' human beings and landscapes. Contrary to literature where characters and settings are often created in the imagination of the reader, film shows them in the frame. However, Bordwell and Thompson warn that "[n]otions of realism vary across cultures, over time, and even among individuals" (113) as well as across genres. In a given filmic frame the setting and characters are constructed and only convey a sense of 'reality.' Hence, this special notion of realism affects the cinematic production, spatial imagination, and audience reception of a given urban space.

Until the mid-1970s The Bronx was only occasionally a subject on screen, especially when compared to the countless films set in Manhattan. One of The Bronx' earliest filmic representations is the 11-minute silent movie "A Bronx Morning." Although the context is the economic crisis of the Great Depression, the avant-garde short film presents a safe, friendly, and bright Bronx. It provides an inside perspective into the neighborhood through de-centered close-up shots of mothers and children. Presenting The Bronx as a communal small-town, "A Bronx Morning" contrasts with avant-garde movies such as "Manhatta" (dirs. Charles Sheeler and Paul Strand, 1921) that construct Manhattan's urban space as an impersonal flow of people and cars. The representation of The Bronx as a rather quiet and unspectacular white middle-class suburb of New York City, however, is also evident in the 1955 production *Marty*. The film focuses on the bachelor Marty (Ernest Borgnine) who struggles to find the girl of his dreams while conforming to traditional Italian American family values. Other examples of the filmic Bronx in the mid-twentieth century are the Warner Brothers cartoon *Boulevardier from the Bronx* (1936), Edgar Ulmer's *American Matchmaker* (1940), and Richard Brook's *A Catered Affair* (1958).

Since the mid-1970s The Bronx as a subject matter in film has gained increasing attention by filmmakers. *The Gambler* (1974, dir. Karel Reisz) represents the beginning of a shift in its cinematic depiction. An adaptation of the novel of the same name by Russian writer Fyodor Dostoyevsky, *The Gambler* centers on the gambling and drug-related downfall of English literature professor Axel Freed (James Caan). The downfall of this male protagonist is symbolic and symptomatic of the downfall of The Bronx as well as the crisis of white masculinity and the American Dream in the 1970s.

The increasing amount of cinematic productions in the second half of the 1970s is a direct response to the extensive news media coverage of the devastation of The Bronx. Released in the late 1970s and early 1980s, these representations can be loosely grouped into three clusters.[1] A first, and perhaps most important, group represent the genres of police, gangster, crime, and horror movies. The police film *Fort Apache: The Bronx* was one of the most controversial movies of this group because it elicited severe criticism from various local community groups (Perez). The gangster film *Gloria* centers on an Italian American ex-mafia woman who escapes the violence of the South Bronx. The horror film *Wolfen* uses the declining urban landscape for a larger criticism of its underlying economic causes. These movies demand a close analysis as they all build on the idea of The Bronx as an unsafe urban frontier space in the era of decline.

A second cinematic cluster in this era is concerned with the emerging hip-hop culture. The PBS documentary *Style Wars* (dirs. Henry Chalfant and Tony Silver, 1983) and the Harry Belafonte production *Beat Street* (dir. Stan Lathan, 1984) engage in the notion of The Bronx as the birthplace of hip-hop culture. *Wild Style*, a cult film and key text of this film genre, will be analyzed in greater detail in Chapter 4. Those films capture the powerful spirit of renewal as they center on local youth who find creative and empowering responses to deindustrialization.

The final cluster consists of gang and youth films. Titles in this grouping include *The Wanderers*, the cult film *The Warriors* (dir. Walter Hill, 1979), and the Italian adaptation of *The Warriors*, *1990: Bronx Warriors*. They are all more or less inspired by Richard Price's cult novel *The Wanderers* which was published in 1974. Juvenile gangs are also a central issue in *Fort Apache: The Bronx*. The films depict gang life as struggle for survival in the urban territory. Compared to the hip-hop films, they are more violent in their competition for urban space and for respect among their peers. At the same time, they suggest new individual and collective social formations as a result of decline.

---

1   Although Martin Scorsese's black-and-white bio pic *Raging Bull* (1980) is set in The Bronx, it does not really fit into the three clusters at first glance. The sports film, which narrates the life of the Italian American boxer Jake LaMotta (Robert De Niro), is set in The Bronx of the 1940s before the era of decline. Analyzing how the film remediates (Bolter and Grusin) the literary success stories presented in Chapter 2 would certainly be a worthwhile endeavor.

This chapter explicates why filmmakers are so fascinated by or even obsessed with the decaying urban landscape. I argue that *Fort Apache: The Bronx*, *Gloria*, and *Wolfen* promote the poetic resurrection of The Bronx by discursively re-connecting it to the cultural narrative of the frontier. First, they re-imagine The Bronx as a frontier space which is marked by conflict, survival, and exploration. Second, they situate and complicate stories of frontier heroes/heroines and villains, colonizers and colonized in the devastated area who reconfigure their identities. Third, they converge (H. Jenkins) earlier frontier themes, genres, and aesthetics in order to remind its audiences of the area's critical and productive potential. The films suggest to a wider cinematic audience outside of The Bronx that the borough is an exciting and adventurous space which provides its settlers with many struggles and challenges, but also with opportunities and possibilities. Thus, they semantically tie the right to civilize the frontier to the right to gentrify The Bronx (and other urban areas for that matter). In re-imagining The Bronx as a frontier zone, the films affirm that the borough is a multifaceted space which is, perhaps most importantly, ready to be gentrified.

Like the success story and the American Dream, the frontier narrative is one of the central myths in American history and culture. Famously described by American historian Frederick Jackson Turner in his groundbreaking 1893 study *The Significance of the Frontier in American History*, the frontier zone refers to the "outer edge of the wave – the meeting point between savagery and civilization" (3). As a zone of contact and conflict (Pratt) between social groups embedded in asymmetrical power relationships, the frontier is a space of domination/subordination, oppression/empowerment. According to Turner, one of the biggest achievements of the frontier experience is that settlers strip away their old European immigrant identities and adopt their uniquely American character (3-4). This character is marked by freedom, individualism, pragmatism, self-reliance, skepticism and democracy (37). Turner also highlights that this transformation process, although the physical frontier is closed at the time of writing, is ongoing and open (2).

The concept of the frontier has also been used to describe new urbanist developments in the twentieth century. Urban studies scholar Neil Smith, for instance, analyzed in his book *The New Urban Frontier: Gentrification and the Revanchist City* (1996) how shrinking urban spaces have become contemporary 'frontierscapes' for disenfranchised residents. As a result of post-World War II global economic restructuring processes, Smith explains how those spaces are again threatened by corporate and private middle-class colonizers through gentrification in order to reclaim their power over American inner cities (6-8, 44).

Because of its ambiguous, open, and transformative character, the frontier narrative has profoundly changed the perception of the American West since the nineteenth century. In his study *Gunfighter Nation: The Myth of the Frontier in Twentieth-Century America* (1992), American historian Richard Slotkin shows how the frontier myth continues to be a central script in the formation of the American identity as its themes, characters, and genres are constantly updated, remediated, and converged into different forms of representation. In the twentieth century, for instance, "the [f]rontier was displaced into genres dealing with metropolitan crime, high-seas swashbuckling, and imperial or 'oriental' adventure, supplemented by a new wave of 'horror films'" (Slotkin 634). The crime, gangster, and horror films to be analyzed in this chapter stand therefore in the tradition of earlier frontier genres.

One of the most pervasive narratives in American literature, culture, and media, the frontier has promoted ideas of exceptionalism, manifest destiny, and a pioneer spirit since the nation's colonial beginnings. *Fort Apache: The Bronx*, my first example to be analyzed in the next section, adapts, converges, and critiques notions of the frontier, heroism, and freedom.

3.1 "It's a fort in hostile territory, you understand?": Colonial Encounters, Irish American Heroism, and Precinct Skepticism in *Fort Apache: The Bronx* (1981)

Fort Apache: The Bronx is perhaps the most widely known and the most controversial movie about The Bronx in the era of decline released in the early 1980s. An adaptation of the famous John Ford western *Fort Apache* (1948) and inspired by the experiences of Bronx detective Thomas Mulhearn and police officer Pete Tessitore (Corry C17), Petrie's Time-Life production was frequently criticized by reviewers and local activist groups such as the Committee Against Fort Apache for its racist one-dimensional treatment of the African American and Latinx inhabitants (see Canby, "*Fort Apache, The Bronx*"; Citron et al.; Perez; Shepard). The controversy surrounding the movie was also documented by local photographer Joe Conzo (Bessa; see also Ch. 4).

Some people defended the movie's racial dramaturgy. Director Daniel Petrie is known for his commitment to racial justice in his oeuvre, for instance in his critically acclaimed adaptation of Lorraine Hansberry's play *A Raisin in the Sun* (1959). Paul Newman, the leading actor, dismissed the accusations by pointing out that "the two villains are Irish cops who throw a Puerto Rican kid off of a roof" (Shepard C5). The debate around *Fort Apache: The Bronx* demonstrates that the film draws a complex and contested cinematic portrait of The Bronx in terms of race, ethnicity, class, and gender in the era of decline. This is also remarked by *New York Times* film critic Vincent Canby. He observes that the movie is "entertaining and very moving, which is not something you can say of most movies about the decline and fall of civilizations" (Canby, "*Fort Apache, The Bronx*").

The controversy surrounding the movie's depiction of ethnic and racial identities and the emotional reactions from audiences and commentators raises questions of how the movie depicts The Bronx and its residents, in what ways it relies on and subverts formulaic figures, and how the spatial, racial, and gender depictions reimagine the frontier narrative in the age of decline. I argue that *Fort Apache: The Bronx* revises the frontier narrative by imagining The Bronx as an urban frontier where the dynamic relationship between so-called civilization and wilderness is complicated. My reading of the film will show how it introduces an ambiguous frontier hero who finds himself in between the causes and consequences of the urban frontier. I demonstrate how the film also reworks the Hollywood western film tradition in order to build on the idea of a morally corrupt apparatus. In doing so, this chapter continues, combines, and expands existing film criticism which addresses the afore-mentioned racial representations (Simpson) as well as its overarching religious aspects (Stacy and Hale; Hatt).

The opening shot foreshadows the highly contested nature of this film. It starts with a "disclaimer" (Simpson 104) which addresses the viewers directly by using the pronoun "you," which problematizes the film's narrative perspective:

> The picture you are about to see is a portrayal of the lives of two policemen working out of a precinct in the South Bronx, New York. Because the story involves police work it does not deal with the law abiding members of the community nor does it dramatize the efforts of the individuals and groups who are struggling to turn the Bronx around.

The title card is written from an omniscient narrative perspective. It aims to justify the dominant police perspective while being aware of excluding "the law abiding members of the community." It was added in post-production following the protests of the local community groups who felt that they had not been represented adequately ("Fort Apache: The Bronx," *Variety Movie Review* 32). This controversy already opens up important questions of who can claim the authority to represent a place in the era of decline and which stories can be accepted from whose perspective. The disclaimer attempts to justify a quasi-colonial perspective of law enforcement in which the 'indigenous' inhabitants including local residents and community activists are excluded. The opening title eventually indicates a different narrative perspective than the first-person narratives of the literary texts analyzed in the previous chapter. While those works exemplified a highly localized inside perspective of former residents which involved different neighborhoods such as Tremont, Highbridge or Kingsbridge, the film's opening constructs the South Bronx from the perspective of frontiersmen who struggle with a metaphorical 'wilderness' in The Bronx.

Resembling an outsider gaze to the neighborhood, the movie consequently introduces the setting of the South Bronx as a semantic entity. A blue-filtered panoramic shot follows the disclaimer. While the camera is firmly positioned in an elevated position above the rooftops in The Bronx thus establishing a particular South Bronx perspective, it slowly tilts and zooms from the Manhattan skyline known to a large national audience to the cultural periphery. This tilted panoramic zoom reveals the roofs of the apartment buildings, a subway station, and eventually a street in the South Bronx. Although the film was shot on location in the actual 41st Precinct Station House, "a stocky stone bunker at 1086 Simpson Street" (Fisher) in the poor south eastern Longwood neighborhood of the South Bronx, individual streets or neighborhoods are never explicitly mentioned or visible. The police headquarters is the most recognizable building for audiences familiar with The Bronx amid its abandoned cityscape. The opening pan reinforces the notion that while the literary examples establish a sense of place by closely situating the stories in individual neighborhoods and personal spaces, the film presents The Bronx as a spatially homogenous declining urban space with little individuality from a colonial frontiersmen gaze.

The one-sided colonial perspective is introduced in the beginning when the declining South Bronx is visualized as a criminal territory inhabited by 'savages.' The plot begins with a crime incident when the drug-addicted African American prostitute Charlotte (Pam Grier) kills two rookie police officers on their day shift. Her name is an intertextual reference to Charlotte Street, one of the worst hit neighborhoods in the wave of arson during the 1970s (Ultan, *Northern Borough* 300). Although the Time-Life movie pays tribute to African American filmmaking in choosing Blaxploitation film icon Pam Grier as an opening character, Charlotte comes across as a de-humanized figure when she moves and hisses like a snake. A snake is a Biblical symbol of evil and corruption and her name as well as her animal-like acting connote personal and urban decay as black. Her appearance fits in with the one-sided representation of the accompanying male African American youth gangs that rob the officers after Charlotte has killed them.

The black youth gang is depicted as a voiceless horde coming out of abandoned buildings. Visible only from the back and lacking any human speech, they are represented as a savage mob and the police as helpless victims. This racialized imagination of violence as black and victims as white draws on common racist stereotypes not just seen in the national news media. It strongly resonates with a larger white middle-class audience in their expectations of the "moral panic" that took place in American cities since the 1970s (Macek viii). As the suburban middle-class feared inner cities with their supposed poverty, crime, drugs, danger, and non-white urban underclass (Macek xv), the representation of black juvenile delinquency is clearly a strong indication of the racism the film has been accused.

As offensively racist as this criminalization of blackness is, it conforms to the genre conventions of the police procedural. Cultural theorist Dominic Strinati understands the police film as being concerned with "law, order and crime" as it is narrated from the perspective of the police or law enforcement institutions (55). As a cinematic form, it appeared in the first half of the twentieth century in film noir and gained importance in the racial, political, and social turmoil of the late 1960s and early 1970s with films such as *Dirty Harry* (dir. Don Siegel, 1971) and *The French Connection* (dir. William Friedkin, 1971) (Rafter 111, 116). Film scholar Neal King affirms the genre's critical and subversive potential. He explains that it addresses the loss of "privileges that so many feel they have lost to moral and economic decline" (2). Film scholar Jack Shadoian takes this idea even further when he states that police and crime genres depict "America as a failure. [...] The frontier is closed; there is no space left" (198).

While this genre addresses issues of race, masculinity, and social (in-) justice, it takes up the narrative perspective of the oftentimes white male police officers, their work of solving of crimes, and their surrounding institutional structures. The opening of *Fort Apache: The Bronx* therefore heavily relies on the police genre in its construction of the South Bronx as a dangerous territory, its criminalizing of youth of color, and its narration of the police force trying to re-create a sense of law and order. Daniel Petrie's police film captures its audiences by constructing the urban space as a frontier zone in which indigenous residents of color are depicted as criminal aggressors and white police as victims. Those aspects are complicated in the remainder of the movie.

The narrative focus of *Fort Apache: The Bronx* is the middle-aged Irish American police officer Murphy (Paul Newman). Murphy is an immigrant settler in Turner's frontier logic who functions as an ambivalent hero. Introduced shortly after the opening sequence, he finds himself in the midst of the sociocultural dynamics of the frontier space. His first name, Murphy, is a typical Irish surname and his job as a police officer is a typical type of employment for Irish Americans (O'Brien 861). He represents the working-class and lower middle-class Irish American population group which, along with Italians, Germans, and Eastern Europeans, were traditionally a strong population group in The Bronx until the second half of the twentieth century (Gonzales 110). Many Irish Americans left for the suburbs in the pursuit of their respective post-World War II American Dreams. As the borough had changed its ethnic, racial, and socioeconomic make-up in the 1960s and 1970s, Murphy functions as a stand-in for the last remaining member of his ethnic group.

Despite the poverty and decline around him, he is comfortable living and working in The Bronx. He has been working in the afore-mentioned 41st Precinct for eighteen years. He is a respected colleague because his work is guided by honesty, sincerity, humor, and de-escalation. While on patrol, for instance, Murphy and his partner, the younger Italian American police officer Andy Corelli (Ken Wahl), manage to stop a young, apparently mad man named Carl (Joaquin La Habana) from jumping off the roof. Murphy solves the incident by humorously renouncing tough masculine police violence as an ultimate means of conflict resolution. The comedy in this scene ridicules the notion of urban decline as a total nightmare and enables the audience to identify with the male protagonist and his style of solving conflict. Murphy and his Irish American and Italian American colleagues in the precinct are a remnant of once dominant European immigration groups in the South Bronx which have slowly been replaced by new generations of people of color.

Murphy cares for the residents of the South Bronx and their situation as he, too, is critical of the one-sided news media coverage of the urban frontier space. While on patrol with Andy, Murphy disapproves of the overreaction of the reporters with regard to the killing of the rookies from the beginning:

> Murphy: "The neighborhood is gonna to be full of stars with all these TV cameras around. People will be blowing each other away just to get on the news. Fires. You see a lot of fires 'cause they'll look real good on the tube."
> Andy: "I am telling you, man, a, cop killing is a media event."

Murphy is much more skeptical and distanced than Andy in this dialogue. While Murphy cynically comments on the news media hysteria regarding the crime in the South Bronx, Andy sees an opportunity to be on the spot: "We get our names in the papers, right? We can be real serious on TV." Murphy is a hero who is aware of the double morality of the media system in the age of decline. His criticism of the news media serves as a self-reflexive comment on the opening crime scene. In addition to being a critical observer, he displays his social activism on duty when he helps deliver the baby of a Spanish-speaking teenager in her family's tiny apartment. Being part of the law and order side of society as a police officer, he simultaneously transgresses the boundaries between cop and street worker, and, on a larger level, between authority figures and the communities for which they are responsible.

Besides introducing an ambivalent frontier figure, *Fort Apache: The Bronx* reimagines the 41st Police Precinct as an outpost in the wilderness. During the era of decline, the station house was even known as "Little House on the Prairie" to the locals because the devastated area lacked buildings and residents (J. Rose). The film's mis-en-scène strategies inside the fort includes indigenous tribal ornaments. While examining the precinct, the new Captain Connolly (Edward Asner) demands that the "Indian junk" that has been brought back by officers from their vacation be taken down.

The wilderness theme builds on the idea that the frontier landscape can be equated with the devastated South Bronx and that its 'Native' inhabitants are the residents of The Bronx. The killing of the two rookies by the African American prostitute and the youth gang in the opening sequence fits very well into this pattern of wilderness vs. civilization. Similar to the white settlers and cowboys in a fort fearing indigenous attacks, the precinct faces outside threats, such as civil disorder, crime, and a drug epidemic which the police seek to gain control over through the use of force. For example, Captain Connolly increases police pressure in order to find the murderers of the two rookies from the beginning of the movie. The notion of wilderness, conflict, and contestation is further reinforced when police officer Applebaum (Irving Metzman) explains to Captain Connolly: "This isn't a police station. This is a fort in hostile territory, you understand?"

The idea of the police precinct as an outpost in Native territory draws on the frontier narrative mentioned earlier. In his study *Gunfighter Nation*, Slotkin defines the frontier as a "conquest of the wilderness and the subjugation and displacement of the Native Americans [...] [as a] means to our achievement of national identity" (10), economic expansion, and the idea of progress in white American culture (10-11). Mastering the wilderness is crucial in creating a common identity and the vision of progress in American society. More than Turner in his late nineteenth-century frontier thesis, Slotkin closely links the notion of progress to violence (11). The frontier narrative affirms a justification of violence in order for a place to grow, develop, and eventually become American. American history has shown that already in the violent domination of whites over Native tribes.

Fort Apache: The Bronx takes up this theme where the police force exerts racially motivated violence on South Bronx residents, but it draws slightly different conclusions. Murphy's colleagues Morgan (Danny Aiello) and Finley (John Aquino) beat up an innocent Puerto Rican teenager who is watching a fight between police officers and locals from the roof of a burning building. Along with Murphy and Andy, the audience witnesses the entire scene from a neighboring rooftop. The officers try to stop the on-going crime by shouting at Morgan who eventually pushes the boy off the roof. The scene is reminiscent of racially motivated riots between white police officers and non-white protesters in the 1960s and 1970s, and it accelerates Murphy's alienation from his job. Murphy sees the racial injustice and the authorities' corruption as Andy advises him to cover for his two colleagues. He cynically summarizes the social double standard on victimization by rhetorically asking Andy: "Another Puerto Rican kid is dead. Why worry about it? [...] Meanwhile, boy, if that kid had been Irish or Italian..." Murphy recognizes that the moral savagery is indeed in the very system he finds himself in. As a consequence, he reports Morgan and Finley as the prime suspects to Connolly while at the same time returning his badge and quitting his job at the end of the movie. Murphy's alienation from his precinct therefore resonates with film scholar Thomas Schatz's observation that the fort in the western genre is a site of conflict and contestation from the outside as well as from the inside (49).

Petrie's movie displays the internal struggles and positions inside the fort of how to deal with a declining and allegedly disorderly neighborhood. When Captain Connolly enters the building in order to take over this new job, the camera shows him passing kids playing games in front of and inside the station house while a police officer moves a young convict through the scene.

Here, the police precinct is reminiscent of a community center more than an orderly police headquarters in a supposedly mostly rundown district of New York City. Connelly, who represents a bureaucratic attitude which neglects the complexities and contradictions of decline, critically remarks to Sergeant Anthony Pantuzzi (Rik Colitti): "Don't you monitor the people who ask to see the commander? What if I was a lunatic with a gun?" The precinct is a place which is simultaneously a police headquarters and a community center, thus affirming that it holds an in-between position between the police officers (civilization) and local inhabitants (wilderness).

The complex dynamics of how to deal with the realities in The Bronx is exemplified by the two Irish captains presiding over the fort, Dugan (Sully Boyar) and Connolly. Captain Dugan is a figure who takes up an inside perspective of the area, whereas his successor represents the hegemonic top-down attitude of the downtown police headquarters. Both elderly male figures are very similar in their bodily appearance. Yet they constitute the ambivalence of the situation which is marked by the local precinct perspective and the perspective of the headquarters. While the new Captain Connolly blames Dugan as the boss of the precinct for "the worst absentee record in the city, most disability claims, the highest percentage of men on sick call, and the least convictions per arrests," Dugan points to the larger socioeconomic causes of the decline:

> Yeah that's right, blame Dugan! Sure, let the politicians and everyone else off the hook. Blame Dugan. That's the easy way. You got a 40-block area with 70,000 people packed in like sardines, smelling each other's farts living like cockroaches, and that's Dugan's fault. You got the lowest income per capita, the highest rate of unemployment in the city and that's my fault! Why aren't I out there getting all these people jobs? Largest proportion of non-English speaking population in the city! Dugan's fault. Why aren't I out there teaching them to speak English? Four percent Spanish-speaking cops on the force! Hey, Dugan, get your ass out in the *barrio* and recruit! Families that have been on welfare for three generations. Youth Gangs. Winos. Junkies. Pimps! Hookers... Maniacs... Cop-killers.

Captain Dugan challenges Connolly's perspective of the South Bronx as a space of civil disorder and the precinct as an inefficient organization. Dugan criticizes the structural inequalities that led to the downward spiral in the area, such as unemployment and low education levels. He points to the larger causes of the decline by explaining that the immense poverty in the area has been growing for a long time and employment opportunities are rare. He criticizes the indifference of city officials and their lack of effort to improve the situation, such as the officers' lack of second-language competencies, police officers who rather go "by the book" (Murphy) and neglect the local circumstances, and accusations that the precinct has failed to manage the situation in The Bronx. Dugan shows Connolly that the causes and consequences of decline can by no means be solved in a bureaucratic way as the problems are multilayered and long-term measures need to be taken in order to resurrect the South Bronx.

It is not surprising that *Fort Apache: The Bronx* revises the long-standing western genre in Henry Jenkins's sense of convergence in order to reimagine The Bronx as an urban frontier space. The movie reworks a specific western: the film's title is an intertextual reference to John Ford's western *Fort Apache*. The extension of *Fort Apache* suggests that the precinct is a military outpost on the border of wilderness and savagery, The Bronx. American film scholar Thomas Schatz explains in his 1981 study *Hollywood Genres: Formulas, Filmmaking, and the Studio System* with regard to the western genre:

> In Hollywood's version the West is a vast wilderness dotted with occasional oases – frontier towns, cavalry posts, isolated campsites, and so forth – which are linked with one another and with the civilized East by the railroad, the stagecoach, the telegraph: society's tentacles of progress. Each oasis is a virtual society in microcosm, plagued by conflicts both with the external, threatening wilderness and also with the anarchic or socially corrupt members of its own community. (49)

Schatz demonstrates that the fort in the western genre is a "microcosm" of civilization in the vast landscape of the wilderness. The fort therefore takes up the function of a Foucauldian heterotopia (see Ch. 1.1) where people living in the fort face similar issues and conflicts as the greater society.

Fort Apache: The Bronx reworks ideas of liberty, love, and freedom of the original John Ford production *Fort Apache*. The 1948 western features a romantic plot between Second Lieutenant Michael 'Murphy' Shannon O'Rourke (John Agar) and Philadelphia Thursday (Shirley Temple). Philadelphia is the daughter of the patriarch Lieutenant Colonel Owen Thursday (Henry Fonda). Thursday symbolizes "caste-snobbery" (Slotkin 339) in disapproving of his daughter's relationship because of O'Rourke's alleged inferior social status: "[A]s a noncommissioned officer, you are aware of the barrier between your class and mine." Yet, while the fort is the arena where the patriarch Colonel Thursday is in charge, the space outside the fort is the arena where Philadelphia and Michael meet first and where they get to know each other better.

Similar to Murphy's experiences in The Bronx, the danger for the couple in the western lurks inside the fort where Colonel Thursday reigns. The danger is to a lesser extent outside of the fort where Native Americans could attack the couple. A panoramic long shot of the vast landscape of Monument Valley reinforces the idea of freedom and liberty where both are free to roam beyond the influence of Philadelphia's father. As the couple meets at the border between civilization and wilderness, the western presents a wilderness which is part of the American imagination and has the potential to be transformed. The desert of the American West is a space of freedom and exploration which provides them an opportunity to start their own relationship and live their own version of the American Dream.

In contrast to Philadelphia and Michael, however, Murphy and his love interests Isabella (Rachel Ticotin) in *Fort Apache: The Bronx* are alienated from their surroundings. The movie extends the narrative beyond Murphy's workplace to his private sphere, allowing the audience to learn more about his personal desires, failures, and his relationship to the Puerto Rican nurse, a plot element which is rather unconventional for masculine genres, such as the police procedural and western. The middle-aged Irish American divorcé, whose three kids live with their mother, finds himself in a crisis as he has been steadily working for many years in The Bronx. He longs for a new relationship and wants to end his loneliness, but that is difficult because of the downfall of the neighborhood. The era of decline has a direct impact on him as he does not find the right woman in the neighborhood for his personal happiness.

The frontier experience results in the couple's unstable, short-lived, and unfulfilled relationship. While sitting in the enclosed space of a car in the nocturnal Bronx after their date, Murphy asks Isabella: "How about we get out of The Bronx?" She replies: "It stays in your head no matter where you go." Her answer affirms that getting out of The Bronx in the pursuit of social upward mobility is not just a process of geographical relocation. Both have a desire to escape and start a new life as an interethnic and interracial couple outside of The Bronx, but it is not possible due to their cultural, ethnic, racial, and class backgrounds as well as the social stigma of the borough. The couple and their relationship appear trapped in Isabella's addiction as a result of the hostile living conditions. Compared to Michael's and Philadelphia's experience of freedom and love relationship in the West, the Bronxites' realities are marked by much more confined spatial and social restrictions.

Escape from the grim realities of the neighborhood is hardly possible except through substance abuse. For instance, Isabella explains her heroin use to Murphy by saying that "[s]mack's like a vacation to me" – a vacation which allows her to temporarily step out of her situation. Her eventual death as well as the senseless murder of the nameless Puerto Rican teenager is a strong metaphor for the individual and collective American nightmares taking place in those declining spaces. The cinematic imagination of The Bronx as a space of limitation, immobility, and hopelessness thus signifies the social limitations which are at work in New York City and the greater United States. This spatial imagination critiques the lack of class mobility which is central to the American project and exists outside of The Bronx as well.

This sense of entrapment is climaxed by Isabella's abrupt passing, which was caused by her drug dealer Hernando (Miguel Piñero) who opposed her relationship with Murphy in the first place. Isabella's death accelerates Murphy's alienation from his job as a police officer, and as a result he quits his job at the end of the movie. Hence, the Irish American police officer is as much a vulnerable victim as the Puerto Rican nurse (Hatt 110). While Philadelphia and Michael find their home as a married couple inside the fort in *Fort Apache*, Isabella and Murphy's relationship is ended violently by her heroin overdose.

The extension of the narrative framework to Murphy's and Isabella's relationship in this urban frontier space is an effect of the melodramatic mode. American film scholar Linda Williams explains this particular mode in her article "Melodrama Revised" (1998) not as a "specific genre like the western or horror film [...] [but as] a peculiarly democratic and American form that seeks dramatic revelation of moral and emotional truths through a dialectic of pathos and action" (42). Compared to the genre of melodrama, the melodramatic mode is therefore much more open and flexible as it appears across many different types of media, texts, and genres (Brooks; Zarzosa). The melodramatic mode gains increasing importance in times of crisis (Smit 81) including economic, social, and urban crisis. The representation of such crises generate dramatizations of masculine and feminine gender identities which help to understand the larger ideological struggles at work.

In *Fort Apache: The Bronx*, the melodramatic mode zooms in on the main protagonists' frontier realities by providing an insight into their personal struggles for survival. It does so by allowing Murphy the most on-screen time, working with (medium) close-up shots of the protagonists to achieve audience identification. While traditional western and police genres mostly present cowboys, military personnel, police officers, detectives, and private eyes as lonesome anti-heroes, Petrie's film moves beyond Murphy's job to show that the drug and violence problems have penetrated not only the public space, but every sphere of life of all residents who live in this decline context. The melodramatic mode appears as a localization strategy in a masculine film genre of law and order seldom associated with such "emotional truths" (L. Williams 42). A clear division between culprit and victim, those out there and 'us' in here is not possible anymore.

Fort Apache: The Bronx reimagines the frontier narrative in the era of decline by introducing a feeling of being stuck. In the nineteenth century, settlers on the Western frontier could move on when they felt stuck and *Fort Apache*'s cinematography celebrates the vast desert landscape. By contrast, The Bronx is not a landscape of hope, growing up, progress, and social upward mobility, but a territory which poses limitations and obstacles to the protagonists which they fail to overcome. Because the South Bronx is depicted as an unsafe public space, Murphy and Isabella are eager to get out of it. Their feeling of being stuck deviates from the myth of the frontier of perpetual (westward) movement to new and open spaces and opportunities. The movie voices criticism of the existing shrinkage processes because even personal relationships are doomed to fail in such an environment and the consequences of decline pervade every level of life. As a consequence, the film criticizes urban shrinkage by breaking it down to a personal micro-perspective and thus raising emotion and empathy for the locals living on the imagined frontier of The Bronx.

However, the film ends on an affirmative note by suggesting that giving up is not an option. Murphy does not resign, but he continues his fight against the crime in the neighborhood. In the final humorous and open-ended sequence which ironically takes up melodrama's deus-ex-machina endings, Andy and Murphy continue chasing the young criminal from the beginning of the film. This time, they act as civilians dressed in casual clothes and are shown driving in Murphy's car. The final freeze frame suggests that when authorities fail to deal with shrinkage, it is up to individuals to take action, thus alluding to one of the central values of individualism in American culture with regard to the pursuit of justice.

However, those individual efforts to counter crime in the neighborhood re-affirm the status quo, as critic Harold Hatt summarizes: "Murphy failed because [he] wanted to help marginalized individuals, but did not see that this requires a change in the system that marginalizes them" (109). Despite his failure to come up with a solution that benefits all residents, Murphy is represented as a fighter and frontier hero who still believes in American virtues and, as a result, does not give up the struggle against a corrupt society. Murphy's destiny thus takes up the promise of the classic western in which the audience knows that the cavalry, settlers, and sheriffs – despite their struggles – eventually manage to conquer the frontier, establish law, and order and build a civic community. As the taming of the frontier was successful in the nineteenth century, *Fort Apache: The Bronx* prophesies that the urban frontier of The Bronx will be tamed and conquered by global capital flows and gentrification. The movie's ironic deus-ex-machina ending along with its larger prophetic message is likely one of the reasons the production appealed to a large audience, raising more than $29 million at the American box office and $36 million internationally ("Fort Apache, The Bronx," *Numbers*).

Compared to the literary protagonists in Chapter 2, Murphy's success story at the frontier is much more ambivalent. While Kate, Danny, and Steven stood at the beginning of their lives and careers when they left The Bronx to pursue their upward movement, Murphy stayed on, grew up and grows old in The Bronx. His identity is closely interwoven with the surrounding frontier space. More than the literary examples, Murphy is a victim of decline (Hatt 110) who is disillusioned about the prospect of class mobility even outside of The Bronx.

However, the main protagonist displays extraordinary and American virtues which help him to succeed amid the poverty, crime, violence, and devastation. Most important is the skepticism displayed towards institutions which fail to improve the circumstances facing the neighborhood. Likewise, resilience, self-reliance, individualism, humor as a coping strategy, and the deep belief that difficulties will be overcome eventually are also salient features of the film. Despite the fact that he lost his beloved girlfriend Isabella, giving up is not an option for Murphy. Just like cowboys and pioneers on Turner's frontier, the film promotes an underlying message that success on the urban frontier means cooperation, learning, and not trusting authorities.

To sum up, *Fort Apache: The Bronx* reconnects The Bronx to the frontier narrative by reimagining its spatial dynamics, its character constellations, and its generic traditions. The movie depicts The Bronx as a frontier zone which highlights the dynamics between civilization and wilderness, colonizer and colonized, conflict and cooperation. Like Turner's and Slotkin's notions of the frontier forming a national identity through violence, *Fort Apache: The Bronx* presents a space that reveals the grim limitations of the American experiment which exclude ideas of enduring freedom and unlimited opportunities in the age of decline. The police precinct is a metaphor for the fort in which the power dynamics of the frontier are spatialized. It is a place of law and order as well as of moral, systemic, and even political corruption where the sworn-in representatives of law and order are savages. The film criticizes the double standard and inability of political authorities as well as the media to deal with the consequences of decline.

The main protagonist Murphy functions as an agent who is frontier hero, street worker, and outcast. He is also the lens through which the audience learns about the complexities and realities of the era of decline marked by death, pain, and suffering as well as American virtues of resilience, self-reliance, love, hope, and humor. His, and on a larger level the film's, solution to the socioeconomic realities of The Bronx posits the continuation of fight on an individual level against neglect on the margins of a sociopolitical system which initially caused sharp inequalities. Murphy's destiny strongly resonates with Turner's claim that the "frontier is productive of individualism" (30). The film's biggest contribution to the era of decline is how it draws on existing decline imaginaries familiar to a white suburban middle-class audience while at the same time deconstructing them by showing that it is a multifaceted and complex phenomenon with many different causes, consequences, and victims.

Despite Murphy's liminal subject position, *Fort Apache: The Bronx* takes up and normalizes a racialized colonial gaze in which the colonizers tend to be round characters and the indigenous populations are rather flat. There are no African American round characters in the entire movie. With regard to Puerto Ricans and Irish characters, however, the film shows that perpetrators and victims are on both sides: the Irish murderer Morgan and the Irish victim Murphy as well as the Puerto Rican drug dealer and murderer Hernando and the Puerto Rican victim Isabella.

Fort Apache: The Bronx constructs the borough for an audience outside of The Bronx. It complicates a white-middle class colonial gaze which builds The Bronx as an unsafe and criminal urban frontier space. Murphy serves as a vehicle to discover its racial, ethnic, gender, sexual, and class dynamics. The film echoes Slotkin's observation that the frontier narrative serves as a gateway to explore how violence is destructive for individuals and communities, but ultimately necessary to a spatial regeneration. It promotes the idea that giving up is not an option for the self-made frontiersmen to suggest that people at this eastern urban frontier should not rely on the state or government to rebuild their borough. It also demonstrates how the shrinking urban space facilitates narrative, generic, and media regeneration and, ultimately, how such a space because of all the aforementioned entanglements, conflicts, and dynamics is an interesting territory worth exploring cinematically, including for commercial exploitation.

Although *Fort Apache: The Bronx* proves to be a complex cinematic text for American audiences with regard to the depiction of urban shrinking processes in the early 1980s, it generated racial and spatial stereotypes for a larger international audience through global convergence (H. Jenkins 113). The American film industry distributed the image of The Bronx as an urban frontier space nationally and globally. In Germany, for instance, both the film and the novel were entitled *Die Bronx* ("The Bronx;" Gould). The translation completely omits the intertextual reference to the John Ford western and reduces the entire borough to a criminal urban territory for German-speaking audiences, thus creating and nurturing a one-sided imagination of this borough for decades to come. *Fort Apache: The Bronx*, along with the film adaptation of Tom Wolfe's *The Bonfire of the Vanities* (dir. Brian de Palma) at the end of the 1980s, has created a rather fixed image of The Bronx as a hostile space in the mind of many Germans until today. Whenever news media have reported about The Bronx in the past decade, those cinematic imaginations were reactivated. More research is needed, for instance, on how the novel and the films were translated and dubbed into languages other than English and in how far these cultural translation processes might have contributed to the global stigmatization of the borough.

Despite the mixed national and international reception, *Fort Apache: The Bronx* allows a useful insight into the struggles of the fictional individuals who live in a declining environment and fight against it. The cinematic era of decline invites audiences to blur societal norms, generic conventions, and spatial boundaries. Shrinkage is a productive urban tendency and aesthetic practice as it introduces complex figures and offers an opportunity to reexamine the state of the American project, its norms, values, and narratives. The gangster film *Gloria* features a female middle-aged protagonist. What is her story and what repercussions does a female outlaw figure have on the notion of the frontier narrative in the era of decline?

3.2 "I hate kids, especially yours": Italian American Domesticity, Frontier Femininity, and Gangster Journeys in *Gloria* (1980)

Gloria draws on the gangster film genre to create the idea of The Bronx as an urban frontier. The movie was directed by filmmaker and actor John Cassavetes. Cassavetes is widely known as the "father of American independent filmmaking" (Carney, "Adventure" 102) inspiring New Hollywood directors of the 1970s and 1980s such as Martin Scorsese and Oliver Stone ("John Cassavetes"). He also starred in Roman Polanski's successful 1968 horror film *Rosemary's Baby*. Although somewhat disliked by critics and the director himself alike (Applegate; Canby, "Cassavetes's *Gloria*;" Carney, *Films of John Cassavetes* 28), *Gloria* was nominated for an Academy Award, inspired other films on the way, and was eventually remade with the same title in 1999 by American director Sidney Lumet.

This chapter expands the existing research on *Gloria* by exploring its take on the urban frontier. *Gloria* has often been analyzed in terms of Cassavetes as an auteur, for instance, by Raymond Carney (*Films of John Cassavetes*; *American Dreaming*) and Ivone Margulies with regard to New American Cinema. The term auteur refers to the idea that a director has a distinctive style of filmmaking which is recognizable across his or her works. With regard to gender and sexuality, Cassavetes's films have been analyzed to a lesser extent (Esposito). I argue that *Gloria* facilitates the poetic resurrection of The Bronx by reconnecting it to the cultural narrative of the frontier. The recombination happens in three ways: first, the Cassavetes movie centers on a specific female frontier perspective in the age of decline; second, it blurs the boundaries between wilderness and civilization in terms of existing spatial and news media imaginaries; and, third, it revises the gangster genre by adding the melodramatic mode. *Gloria* bears similarities to *Fort Apache: The Bronx* in how each presents a more ambivalent frontier narrative: both present shrinkage as an opportunity to revise existing spatial imaginaries about The Bronx, highlight anti-essential and relational identity formations, and promote cultural and generic creativity as a consequence of decline.

Gloria's opening introduces New York City as an ambivalent frontier space where the boundaries between civilization and wilderness are blurred. Similar to *Fort Apache: The Bronx*, *Gloria* starts off with the Manhattan cityscape before shifting to The Bronx. An aerial shot of illuminated Manhattan's skyscrapers at night is followed by an upward tilt shot of the nocturnal Yankee Stadium. The stadium framed in the center as a glowing entity is not only one of the most famous landmarks of The Bronx, but also signifies the South Bronx setting. Illuminated with a cold bright blue light, the baseball stadium glows in the dark urban landscape and evokes associations to a fort in the urban wilderness. As noted earlier (see Ch. 1.3 and 3.1), news media depictions of The Bronx draw a rather sharp distinction between the alleged savage territory of The Bronx and the civilized rest of New York. The opening shots establish the idea of New York City as a fluid space, a space of movement and journey between civilization and wilderness.

However, and contrary to the popular imagination of the urban frontier, Yankee Stadium is positioned by way of cross-cutting as a pivotal monument that belongs to the New York cityscape as much as the Statue of Liberty and the World Trade Center. A series of vespertine helicopter shots show the Statue of Liberty, the southern tip of Manhattan's skyline, the World Trade Center as well as the Brooklyn and Manhattan Bridges early in the morning. Spatial and temporal in-betweenness is further conveyed in the time of shooting. Dawn as a transitional time between night and day is neither night nor day, exclusively. As a result, all of New York City in the early morning hours appears as an unfamiliar territory and estranged cityscape to the audience. The fluidity of the frontier space in the film frame is medially achieved through mobile framing, such as aerial helicopter shots, panoramic shots, or tilts, of water, such as the East River, the two bridges, and vehicular traffic.

The exposition suggests a (film) *noir* atmosphere of New York City which is not only reinforced by the blue color filter, but by a melancholic saxophone tune in the soundtrack. This atmosphere is further underlined by the nocturnal gloom where the Statue of Liberty, the symbol of the American Dream, is framed as a rather dark monument – not even her glowing torch manages to light up her surroundings. The torch's weak illumination embodies the weakness of the American Dream narrative in this city. Similarly, the city's skyscrapers are surrounded by an early morning gloom evoking a melancholic and subdued feel rather than the image of a bustling 'city that never sleeps,' a metaphor for New York City that resonates with people around the world and domestically.

After establishing New York City as a global, fluid, and gloomy frontier space in the opening sequence, the film firmly localizes the narration in the urban 'wilderness' as the movie camera eventually arrives in The Bronx. The film's perspective changes from aerial views of the Manhattan cityscape evoking an omniscient gaze to the streets of the indigenous residents in The Bronx after sunrise. The camera, already positioned in the 'Native territory' of the

South Bronx, zooms in on a bus crossing Manhattan's Macombs Dam Bridge. A tilted pan over Yankee Stadium demonstrates such a localization strategy as the stadium in the lower part of the film frame is clearly recognizable as one of the pivotal sights of the South Bronx. The famous baseball stadium, a symbol of baseball and 'America's favorite pastime' is used as a powerful geographic marker to indicate the main setting of the film. *Gloria* subverts one-dimensional ideas of The Bronx as a space of terror, violence, and disorder when it presents a lively, positive, and vibrant urban community in the inside shot of the rumbling bus and its energetic passengers. Compared to Petrie's opening incident which echoed dominant discourses of fear and dystopia (Ch. 3.1), *Gloria*'s opening redefines The Bronx as an urban wilderness by making it less threatening.

This process of localizing and 'going native' is completed when the female passenger and minor character Jeri Dawn (Julie Carmen) exits at a bus stop and enters the dark entrance hall of her apartment building. While the name of the building is not explicitly mentioned, its destiny is exemplary in the age of decline in The Bronx. The on-location setting (Carney, *American Dreaming* 274) is the former and, at the time of shooting, rather empty Concourse Plaza Hotel on Grand Concourse and 161st Street near Yankee Stadium. Once one of the most elegant hotels in the early twentieth century, "[the] former symbol of Bronx greatness [...] went from housing the Yankees and visiting dignitaries to housing drug addicts and welfare families" (Gonzales 129). Connoting the downfall of the borough since the 1960s, the hotel is located in a low-income area where mostly marginalized African American and Latinx people lived in the 1970s (Gonzales 129). Later sequences also reveal the run-down character of the building which alludes to a space of wilderness, neglect, and social disorder. Deconstructing the meaning of the building presupposes knowledge and is perhaps less accessible to an audience outside of the borough. A sense of place in *Gloria* is therefore mostly established via mis-en-scène by attributing buildings with a narrative relevance that have a local significance in the era of decline.

The film's opening deconstructs the public imaginary of The Bronx as an urban wilderness by suggesting that it is a home as well. The camera is positioned at Gloria Swenson's window (John Cassavetes's wife Gena Rowlands), the movie's female protagonist. The middle-aged woman represents an outsider character who lives by herself in an apartment in this run-down building. The camera movement reveals that her home is modestly decorated with many paintings on her walls and pictures on a drawer. The pictures indicate that her closest companion is her cat because they are prominently featured in the film frame. Her lower Italian American middle-class lifestyle demonstrates that the maverick made herself comfortable in her "cozy nest" (Carney, *American Dreaming* 274) situated in this declining neighborhood – a benefit of this shrinking frontier place. For Gloria, the urban wilderness has become a space of comfort and home where she can live her outlaw life much more freely away from rigid social conventions and conventional gender expectations.

Her outlaw identity is underlined by her cultural background. Gloria is part of the Italian American population group in The Bronx who used to live in the Melrose neighborhood near Yankee Stadium in the early twentieth century along with German, Irish, and Eastern European immigrants as well as older Anglo Americans (Gonzales 76, 98). The Italian American woman does not live according to traditional Italian family values as seen in the 1950s movie *Marty*. Marty's mother was depicted as a matriarch who likes to cook, enjoys having a large family, and raises her grandchild. Gloria challenges this cultural stereotype openly: "I don't like kids. I hate kids […]." When talking to her ex-boyfriend, mafia boss Tony Tanzini (Basilio Franchina), Gloria cynically explains: "Me, I'm not a mother. I'm one of those sensations. I was always a broad. Can't stand the sight of milk." She clarifies early in the film's plot that she opposes traditional ideas of womanhood dedicated to motherhood and family.

Her feminine identity is a mixture of gangster toughness, cowgirl swagger, and aged glamorous femininity. In the movie poster she wears a black satin jacket, knee long skirt, and high heels. Her gaze is directed to the observer of the poster while her body language conveys a self-confident and aggressive attitude. Her blonde shoulder-long hair, held by clips, is formed like that of Gloria Swanson, the American silent film icon her name references. Swanson is perhaps best known as the aging Hollywood movie star Nora Desmond in Billy Wilder's highly acclaimed film noir *Sunset Boulevard* (1950) who fails to recognize that the zenith of her professional career has passed. Swenson's glamorous hair and her fine-quality clothing signify the grandeur of the Hollywood era, but in contrast to Nora Desmond, Gloria appears as a tough, gun-wearing ex-mobster woman who knows how to defend herself.

Analyzing Gloria's liminal femininity, American sociologist Dawn Esposito states that her "masculinity [is] coded as an extension of her femininity" (105) and goes so far as to attribute Gloria with a lesbian identity (107). More than the aging heterosexual Irish American police officer Murphy in *Fort Apache: The*

Bronx, Gloria is presented as a maverick figure in terms of her age, gender, and sexual identity. Her social status as a retired mobster woman and her masculinized femininity deviate from hegemonic and heteronormative white Anglo American middle-class norms of motherhood, age, and sexuality. The film suggests that context of decline provides a space where such alternative gender identities can be lived more freely as conventional norms and post-war conformist middle-class values are disappearing.

Although The Bronx is a comfort zone for Gloria, just as it is for Murphy in *Fort Apache: The Bronx*, the Cassavetes' movie buys into the public imaginary in the era of decline as its main message: even for cultural outlaws, The Bronx is an unsafe urban frontier territory. Crime is the reason why Gloria, a former gangster woman herself, eventually has to leave her apartment. Her Puerto Rican neighbors, the Dawns, are brutally murdered by her mobster friends at the beginning of the movie. Prior to their murder, the Dawns ask her to take care of their six-year old son Phil Dawn (John Adames). The father, Jack Dawn (Buck Henry), gives his son Phil a secret book. This book contains "names, dates, money, account numbers," as the mafia boss Tony Tanzini later states. Gloria, like Murphy in *Fort Apache: The Bronx*, is affected by violence on the frontier, but the crime affects the Puerto Rican characters more than the Italian American and Irish American protagonists. The murder of the Dawn family affirms that the violence in the neighborhood comes from Gloria's own cultural group who is in a superior power position as violent and law-breaking settler/colonizers. Consequently, Gloria and Phil have to escape from their home/urban wilderness, thus being forced to reconfigure their liminal identities and unusual relationship to one another.

Their journey through the city opens up the possibility to renegotiate their identities. Before his murder, Jack urges his son Phil to adopt a *machismo* attitude: "Be a man. Always be tough. Don't trust anybody." This leads to Phil's attempt to exercise his new forced-upon role towards his Italian American neighbor by telling her in the run-down stairway of their building that "I am the man!" Although he is a child, he wears clothes that are typical for men's fashion of that time: black bell-bottom pants and a buttoned large-print shirt. His attitude as well as his clothing suggests that the boy struggles with his identity establishing him also as an in-between character.

During their journey the two take up different constellations which underline the relationality of their identities (Carney, *American Dreaming* 304). As their itinerary changes from the Upper East Side in Manhattan, to a hotel in Queens, and Penn Station in Manhattan, Gloria's and Phil's relationship also changes. A comparison of street scenes reveals how Gloria rejects Phil and leaves him on Bronx streets while she accepts him by carrying him through Manhattan. Their involuntary journey caused by the violence on the frontier allows Gloria to come to terms with her responsibility of taking care of Phil even though she is not fond of kids. Phil in turn learns to accept Gloria as his new guardian.

Because their constant identity re-configuration is influenced by the journey through the city, the film echoes Turner's claim that the frontier experience fueled the formation and regeneration of individual identities. *Gloria* thus suggests a relational identity formation similar to Kate's in *Bronx Primitive*, Danny's in *Growing Up Bronx*, Steven's in *The Old Neighborhood*, and Murphy's in *Fort Apache: The Bronx*. Because of the age of decline, Gloria and Phil are forced to leave their home on the frontier, but their departure is nevertheless productive because it allows them to rework their relationship to each other starting a learning process about themselves.

Their identity transformation is completed when both leave the frontier space of New York City at the end of the movie. After Gloria has met the mobsters to give them the book (while admitting that she has read the content), Phil and Gloria separately go to the steel city of Pittsburgh where they reunite at Carson Memorial. Pittsburg is presented as a sunny, friendly, and economically intact place in contrast to gritty New York. The city offers a safe space for the protagonists and evokes allusions to a strange and dreamy "fairyland" at the same time (Carney, *American Dreaming* 287). The representation of Pittsburg is ironic because in the early 1980s it suffered from similar deindustrialization and population shrinkage as the South Bronx and other former industrial centers of the Northeast. Having escaped from New York City, their positions within the substitute family finally stabilize: Gloria takes over the role as sort-of grandmother indicated by her grey wig and dark clothes, and Phil accepts his role as a sort-of grandson as the movie's final sequence illustrates. While they are united, their gender identities still differ from the heteronormative white Anglo American middle-class ideal of the nuclear family. From this hegemonic point-of-view, they are still liminal characters, but they have found a way of relating, caring, and supporting each other. *Gloria* ends with a humorous twist on the protagonists' regeneration. This is further underlined by the setting of their unification, a cemetery. Their unconventional unification ironically subverts conventional Hollywood happy endings. Just as the final humorous freeze frame sequence of the new civilian Murphy chasing a thief in *Fort Apache: The Bronx* promotes an individual solution to deal with dynamics on the urban frontier, so does the final surreal slow-motion sequence of Gloria's and Phil's reunion in *Gloria*.

Gloria reworks the conventional gangster film genre in order to create The Bronx and New York City as a contemporary urban frontier. The movie's generic framework is important because it stands in the tradition of the western film in its character constellations, narrative and audio-visual styles, larger politics, and its treatment of the frontier myth (Slotkin 260, 265). Slotkin argues that the gangster film is a continuation of the western genre in its take on the frontier, but its audio-visual style is urban, grittier, and more contemporary (265). Gangster films have a long tradition in American cinema as they emerged in the 1930s when filmmakers translated the Western myth into the grim realities of the Great Depression (Slotkin 265). Historically, they used the genre to critique notions of progress, success, and growth on the urban frontier as well as the double moral standards of the 1920s (Slotkin 259). The revival of the gangster film as an urban frontier genre in the 1970s affirms that there are "particularly close affinities between the genre maps of the 1930s and the 1970s" (Slotkin 634).

Cassavetes's movie revises the spatial conventions of the gangster film genre. Oftentimes, gangster films are based on the idea of the American city as a labyrinth. Since the genre's inception in the wake in the early 1930s, movies like *The Public Enemy* (dir. William A. Wellman, 1931), for example, create an urban space which is marked by danger, unpredictability, and instability. Film scholar Edward Mitchell describes the urban setting in his genre study of the American gangster film as "a violent and hostile environment, a labyrinth of dark alleys and concrete canyons, a warren of mean streets from which danger constantly threatens" (259). The urban space in the gangster film is marked by strict boundaries, restrictions, limitations, and non-redemption (Slotkin 634).

Gloria reworks the gender politics of the gangster genre by focusing on a specific female experience in an otherwise hypermasculine gangster or crime setting. Both, the gangster and the western film prominently feature (white) male outlaw figures who are modeled after the "good-badman action-formula" whereas female figures merely assist them (Slotkin 260). The gangster genre traditionally centers on male mobsters and their stories as it "concentrates as much on power and corruption and the ambiguity of law enforcement as it does on the need for justice to prevail and for the gangster to be punished" (Strinati 55). *Gloria*, by contrast, shifts the perspective to highlight the struggles of an ex-mafia woman and her sudden role as a mentor and substitute mother which are the costs of a specific masculine regimes of violence and power.

The inside perspective on this relationship between a tough mafia woman and her neighbor's son at the frontier is established through the melodramatic mode (see Ch. 3.1). Film critic Thomas Elsaesser defines melodrama as a cinematic genre which is concerned with issues of domesticity, love, family, or an unfulfilled love interest (446). Oftentimes, the setting of melodrama is the home and private spaces because this is traditionally the sphere of women and the family (Neale and Gledhill 157). *Gloria* reworks this generic convention by transferring the alternative family formation to the public sphere because the South Bronx home has become an unsafe space. Instead of negotiating the heroine's femininity in the private sphere of her apartment, *Gloria* promotes that the cityscape facilitates the heroine's identity regeneration. Hence the protagonists' journey through the streets of New York City as a consequence of the unstable living conditions in the South Bronx 'wilderness' allows reconfiguring their gender and family identities.

The melodramatic mode in *Gloria* presents an alternative character constellation similar to *Fort Apache: The Bronx*. Both film's main protagonists are characters who do not seem to fit in their immediate environment. Both subject positions are rooted in and affected by the drug crime and mafia violence of the frontier space of the South Bronx. Both films direct the viewers' attention to the private spheres and to personal relationships of their protagonists in the era of decline. While the melodramatic mode in *Fort Apache: The Bronx* provided an insight into an unfulfilled love interest and a broken male hero, *Gloria* highlights a non-traditional Italian American woman and the emergence of a substitute family constellation. This mode illuminates how the characters deal with the consequences of living in this declining neighborhood, such as the loss of loved ones, being a victim, and finding a new outlook on life. The melodramatic mode soothes the dark character of the urban frontier and works to 'downgrade' the intensity of violence in the city. As a creative mode for describing decline, the film reconfigures traditional gender, sexual, and family identities by introducing new, relational forms of interpersonal relationships and lifestyles. Hence shrinking becomes productive: The urban frontier allows new possibilities to imagine, revise, and create more diverse social and familial relationships.

In *Gloria*, the cityscape is depicted as a frontier where female-coded civilization (Gloria) and male-coded savagery (mob) meet. Gloria succeeds in this dynamic frontier space because the heroine is smart, witty, self-determined, strong-willed, and self-reliant. The Bronx and Manhattan are represented as less dangerous than in other gangster movies despite the frequent portrayal of violence. Although Gloria and Phil are chased by the mafia, and she acknowledges that the mobsters "have everything covered. Trains. Planes," she knows how to defend herself physically and intellectually to get the two of them ahead of the Mafiosi. The strong woman demonstrates that she succeeds in this endless frontier-space of New York City which is marked by the blurring of clear borders and boundaries between civilization/savagery as well as colonizer/colonized. As a result, *New York Times* film critic Vincent Canby observes that "[t]he streets are cluttered and filthy but never threatening" ("Cassavetes's *Gloria*").

Gloria engages in a frontier discourse of journey and freedom similar to *Fort Apache: The Bronx*. While in *Fort Apache: The Bronx* Murphy and Isabella are stuck in their urban and social environment, Gloria and Phil are forced to leave the apartment building because of the mob violence in the neighborhood. They leave The Bronx not because of their dream of social upward mobility and personal freedom as the literary examples suggested before, but because their home is not safe anymore and they have no other choice. Here the South Bronx functions as a departure point which forces them out yet opens up the possibility of a fresh start at the same time. Hence, Cassavetes's film revises the aforementioned spatial and ideological limitations of the gangster film.

With regard to the protagonists' urban journey, film critic Raymond Carney explains that "only in free movement [...] exploration, discovery, and growth is possible" (Carney, *American Dreaming* 283). Carney attributes a positive side effect of their forced journey out of The Bronx as their roaming of the streets allows them to advance in their identity formation. He even elevates the significance of escape as a way of dealing with the shrinking city when he states that "[m]ovement has become the last remaining expression of personal freedom and independence. It has become a last-ditch strategy of survival under fire" (Carney, *American Dreaming* 281). Hence, The Bronx takes on a double function in the era of decline. In the beginning of the movie, Gloria's apartment is a private space and a zone of personal freedom to live her maverick identity. Once the protagonists have to leave the neighborhood because of the violence, their journey away from it allows them to rework their relationship to each other more freely. The Bronx is order and disorder, familiar and unfamiliar, liberation and threat, regeneration and violence at the same time.

This proposition has two implications. First, the movement through and eventually out of the city alludes to the frontier myth where leaving the old settlements of the East and going West is an opportunity to reconfigure one's identity (see Ch. 2.3 and 3.1). Gloria and Phil leave their familiar comfort zone in order to regenerate their identities somewhere else. *Gloria* therefore varies the earlier literary and filmic frontier narratives. While Steven Robbins returns to The Bronx in order to overcome his crisis of masculinity in *The Old Neighborhood* and Murphy never left his frontier space in *Fort Apache: The Bronx*, Gloria and Phil have to leave the borough to overcome their crisis. Their 'outbound' journey allows the regeneration of their identities. Cassavetes's film thus extends the South Bronx as a frontier space by reworking the idea that in addition to the declining Bronx the entire inner-city functions as a place for identity reconfiguration as a basis of the protagonists' alternative success stories.

Second, the film promotes an individual strategy of dealing with the downfall in the era of decline: Gloria and Phil's departure from The Bronx reinforces the status quo of the neighborhood. Similar to *Fort Apache: The Bronx* where Murphy left the police force, Gloria leaves the struggling residents behind. This individual survival strategy resonates with the neoliberal logic where the state and political bodies retreat from their responsibilities of ensuring their people's decent standard of living. Both cinematic protagonists do not interrogate or try to change the systemic failures that led to the decline.

In conclusion, *Gloria* presents an ambivalent variation of the frontier narrative in the age of decline. First, *Gloria* constructs The Bronx as a multifaceted and ambiguous frontier zone which contains civilization and wilderness, freedom and violence, colonizers and savages alike. Similar to *Fort Apache: The Bronx*, *Gloria* establishes The Bronx as home, hiding place, and as a comfort zone for the female protagonist as well as point of departure to explore new interpersonal constellations and identity formations in the light of urban shrinkage. The movie extends the frontier zone to the entire city in order to show that the urban landscape of New York City is a territory where civilization and savagery meet. Extending the frontier to the entire city, *Gloria* subverts popular news media imaginaries which suggest that the border between wilderness and savagery in The Bronx is largely disconnected from the rest of New York City. *Gloria* therefore resonates with some of the central features of the frontier narrative, such as democracy, individualism, and freedom, by demonstrating that the entire city is an urban territory where civilization and savagery meet and where violence is the first step of a spiritual and spatial rebirth. Because of this ideological continuity, *Gloria* establishes that The Bronx is not just a frontier space, but an American space as well.

Second, *Gloria* updates the hypermasculine gangster film tradition by introducing white female agency to the frontier narrative. The strong Italian American frontier heroine showcases virtues and characteristics typical of the male-dominated frontier experience, such as self-determination, self-reliance, resilience, smartness, and optimism, to overcome challenges. Gloria and Phil's journey through the frontier territory allows them to re-configure their own subject positions and identity formations in new, relational, and performative ways. The movie therefore promotes sexual, gender, and family constellations which are chosen and created rather than born into – a central idea of Turner's frontier thesis where the frontier space facilitates individual regeneration.

Gloria shifts the attention to the destiny of white immigrant settler women in the era of decline by showing that not just men struggled and survived in the urban frontier. Gloria, like Murphy in *Fort Apache: The Bronx*, is an outlaw figure who embodies cultural Otherness. Neither character fits the dominant white Anglo American value system nor their immediate urban environments. Gloria has been part of the institution of the mob, but as an ex-mob wife she also suffers from the violence in the borough. However, Gloria and Murphy are more privileged in terms of their ethnic and racial identity than their Puerto Rican peers because they are only indirectly affected by the violence in the neighborhood.

Because Gloria is presented as a cool, tough, strong, and feminine frontier heroine, a larger suburban audience learns about the complexities and realities at the urban frontier. Although little is said about how long she has lived in The Bronx, she can be interpreted as a new kind of urban pioneer who appreciates her neighborhood as a space where she can live her alternative gender, sexual, ethnic, and class identity. Gloria shows a larger filmic audience that The Bronx has the potential to become a space of home, freedom, and colonial exploration for liberals and artists. She embodies the first wave of white (queer) female gentrifiers who are often members of the cultural avant-garde and the queer community for whom shrinking spaces are zones of freedom and exploration (N. Smith 16).

Third, *Gloria* converges the western and gangster genres, motifs, and figures as well as the melodramatic mode in order to convey the complexities of the frontier experience. Both *Gloria* and *Fort Apache: The Bronx* rework cinematic genres of crime and gangster that initially suggest that the South Bronx is an urban space of violence, crisis, and disorder in order to introduce complex stories, character constellations, and social critique. Both films also employ the melodramatic as a mode to rework spatial imaginations and to humanize the urban experience. The melodramatic mode in *Gloria* serves to personalize the urban space by introducing a strong-willed female heroine who is forced to take care of a child as a result of gangster violence in her building. This mode enriches gangster violence, a stable element in the longstanding gangster genre which is concerned with traditional gender and power hierarchies, with issues of alternative family, motherhood, and childhood in the South Bronx. This mode transfers issues of domesticity, femininity, and family which traditionally take place in domestic spaces to the road. Hence, the melodramatic mode in *Gloria* zooms in on the micro-level of the fictional characters in a similar way as *Fort Apache: The Bronx* in order to present their struggles in the context of an urban space in crisis. It also shows a wider audience that The Bronx as a frontier space facilitates generic and artistic creativity.

The Cassavetes production uses the frontier narrative to convey the complexities and realities of the urban frontier to a larger audience. On the one hand, *Gloria* is skeptical about the promise of Turner's frontier thesis because it points to the frontier's limitations as the protagonists must leave the area without really having the option of changing or even improving their situation. The heroine has to leave The Bronx not because she wants to pursue her path of social upward mobility as seen in the literary examples in Chapter 2, but she is ultimately forced to leave because of the socio-economically unstable situation in the borough. Leaving means accepting the limitations of living in a shrinking space and reinforcing the declining status quo of the neighborhood. Gloria and Phil along with Murphy and Isabella are the victims of the era of decline: While Murphy and Isabella's love affair fails in *Fort Apache: The Bronx*, Gloria and Phil lose their home in *Gloria*.

On the other hand, like *Fort Apache: The Bronx*, *Gloria* also has its empowering moment because it suggests an individual way out of shrinkage, crime, and violence. The empowerment of the individual amid the decline in the neighborhood is a very American reaction to the transformation processes on the frontier. Neither Gloria nor Murphy trust an official apparatus, but they manage to succeed in their challenges by virtues of self-reliance, resilience, and strength. In contrast to the literary works where The Bronx was the departure point to the protagonists' success stories, it is Gloria's journey out of The Bronx and movement across the city which allows her personal development. Here, the protagonists' urban journey reveals its productive side as it helps them find their relationship.

Gloria also suggests that violence is necessary for the spatial and individual regeneration of the borough (Slotkin). The movie's accomplishment is therefore the insight that a decline context triggers anti-essential, relational, and postmodern identity formations which, in turn, empower its characters.

As a result, a cinematic audience outside The Bronx can understand the complexities behind the dystopic news media images and might become personally and eventually financially interested in this special frontier space. By introducing fictionalized frontier stories of people who struggle to live in The Bronx, both films discuss various insider and outsider positions. They eventually make the individual struggles in the era of decline accessible through the use of familiar narratives, such as the frontier narrative, emotional structures of feeling (R. Williams, *Marxism*), and through generic convergence and creativity. As such, they raise empathy and understanding and contribute to the poetic, spatial, and economic resurrection of The Bronx. But how does a horror film such as the critically acclaimed *Wolfen* rework the frontier narrative in the era of decline and generate empathy for its residents?

3.3 "South Bronx and Wall Street: They are both dead": Gothic Ruins, Supernatural Creatures, and the Postcolonial Politics of Decline in *Wolfen* (1981)

Wolfen takes the frontier narrative even further by combining gothic and horror traditions in order to center on the perspective of the colonized. The movie was directed by Michael Wadleigh who is perhaps best known for his *Woodstock* (1970) documentary. Based on the novel *Wolfen* (1978) by Whitley Strieber, the film adaptation is a mixture of "horror noir" (Meehan 222), "werewolf movie, police procedural, and serial killer thriller" (Kinkle), "sci-fi, and political thriller genres" (McCormick 60). *Wolfen* intrigues and haunts the audience by revealing an explicit gaze on the devastated Bronx cityscape in its opening sequences. However, the movie's larger message is even more political than that of *Fort Apache: The Bronx* and *Gloria* as it criticizes mechanisms of capitalist exploitation which are guided by the frontier ideology of regeneration through violence (Slotkin). How does the film achieve this ideological criticism?

Similar to *Fort Apache: The Bronx* and *Gloria*, *Wolfen* establishes The Bronx through Manhattan as the geographical point of reference. The movie starts off with a tilted pan over Lower Manhattan. The Twin Towers are filmed from a lower camera angle against the sunset. They appear as empty buildings, void of any human activity. While the worm's eye perspective underlines the vertical composition of the Twin Towers in the screenshot and portrays them as powerful symbols of global capitalism, the late afternoon atmosphere in the panoramic shot suggests a declining civilization. This notion of civic decline and urban corruption is underlined by a piercing musical score which suggests that something is not right.

After the establishing panoramic shot of Lower Manhattan, the opening scene continues with a helicopter flight over the devastated landscape of the South Bronx, including empty lots and an abandoned church. This sequence, by contrast, is shot from a bird's-eye view, which highlights different power hierarchies. The aerial view over a seemingly dead cityscape reminds of vultures searching for dead animals in the desert. This gaze renders the audience as vultures because they enter this space through the cinematography. It also resembles the hegemonic colonial gaze of those in power who see the abandoned area as an open space for their new ventures to maximize their profits. Another shot reveals that this point of view belongs to powerful men like Dutch American Christopher Van der Veer (Max M. Brown), New York City's most influential real-estate mogul who attends a groundbreaking ceremony in the South Bronx and is killed shortly afterwards. Surrounded by city officials and media representatives from outside The Bronx, the real-estate tycoon hosts the inaugural ceremony for the construction of the exclusive luxury Van der Veer Tower condominium complex, "the largest urban renewal project since the early '70s [which] marks the beginning of the rebirth of this city" (voice-over). While Lower Manhattan is established as a rich, corrupted power center from a low-angle point-of-view of the colonized, the South Bronx landscape is represented as a space of subordination and commercial exploitation from the colonizer's position. The devastated church in the screenshot above underscores that religion, faith, morals, and hope have been abandoned. Urban decline and moral decline are closely connected. Hence, the film's beginning reinforces an outside colonial perspective onto the frontier space of The Bronx by contrasting asymmetrical power hierarchies between rich and poor within a few miles of each other in the same city.

The urban landscape presented at the beginning of *Wolfen* evokes fear more than the opening sequences of *Fort Apache: The Bronx* or *Gloria*. In *Wolfen* the opening sequence is followed by a set of freeze frames of ruined tenements, abandoned buildings, and piles of rubble suggesting a place void of human occupation. Low-angle shots show streets and apartment buildings against a clear blue sunny afternoon sky while a voice-over counts down from ten. The audience sees The Bronx through the eyes of the colonized in these takes. The gaze of the colonized evoke a graphic match to the worm's-eye perspective of the skyscrapers of Lower Manhattan. However, the infrastructure in The Bronx is destroyed and the buildings do not connote economic power, but the eerie power of death, destruction, and decay.

The various shots and takes highlight the enormous dimension of the devastation. The fact that there is hardly any camera movement in those sequences allows an unobstructed, voyeuristic outside gaze towards the devastation. Here, the horror results in the explicit and exploitative images of the actual declining South Bronx cityscape in contrast to an uncanny fictional monster in a classic nighttime horror flick, or as film critic Paul Meehan states: "[T]his very real image of fallen faith and urban desolation is ultimately more terrifying than any Hollywood monster" (224). At the end of the countdown, an empty old house is demolished which reveals an unobstructed view of the abandoned church. All of the shots of the destruction evoke an overall ambivalent atmosphere of the urban frontier; they show decay, but are filmed during a bright, sunny day. The bright sunlight references other classical horror films of the 1970s such as *The Texas Chainsaw Massacre* (dir. Tobe Hooper, 1974) where the monster escapes to the street under sunny skies.

This hauntingly decaying cityscape strongly references the gothic genre, another fictional genre which converges with the frontier tradition (see Mogen, Sanders, and Karpinski). Gothic spaces are traditionally marked by darkness, cursed castles (*Nosferatu*; Walpole) and falling aristocratic mansions (Poe). With regard to *Wolfen*, this has now changed. As literary scholar Seymour Rudin observes:

> [T]he old Gothic creatures, the blood-drinking, flesh-eating, sometimes shape-changing entities, vampires and werewolves and their kith and kin, have shifted their locales. The horrors that once stalked the castle of Otranto or Dracula's lair in Transylvania or sometimes even the country houses of Saki are now to be found and feared in the South Bronx. (116)

In his analysis of the American urban gothic, Rudin emphasizes that in cultural representations of the 1970s and early 1980s, a transfer of gothic settings from an old stock of European aristocratic architecture to the American declining inner city takes place. Whereas remote frontier wilderness and rural places were the source of terror, now the former bustling center of America's cities takes up this position. In *Wolfen*, the verbal countdown and musical score work to undermine the bright mood mentioned earlier, foreshadowing that something is not right and the horror is about to come. This fear-invoking opening further draws on the conventions of the gothic and horror genres by building on a feeling of fear and fascination of what the viewer knows and does not know. The South Bronx is, therefore, represented as a dual space, the space of the known and the space of the unknown.

Wolfen converges and updates the spatial imagination of the gothic. Literary scholars Anna Powell and Andrew Smith explain the gothic as an open and flexible phenomenon: "Gothic is a vibrant, flexible mode, mutating to fit changing cultural and ideological dynamics" (2). In subverting existing societal hierarchies, "the Gothic mode allows for a demystified and thereby skeptical reading of [legal and economic structures], encouraging the reader to see the horror implicit in seemingly mundane systems of oppression" (Bienstock Anolik 34). While the melodramatic mode critiques existing power inequalities by individualizing, embodying, and dramatizing, the gothic mode employs more abstract narrative perspectives and aesthetic techniques to expose social, ethnic, class, and gender inequalities during moments of crisis. The gothic mode in Wadleigh's movie works to articulate criticism of urban decline, not through failed love or substitute family relationships as in *Fort Apache: The Bronx* and *Gloria*, but through criticism of the capitalist forces symbolized by the murdered Van der Veer couple. The South Bronx frontier (and with it Manhattan to some extent) is represented in a much more horrifying manner than in *Fort Apache: The Bronx* and *Gloria*.

While the opening helicopter scenes reinforce a hegemonic colonial neoliberal gaze, the film establishes an inside perspective of the South Bronx shortly afterwards. This indigenous point of view is most notable in an interior shot of the abandoned church. The indigenous gaze is established through a point-of-view shot which is situated inside of the abandoned church marked by the green and purple solarization images as well as distorted sound effects. These images highlight what Henry Jenkins refers to as technological convergence as older forms are incorporated into new media technologies (16). The point-of-view shot in connection with the distorted sounds, "false-color thermography techniques," and "SteadiCam hand-held camera" (Meehan 224) suggests a different frame of reference in comparison to the earlier sequences. The local gaze enhances the notion that this South Bronx resident is not of flesh and blood but a non-human creature. The film style underscores the creature's position as the audience seems to see through its eyes without seeing the creature itself. The audience becomes the creature.

The creature is the wolfen, a type of urban werewolf figure who defends its declining hunting grounds. One of the main shapeshifter protagonists in the film is the Native American Eddie Holt (Edward James Olmos) who eventually lifts the secret around the wolfen's existence. Although the horror movie closely associates werewolves with Native Americans (E. Lawrence 105), the term wolfen does not have any meaning as such when the audience starts watching the movie. The term reminds of the German noun *der Wolf*. It alludes to German vernacular and folk tales, sagas, and legends about wolves, shapeshifters, and werewolves. Inspired by gothic traditions in Germany, "wolfen" situates the film's story in a European gothic tradition and re-works it into an American urban gothic context. As an empty signifier to a larger American audience, it could refer to a wide variety of marginalized population groups in the South Bronx, such as Native Americans, African Americans or Latinx people, the poor, or other displaced victims of urban renewal processes and of the neoliberal expoitation in the 1980s.

This personalization strategy differs from those of *Fort Apache: The Bronx* and *Gloria*, whose frontier figures are immediately visible to the viewer through medium close-up (Murphy) or long shots (Gloria). In contrast to the two earlier films where the audience can *look at* Murphy and Gloria's fate in the declining South Bronx, *Wolfen*'s audience is put in the position of the supernatural creature by taking up its very gaze, thus, *seeing trough* their very eyes. The audience does not just observe cultural difference on the safe movie screen but becomes the Other audio-visually by being forced to take up its point of view, which is an uneasy, unpleasant, and highly distorting experience. *Wolfen* thus blurs the boundaries between the melodramatic mode and the gothic mode by overdoing the subjective narrative perspective of the alleged monster. Narrative and aesthetic exaggeration which symbolizes "heightened dramatization" (viii) is one main feature of this mode as Peter Brooks writes in his study *The Melodramatic Imagination: Balzac, Henry James, Melodrama, and the Mode of Excess* (1995). The distorted visual and aural effects along with the extreme subjective camera perspective are used in excess to emphasize the perspective of the colonized subject in the urban wilderness, to sympathize with their experience, and to make a more political overall statement on the causes of decline.

The gothic mode therefore foregrounds a more direct, political criticism of the economic framework of larger population groups in contrast to *Fort Apache: The Bronx* and *Gloria*. Both movies show the consequences of a capitalist system running amok merely on an individual level. *New York Times* film critic Vincent Canby notes in his review that "Mr. Wadleigh makes even better use of the devastation of the South Bronx than did *Fort Apache: The Bronx*, and he delights in contrasting these lost-looking locations with posh penthouses, pretty little apartments overlooking Riverside Drive and a spectacular police-security center" ("*Wolfen* with Finney"). This observation on the film is striking, because *Fort Apache: The Bronx* was severely criticized as a one-dimensional representation of the area and its inhabitants (see Ch. 3.1). One reason can be found in the fact that *Fort Apache: The Bronx* offers clearly recognizable and identifiable villains: the inhabitants of The Bronx. *Wolfen*, by contrast, blames larger social and economic forces for the downfall of the place. Here, the villain figure is abstract and works on a metaphorical level rather than an individual one, which is perhaps not as easily recognized by the audience.

Although the audience takes up the point of view of the werewolf figures, its destiny is only fully accessible through a mediator, the white Anglo American police detective Dewey Wilson (Albert Finney). Dewey, a resident of Staten Island, is a well-respected cop and an idiosyncratic outsider figure. In the beginning of the movie Dewey is not working in his job as a police detective. Warren (Dick O'Neill), his superior, explains Wilson's absence: "He had a lot of family problems. He started to drink a little too much. Police work piled up on him. He's a good man." Dewey only returns to his work and the film to the genre conventions of the police procedural when Warren asks him to solve the murder of the real-estate mogul Christopher and his wife Pauline Van der Veer (Anne Marie Photamo). Wilson has an affair with his colleague Rebecca Neff (Diane Venora), but apart from that the audience learns very little about his personal life, his masculinity, or their love relationship. The melodramatic mode functions differently in *Wolfen* as it is serves to provide an extremely subjective view of the indigenous Other in the South Bronx, not the detective from Staten Island.

Yet the detective is a variation of the frontier hero figure as he transcends geographical and cultural boundaries between civilization and wilderness, police and werewolf spaces. Although Dewey uses enlightened police methods of logic, rationality, and reasoning in his work, he is the only one who transcends technology-enforced police methods and meets up with the Native Americans on their territory "of the bridges and skyscrapers" (Wilson). Dewey's fashion and clothing style underline his mediating position between police/technology/authority and wolfen/nature/the oppressed. When Dewey arrives at the crime scene of the Van der Veer couple at Manhattan's southern tip, Battery Park, he wears brown sweatpants, a dark green hooded zip shirt, and a red headband in the medium-long shot. His casual outfit bears more similarities with Eddie Holt whom he later meets on Brooklyn Bridge than with the more formal clothing style of his superior Warren. Warren is dressed in a long coat and gloves. Holt mirrors Wilson's clothing as he also wears brownish corduroy pants, a brownish sweater, and a red headband.

Wilson's mediating identity between official authorities and marginalized locals is therefore comparable to Murphy in *Fort Apache: The Bronx*: just like Murphy's experiences of police violence and drug violence in the South Bronx, Dewey's conversations with the Native Americans lead him to a change of perspective and he eventually takes sides with the oppressed. Both Dewey and Murphy are frontier heroes who navigate between fort/police station and desert/deindustrial landscape, civilization/wilderness, colonizer/colonized, and they allow an insight into the complex dynamics at work in shrinking urban contexts in their function as contemporary reincarnations of this American character.

Detective Dewey eventually uncovers the story behind the killing of the Van der Veer couple by cooperating with indigenous people. Wilson meets Holt and other Native Americans in their South Bronx bar "Wigwam." Here, Eddie explains the supernatural phenomenon of the wolfen to Dewey:

> Eddie: "It's not wolves. It's Wolfen. For 20,000 years, Wilson, 10 times your fucking Christian era, the skins and the wolves, great hunting nations, lived together. Nature in balance. Then the slaughter came. The smartest ones they went underground. Into the new wilderness. Your cities. Into the great slum areas, the graveyard of your fucking species. These great hunters became your scavengers. Your garbage, your abandoned people became their new meat animal."
> Dewey: "But they're only..."
> Eddie: "Animals? Are you sure, Wilson? They might be gods. In their eyes you are the savage. You got your technology, but you lost, you lost your senses. They can see two looks away. They can hear clouds pass overhead. In their world, there can be no lies, no crime. No need for detectives."

Dewey finally starts to understand the character of the wolfen who kill "[t]he sick, the abandoned. Those who will not be missed" (Holt). Eddie explains that according to the spirit there is no waste, but a continuing cycle of life and death, devastation and renewal. His explanation affirms that the ruins of the South Bronx reveal a productive side as they constitute the hunting ground for the wolfen. As Van der Veer's urban renewal project posed a threat to their habitat, they started to kill those "neoliberal" intruders (Kinkle).

These considerations strongly remind of the frontier narrative discussed in *Fort Apache: The Bronx* (see Ch. 3.1). Both cinematic settler figures are analogies to lower-class people of color who live in the "new wilderness" (Holt). Both white male heroes fight for disenfranchised groups. Murphy helps locals and Dewey is the mediator through whom the audience learns to take up the perspective of the shapeshifter creatures. Both also understand violence as a regenerating practice in order to create an American identity in Slotkin's and Turner's sense. In *Wolfen*, violence is exerted by corporate institutions. Carried out in the name of urban renewal and the post-World War II regeneration of American cities, this corporate violence displaced long-standing communities and demolished entire neighborhoods. In contrast to *Fort Apache: The Bronx*, *Wolfen* is much more skeptical about the spatial regeneration processes of the urban frontier exerted by corporate violence because only the colonizers profit from this cycle. Finally, both films transgress the conventions of the frontier myth.

Wolfen extends the frontier theme of *Fort Apache: The Bronx* by introducing a symbolic empowerment of those marginalized groups. Dewey destroys the plaster model of the apartment complex at Van der Veer's penthouse on Wall Street watched by the wolfen. He even protects the shapeshifters by not telling his superiors about their whereabouts as he leaves them to believe that the international terrorist group Götterdämmerung, named after a Richard Wagner opera, instigated the murder of the real-estate tycoon. He symbolically smashes the capitalist, profit-driven, neoliberal restructuring forces that attempt to start a new cycle of economic exploitation and marginalization in the South Bronx. Finalizing the transformation of the audience's gaze, the wolfen are depicted as strong, dignified, "beautiful and intelligent animals" (Mackenthun 106) at the end of the movie. *Wolfen* argues for native sovereignty and native rights to the city as they have been formulated in American Indian and indigenous liberation movements since the late 1960s.

Observing this new spatial and ethnic agency symbolized by the wolfen, American Studies scholar Gesa Mackenthun argues that "*Wolfen* displaces the

topic of territorial dispossession from a colonial-imperial context to an eco-
logical narrative about a nature that reclaims territory from a rotten civilization" (105). Instead of being marginalized and silenced by the colonial gaze,
Native Americans become agents of nature's revenge in 1980s neoliberal society (Mackenthun 105). In attacking the police force's reliance on "technology"
and their lack of using their "senses," Eddie and *Wolfen* ultimately criticize
the dominant discourse of an enlightened, technocratic (Western) American
society.

The movie therefore voices a larger criticism of neoliberalism and impe-
rialism in the age of decline than *Fort Apache: The Bronx* and *Gloria. Wolfen*
equates the devastated South Bronx to the corrupt financial world of Wall
Street: "South Bronx and Wall Street. What's the connection?," asks Dewey.
"They're both dead," replies his colleague Baldy (James Tolkan). By equating
Wall Street and the South Bronx, the movie creates a direct link between the
neoliberalist framework and the downfall of the inner city. The South Bronx
has been destroyed by the profit-driven endeavors of the private real-estate
sector burning down houses in order to obtain insurance money. Wall Street,
embodied by the Van der Veer empire, puts a capitalist 'anything goes' mentality in action which does not hold on to moral standards. As such *Wolfen*
highlights the failure of American progress narratives as it creates a vision
where capital reigns supreme, the symbolic elevator which anticipates social
upward mobility is defunct, and a sustainable and grassroots growth of cities
is categorically ruled out. Questioning American values of progress, equality, and freedom on top of lacking a high-profile star such as Paul Newman
could be one of the reasons why the low-budget horror production was less
easily accessible to a larger commercial audience. Shortly after the theatrical
release, *Wolfen* was distributed as a Warner Home Video and thus disappeared
into (horror) film lovers' suburban homes and private TV screens.

At the same time, however, *Wolfen* emphasizes positive aspects of the frontier experience by adding an ironic twist in the infinite cycle of renewal, decline, and resurrection. While the werewolf figures perform the perspective of
the oppressed, they simultaneously engage in a "symbiotic relationship with
capitalist urban planning in the sense that they thrive in the new wilderness
created by urban collapse" (Kinkle). They profit from urban decline, thus help-
ing the real-estate business to eventually redevelop the area. Although constructed as the colonialized Other, they are indeed part of the capitalist cycle of decline, resurrection, and eventually gentrification. Cultural Studies
scholar Jeff Kinkle goes even as far as calling the wolfen the "shock troops

of gentrification." As a result, *Wolfen* prophetically envisions and symbolically foreshadows the spatial resurrection of the South Bronx in the late twentieth and early twenty-first centuries.

Wolfen reveals the frontier's violence-induced cultural productivity as an important element of urban shrinkage processes. Mackenthun attributes the horror noir film with an innovative character as it "giv[es] a voice and a certain degree of agency to the bearers of subjugated knowledges" (105). For her, the movie is one of the few examples produced by Non-Native American artists that address their experience of marginalization and displacement. Meehan and Rudin both note the generic innovation of the longstanding horror genre which consists of the transfer of the gothic and horror genres to the declining inner city (Meehan 222; Rudin 125). Meehan declares *Wolfen* one of the most "memorable" horror noir films (236) and a "modern urban update" of the werewolf genre which contributed to its revival in the 1980s (222).

The explicit depiction of spatialized violence, decline, and decay especially in the beginning of the film also foretells the tendency of ruin porn photography. Coined by John Patrick Leary ("Detroitism"), ruin porn photography emerged as a genre in the early 2000s which is marked by colorful urban ruin landscapes (of Detroit), such as abandoned industrial buildings and private homes, usually void of people. Camilo José Vergara, for instance, took pictures of declining cityscapes in The Bronx, Newark, Gary, Indiana, and Detroit (*American Ruins*; see Ch. 1.2;). The freeze frames in *Wolfen* anticipate this new genre, highlighting contemporary fascination with urban blight.

In sum, *Wolfen* updates the frontier narrative by shifting to the perspective of the indigenous. The movie affirms the frontier logic that violence is necessary to spatial and economic resurrection and echoes its productive, generic, and innovative aspects such as the notion that violence generates an identity reformation. Taking on an extremely subjective camera point-of-view and incorporating new visualization technologies of the early 1980s, it establishes a particular empowering indigenous gaze.

Wolfen also voices a stronger critique of the downside of the modern frontier experience and the economic mechanisms that lead to the age of decline. The mix of horror, werewolf, and police procedural genres presents a fear-invoking version of the South Bronx as home to a monstrous creature. Its urban wilderness iconography of burned-out buildings, empty streets, and piles of rubble is much more horrifying than in *Fort Apache: The Bronx* and *Gloria* because of its verisimilitude. Strongly inspired by the gothic mode which focuses on the ruins and presents the South Bronx as an ambiguous frontier space which is both known and unknown, *Wolfen* shifts the attention from individual protagonists to repressed population groups in The Bronx which are symbolized through the supernatural wolfen creature.

This abstraction from individual subjectivity to collective and systemic mechanisms results in the fact that the horror film is much more critical of progress narratives such as the frontier and ultimately much more skeptical and political in its larger message. The Wadleigh production creates a portrait of a corrupt neoliberal and neo-imperial society marked by greed for profit at the expense of colonized citizens. *Wolfen* is skeptical of who is going to profit from socio-economic regeneration processes as it points out that the colonized are trapped in this ongoing capitalist cycle of urban destruction and redevelopment and sees the historic continuities and present-day dangers of new racial, ethnic, gender, and class exploitations.

While all three films analyzed so far display genres that present an unstable urban frontier space, such as police procedural, gangster, gang, and horror, *Wolfen* uses the notion of the South Bronx as a place of fear and terror in order to voice ideological criticism of the causes and consequences of capitalism. In contrast to Murphy in *Fort Apache: The Bronx* and Gloria in *Gloria*, we hardly get to know the frontier hero Dewey Wilson beyond his work as a police detective. Instead, *Wolfen* shifts the focus to the repressed, thereby criticizing "the strategy behind the abandonment of these neighborhoods, the (re)development behind the dereliction" (Kinkle). In pointing out the influence of corporate capital on the rebuilding of the South Bronx, *Wolfen* foreshadows the gentrification and commodification tendencies of the South Bronx since the 2000s.

3.4 Conclusion

Fort Apache: The Bronx, *Gloria*, and *Wolfen* symbolically reconnect The Bronx to the frontier narrative in the age of decline. As declining and shrinking spaces are zones of violence, terror, and loss as well as identity formation, renewal, and regeneration in the logic of the frontier discourse, the films articulate complex scenarios about the causes and consequences of decline and affirm that such spaces nevertheless open important opportunities for spatial, individual, collective, spatial, media, and technological innovations. The films respond more directly to the frontier ideology formulated in the news media coverage during the era of decline than the literary texts discussed earlier and underline that decline is indeed productive.

First, *Fort Apache: The Bronx*, *Gloria*, and *Wolfen* explore the individuals' transformative potential on the frontier. Similar to the literary examples in Chapter 2, the films introduce interethnic and interracial friendships and relationships, anti-essential family constellations, and provide greater agency to ethnic, gender, racial, and social Otherness figures as a result of the frontier experience. The protagonists take up complex subject positions which are situated in between the colonizer and the colonized.

The characters are directly or indirectly affected by violence at the urban frontier which threatens to destroy their homes and their relationships. Experiencing oppression caused by corporate (*Wolfen*), bureaucratic (*Fort Apache: The Bronx*), or criminal colonizers (*Gloria*), they undergo a development in the course of the narration because they possess American virtues such as resilience, strength, adaptability, and individualism. Especially *Gloria* and *Fort Apache: The Bronx* find highly individualized ways of resisting the challenges of the shrinking Bronx and the industries responsible for its political neglect, moral downfall and urban demolition. The films thus echo one of the main benefits of Slotkin's frontier mythology that violence is destructive but necessary in order to regenerate one's identity. As the American character originated at the frontier in Turner's sense, The Bronx becomes such an urban frontier space in the cinematic imagination where renewed versions of American identities are formed.

Reformulations of individual and collective identities as a consequence of the frontier experience are also evident in youth and gang films released during the late 1970s and early 1980s, such as Walter Hill's cult film *The Warriors* or the Italian science-fiction adaptation *1990: The Bronx Warriors*, and *The Wanderers*. *The Warriors*, to give one example, is about a male gang of the same name that returns from a gathering in the South Bronx to their home turf on Coney Island. On their way home from The Bronx they encounter conflicting gangs and cross different gang territories. Similar to Gloria's journey across the urban frontier, the gang's trip home also showcases "the teenagers' struggle to establish a strong identity, and [...] the ethnic and economic fragmentation that characterizes large cities" (Rafferty 20-21). *The Warriors* experiments with alternative social structures which "are neither a complete family nor a complete state, but, rather, some hybrid creation" of both (Roth 134). Eventually, the journey through the nocturnal urban frontier becomes the Warrior gang's quest for a masculine group identity. The characters' quest affirms the regenerative potential of the frontier marked by relational, anti-essential individual and group identities seen in *Fort Apache: The Bronx, Wolfen,* and *Gloria.*

Secondly, the films cinematically engage, depart from, and expand long-standing visual and narrative frontier traditions by converging, mixing, and blurring the boundaries between classical and modern frontier genres which stand in the tradition of frontier fiction, such as gothic/horror (*Wolfen*), gangster (*Gloria*), police procedural (*Wolfen; Fort Apache: The Bronx*), and western (*Fort Apache: The Bronx*). They combine them with modes and converge them with new media technologies. Modes function as particularly productive narrative and aesthetic strategies to update the frontier genres in this regard. The melodramatic mode in *Fort Apache: The Bronx* and *Gloria* breaks down the frontier experience to the white male and female outlaw protagonists' micro-level, thus offering identification potential, empathy, and understanding of the causes and consequences that led to the downfall of the entire area. *Wolfen* uses the gothic mode to provide the perspective of the Natives and/or a more general cultural Other. The gothic mode converges ruin aesthetics of earlier literary and cinematic gothic imaginaries and articulates a larger ideological criticism and the causes for colonized.

The films demonstrate that age of decline allows filmmakers to experiment with existing media and genre conventions. As media convergence changes relationships between media, genres, and narratives (H. Jenkins 15-16), urban decline facilitates those innovations and changes relationships between cultural narratives and how they are historically narrated. *Wolfen* is one of the most innovative movies analyzed so far in terms of media and "technological convergence" (H. Jenkins 16) as it uses highly subjective and at the time cutting-edge special-effects-enhanced camera perspectives in order to establish the experience of the colonized in this urban frontier.

The updating of genres, modes, and media technologies attract new audiences. As *Gloria* introduces a female gangster figure and frontier heroine and codes the urban frontier as female (see N. Smith 16), white female audiences can identify with the protagonist. While lacking larger commercial success, *Wolfen* is an artistic masterpiece which generated interest in The Bronx especially for pop culture nerds. Because the movies are released in a transnational media context, they circulate the image of The Bronx as an urban frontier among new global audiences though mechanisms of global convergence (H. Jenkins 113).

Thirdly, the films analyzed in this chapter rework The Bronx as a frontier space by diversifying its spatial functions in the age of decline. The movies draw on the binary frontier imagery created by corporate news media (Ch. 2.3), but they complicate the experience of frontiersmen and women. White frontier heroes Murphy and Gloria are comfortable with their frontier life especially in the beginning of the movies. They echo experience of European pioneers and settlers for whom the frontier once became their home turf (Turner). Their comfort builds on Marshall Berman's notion of the home (Ch. 1.2), but unlike Berman who argued that the postmodern avant-garde rediscovers home of the past as a response to deindustrialization (333), home here refers to the characters' present lives in the urban frontier.

The films use the shrinking frontier space as an opportunity to critically reflect on the mechanisms of American capitalism. Because the films begin with Manhattan as a geographical frame of reference, they reveal the striking political, social, and economic inequalities that exist in New York City. By establishing a close link between The Bronx and Lower Manhattan in particular, the movies medially point to the financial and public institutions which are responsible for the downfall of The Bronx. Without Manhattan there is no Bronx. The movies are therefore skeptical about the economic-driven violence caused by corporate America and the medial exclusion and strategies of Othering as a result of this process.

The filmmaker's exploration of the urban frontier, liminal characters, and skepticisms of the ideology of growth bears striking similarities to the long tradition of social critique and reform in American culture at the end of the nineteenth century. In their novels, naturalist writers such as Theodore Dreiser or Stephen Crane created fictitious laboratory situations in which they exposed existing social, class, and gender structures and examined the fall of heroes who seem to be firmly established in their social milieu and gender identity. Dreiser's novel *Sister Carrie* (1900), for instance, zooms in on the middle-aged male protagonist Hurstwood and narrates his economic decline and crisis of masculinity. The films analyzed in this chapter adapt those naturalistic aesthetic strategies in order to highlight race, gender, sexuality, class, ethnicity, and ideological conflicts in the urban frontier.

The on location shooting in all three films reminds strongly of the cultural practice of slumming which was popular when the social inequalities in rapidly industrializing New York City were especially grim. Upper-class residents would stroll to frontier spaces marked by industrialization, urbanization, and poverty for voyeuristic pleasure, looking at the living condition of immigrants and/or paupers in the late nineteenth and early twentieth centuries (Heap 2). Writers such as Theodore Dreiser, Stephen Crane, or muckracker journalists such as Jacob Riis addressed the social inequalities in Manhattan by centering their narratives on lower class residents, immigrant groups, and victims of urbanization in their novels, short stories, and novellas. They showcased a severe criticism of late nineteenth-century growth visions in the age of industrialization (see Fluck, "Realism" 569). More than the writers in the second Chapter who re-remembered how the now declining Bronx was once the starting point for their individual growth, empowerment, and success narratives, the filmmakers chose the contemporary Bronx of the early 1980s as the location for the narrative's criticism and situate their films within this larger historic context of the urban frontier.

Wolfen as the most aesthetically explicit and politically most outspoken film in this group is the most persuasive in exposing the mechanisms of the capitalist-driven real-estate market in the downfall and demolition of urban spaces and calling out to reforms. It interrogates the neglect of the poor in favor of enhancing the wealth and influence of the rich. It probes causes of the downfall as well as symbolic scenarios of revenge. Although *Wolfen* introduces werewolf killers, the real monsters are the real-estate tycoons who both reduce the shrinking spaces of New York City and The Bronx to morally and physically dead spaces. *Fort Apache: The Bronx* and *Gloria* work towards *Wolfen* in that they build on spatial binaries first to blur their boundaries: there is no way out and there are outlaws everywhere. Similar to Jacob Riis' *How the Other Half Lives* (1890), *Wolfen* points to the socially conscious muckracker movement which aimed at exposing social inequalities and improving the living standards of the urban poor. The Bronx films of the early 1980s draw on this tendency, warning of the repetition of urban history in the age of deindustrialization.

Despite their economic critique, the films affirm the frontier narrative and its underlying spatial, ideological, and economic mechanisms in the age of shrinkage. They echo the frontier ideology that violence is necessary for individual and collective renewal (Slotkin). As *Fort Apache: The Bronx*, *Gloria*, and to a certain extent *Wolfen* come up with individual solutions to the demolition, they also affirm the status quo of the capitalist economic system which led to the downfall of The Bronx in the first place. They thus establish The Bronx as a uniquely American space, a spatial and narrative construction similar to the literary works analyzed in Chapter 2.

Because The Bronx is represented as an aesthetically rough frontier space which nevertheless provides individual freedom, the borough becomes appealing and interesting for a larger commercial audience (see N. Smith 18). The films' postmodern outlaw characters and their popular genre bricolage appeals to liberal nerds, pop culture aficionados, and "early adopters" (18). They highlight the role of the movie industry in the poetic resurrection of The Bronx as directors, film crews, and production companies came to The Bronx as modern day slummers and/or colonizers who were inspired by and more or less commercially exploited the deindustrialized frontier-space. The films therefore suggest that The Bronx is ready to be spatially resurrected and eventually gentrified. The cinematic frontier narrative examined here helps justify the social exclusion of its residents as a result of a new urban re-colonization process (see N. Smith 17-18, 27) in which corporate capital takes on the role as colonizer/settler and locals are pushed again into the role of the colonized/indigenous. The films therefore update the ideological function of the frontier narrative: narratively "to tame the wild city" as Neil Smith put it (43) in preparation to re-colonize (27), recapitalize, and commercially exploit the urban 'wilderness' north of the Harlem River. If literature updates the success story in order to facilitate a poetic resurrection of The Bronx, and films revise the frontier narrative, what is the function of hip-hop culture in this regard?

Chapter 4
Creating a New Popular Culture:
Re-Imagining the American Dream in Hip-Hop

Hip-hop culture is one of the main forms of representations connected to the shrinking Bronx in the 1970s and 1980s. African American studies scholar Tricia Rose explains in her pioneering study *Black Noise: Rap Music and Black Culture in Contemporary America* (1994): "Hip hop is a cultural form that attempts to negotiate the experience of marginalization, brutally truncated opportunity, and oppression within the cultural imperatives of African-American and Caribbean history, identity and community" (21). Hip-hop is thus not only a musical style, but a broader series of cultural practices with a strong political dimension directed against racism and discrimination that can empower disenfranchised demographic groups. A "mix of fun and socially conscious music and discourse" (Gosa 64), hip-hop commonly consists of four elements: DJing, MCing, graffiti, and breakdance (see, for instance, Forman and Neal; J. Williams). DJing refers to the use of the turntable, traditionally a device for playing back sound recordings, as a musical instrument via spinning and scratching – that is, rhythmically moving a record's stylus back-and-forth on a vinyl record. MCing is the act of rhythmically rapping over the beats played by the DJ. In some cases, MCs or rappers use their voice to articulate and protest against the invisibility and discrimination of African American youth. Graffiti refers to painting surfaces, walls, or subway cars with spray cans. Breakdancing is a dance performance involving robotic arm or leg moves or the body spinning on the floor to the sound of the DJ. Breakdancers create a makeshift stage when they perform on the sidewalks of streets. All of these four elements serve to "symbolically appropriate[...] urban space" (Rose 22) and conventional genres and media forms. Their protagonists are "alternative cartographers" (Forman 71) who draw on a variety of styles, urban practices, production technologies, and cultural traditions to recreate the urban space according to their rules. They constitute hip-hop as a multi-medial postmodern urban phenomenon. Hip-hop is finally a "participatory culture" (H. Jenkins 3; see Ch. 1.2) where hip-hop practitioners and audiences actively engage in the production of texts, tracks, and clips.

Building on its musical foundations, referred to as rap, hip-hop is a hybrid form where a variety of media such as film, photography, music video, and even fashion converge. Rap music can also unfold as a three-dimensional phenomenon, when it comes out of radio speakers in a room or from a car stereo. As a holistic soundscape consisting of rapped words and music, it can fill a public or private space with melodies, beats, and vocals. What, then, is the impact of hip-hop as a specific genre on the construction of The Bronx? Which figures, spatial discourses, and modes can we identify and how do they reconfigure the American Dream narrative?

I will show how a mostly younger generation of artists and performers of color actively engaged in rap and hip-hop as a local response to the decline by establishing The Bronx was a cultural and creative hotspot in the mid-to-late 1970s. The case studies revive the cultural narrative of the American Dream (see Ch. 1.4) celebrating The Bronx as a mythic place of creativity, community, and innovation. In doing so, hip-hop renews the promise of The Bronx as a site of the American Dream much like the narratives voiced by the older Jewish American writers in their autobiographical success narratives (Ch. 2).

Three texts will serve as corpus in this chapter in order to show how hip-hop creates The Bronx as a place of creativity. First, the film *Wild Style* affirms The Bronx as a creative space for Puerto Rican characters characterized by innovation and community spirit. Second, the film will be discussed alongside the music video "The Message" which, in my reading, suggests critique and skepticism as well as humor and optimism of the American Dream narrative from a young, male, African American point of view. The film, the song, and the music video all provide an inside perspective of disenfranchised population groups living in The Bronx. They shift the cultural narrative of the American Dream to a younger generation of people of color who have been silenced at best and, at worst, demonized in the dominant discourse of the shrinking Bronx.

Finally, the 2007 photo book *Born in The Bronx: A Visual Record of the Early Days of Hip-Hop* features photographs of the emerging hip-hop culture of the late 1970s and early 1980s. This photo book affirms my thesis that all of the texts discussed in this chapter function as a means to personify the urban crisis by emphasizing the experience of individuals, activists, and performers. Beyond Marta Cooper's and Henry Chalfant's 1984 cult photo book *Subway Art* which documents the New York City graffiti scene, *Born in The Bronx* demonstrates a new type of discourse on the American Dream which has been at work since the early 2000s, the legacy discourse. This retrospective discourse celebrates the (South) Bronx as the birthplace of hip-hop, thereby nostalgically remembering the cultural legacy of the decline era while simultaneously showing that the urban crisis in the South Bronx is a myth that can be commercially exploited.

4.1 "We are all graffiti artists": Visual Creativity, Puerto Rican Romance, and a Local Success Story in *Wild Style* (1982)

Wild Style is one of the key films that establish the devastated Bronx as a creative space. It was directed by artist, filmmaker, and writer Charlie Ahearn who received funding for the project from the British TV station Channel 4 and the German public TV broadcaster ZDF (Jaehne 4). Although it is not Ahearn's only film, *Wild Style* is certainly his most famous work, and it introduced hip-hop culture to a wider American and global audiences (see Charry for Africa; Condry for Japan; Nitzsche and Grünzweig for Europe). Its success undoubtedly lies in the detailed depiction of the bottom-up story of hip-hop culture since the film reconfigures the shrinking urban landscape of the Morrisania section of the South Bronx as a space of artistic production and communal creativity (see Naison, "Rap: Morrisania Roots"). The Ahearn production demonstrates the productivity, innovation, and creativity of a mostly younger generation of residents of color, and – on the level of form and media – reworks established cinematic genre and narrative conventions.

Wild Style's unique generic hybridity has been observed by film critics (Canby, "*Wild Style*;" Grabel; Palmer; Stein) and academics alike. In her convincing study of the Ahearn production, to date one of the few comprehensive scholarly analyses of the film besides Nitzsche ("Hip-Hop Culture"), performance scholar Kimberly Monteyne argues that in combining the genres of Hollywood musical and documentary, *Wild Style* addresses social problems of urban spaces in the early 1980s (122). This chapter expands Monteyne's analysis in order to discuss the ways in which the film, hip-hop culture, and especially urban shrinkage intersect in *Wild Style*, how the film constructs the area as a creative space, and, ultimately, which repercussions this particular cinematic representation has on the cultural narrative of the American Dream. I argue that the film responds to the decaying South Bronx by presenting it as a communal and creative urban space and its younger black and brown residents as creative agents of change who stress the importance of staying in The Bronx. By doing so, *Wild Style* believes in its *in situ* resurrection thus renewing the American Dream as a local narrative.

The idea of The Bronx as a creative space is already affirmed in the film's opening sequence. *Wild Style* starts with a straight-on angle of a graffiti-covered wall somewhere in a subway yard somewhere in the South Bronx at night. The opening frame shows a train yard which is commonly overlooked by many Americans. The audience assumes the perspective of an on-location observer as the blurred fence in the image's foreground suggests. Colored in orange and yellow shades, the term graffiti is prominently written in the background on the wall in "softer and more readable bubble style letters of the late 1970s" (Monteyne 89). This graffiti piece affirms the appropriation of an industrial and rather pragmatic urban space as raw material for artistic production. Compared to the literary and filmic texts discussed earlier, it also foreshadows a new take on the discourse of decline: repurposing the urban space instead of abandoning it.

This opening sequence introduces graffiti culture as one of the most important artistic practices in The Bronx. Graffiti is a form of writing and spraying letters, groups of letters (tags), and pictures on walls or subway cars. As an ancient artistic practice, it ranges from prehistoric cave paintings (Hoban 35) to mural art of the early twentieth century and merges these influences with industrial painting technology. In contrast to fine arts, graffiti is much more bulky and cannot be moved easily to an indoor exhibition. Geared towards the street and the public urban space, graffiti is an urban practice that engages the surfaces of a city by adding colors and shapes, adding another layer of meaning onto the existing fabric of a city. Thus, it reclaims the urban space by making visible particular social groups and aesthetic discourses that are mostly invisible in the city.

The central function of graffiti as a creative urban practice against devastation, however, is to challenge and interrogate existing aesthetic and spatial conventions. This is also reinforced in the film's title. The term wild style refers to a "complicated construction of interlocking letters" (Cooper and Chalfant 27) outside conventional writing styles, thereby questioning their validity. The title *Wild Style* can be interpreted as a transgressive urban practice that aims at questioning conventions with regard to film genres, music and art traditions, and spatial relations and that aims at creating a new urban community on the other (Pennycook).

The narrative of *Wild Style* centers on a member of such marginalized social groups invisible to a white suburban middle class in the figure of the Puerto Rican graffiti writer Raymond Ray 'Zoro' ('Lee' George Quiñones). In the film's opening scene, 'Zoro' (the main protagonist) is dressed as a mysterious sprayer in black pants, sweater, and cap. With the non-diegetic instrumental "Subway Theme" by DJ Grandwizzard Theodore playing in the background, he sprays the figure of Zorro on a subway train. Ray's graffiti nickname, 'Zoro,' is an intertextual reference to Zorro. The Mexican literary character is a cool and mysterious superhero figure in American popular culture who fought villains, as portrayed for instance in the 1950s Walt Disney TV series starring Guy Williams. With his masculine and disguised appearance, Zorro is a pivotal figure for graffiti culture including the Puerto Rican graffiti writer 'Zoro.' A medium long shot affirms that the Mexican icon serves as a role model for Ray as both are positioned in a parallel way suggesting Lacan's mirror stage. The mirror stage refers to a model of identity which is imitated by another (younger) person in order to find one's identity (Lacan). Creating an image of Zorro with paint as graffiti, Ray aims to achieve Zorro's iconic status, Robin Hood-type aura, and *machismo* identity. As a graffiti writer, Ray also does not want to be identified by the police or law enforcement authorities, but instead wants to be known by his peers in the neighborhood.

Whereas the Mexican pop culture hero is a strong and masculine figure who fights for the poor and marginalized, the Puerto Rican figure Raymond 'Zoro,' by contrast, does not (yet) quite fit this notion. His graffiti nickname lacks one letter and instead of crusading for the marginalized, Ray is striving for his own recognition, fame, and respect among his peers in the South Bronx. Ray's fascination with Zorro expressed in the visual composition of the take elevates the protagonist's cultural background thereby linking his existing transnational identity as a Puerto Rican young man growing up in The Bronx with that of the literary and filmic main protagonists discussed earlier. In appropriating the superhero figure Zorro, Raymond assumes American, Puerto Rican, and Latinx layers of identity. Thus, the intertextual reference to Zorro is an ironic comment on the protagonist's struggle for fame and respect as well as an important cultural reference to American popular media and transnational ethnic heritage.

Wild Style deconstructs the idea of the South Bronx as a place of urban disorder by depicting Ray as a creative young Puerto Rican artist. At first glance, Ray's dark appearance and unlawful nocturnal activity matches common imaginations of racialized crime (see Ch. 3.1). However, 'Zoro' is not presented as a criminal gang member like those in *Fort Apache: The Bronx*; rather, he is shown as a character who inscribes his subculture on the American urban canvas. The film takes on the local perspective of the abandoned residents which serves as an adventurous playground for a younger generation of locals. This shift away from racialized juvenile delinquency seen in the opening sequences in *Fort Apache: The Bronx* and, to a lesser extent in *Wolfen*, to the local youth as productive actors breaks with the prevalent film conventions examined earlier. Hence, *Wild Style* reworks the image of African Americans and Puerto Ricans as pimps, maniacs, criminals or drug addicts by inscribing Ray with creativity. *Wild Style* can therefore be read as a response to the more popular cinematic representations of The Bronx discussed earlier, to the dominant news media discourse of the inner city of the 1970s which presents young people of color as perpetrators as well as, on a cinematic level, to the youth gang films of the early 1960s, such as *West Side Story* (dirs. Jerome Robbins and Robert Wise, 1961) (Jaehne 4).

Like the protagonists in *Fort Apache: The Bronx*, *Gloria*, and *Wolfen*, Ray 'Zoro' is a liminal figure with regard to his ethnicity, his masculinity, his family, and among his own peer community. He represents a new generation of poorer Puerto Ricans who replaced the middle-class Eastern European Americans, Irish Americans, and Italian Americans in the 1960s that had moved to the suburbs to pursue their version of the American Dream (Gonzales 118). The number of black, Puerto Rican, and Latinx residents increased from 11.1 per cent in 1950 to 63.7 per cent in 1980, making this entire group the biggest population group (Gonzales 110). As an outsider, Ray neither fits the working-class context of his family, nor the group of fellow artists who are friends of his ex-girlfriend Rose (Sandra 'Lady Pink' Fabara). Ray's passion for writing causes conflict with his "paternalistic" (Monteyne 103) brother Hector (Carlos Morales) who admonishes him to finally grow up in a two-shot: "Stop f*** around and be a man. There is nothing out here for you." 'Zoro' replies in pointing to the graffiti-covered wall in his bedroom "Yes, there is – this." While Hector joined the army as a solution to the difficult situation in his neighborhood, Ray's objective is to become an artist and to eventually gain fame and respect among his peers inside and outside of his home, the South Bronx.

Wild Style builds on the local as an idea by placing the plot mainly in public spaces (see Monteyne 103). Similar to the cinematic texts discussed earlier, the movie setting includes streets, blocks, and parks which are only recognizable by a local audience because they are never explicitly mentioned. The South Bronx is created as a spatial entity from an inside perspective. Graffiti writers Ray and Z-Roc (Andrew 'Zephyr' Witten), for instance, walk by empty lots and abandoned apartment buildings near the Dixie Club on Freeman Street in the Crotona Park East neighborhood. While they walk the streets in a long shot, their conversation about the increasing interest of downtown journalists and art promoters in graffiti is not interrupted. The camera follows them from behind in the distance creating a horizontal pan of the young men walking in the devastated area, thus allowing the audience an unobstructed gaze onto the landscape of decline. While they are walking down the street, a black lady crosses the street with her shopping trolley on the right-hand side of the frame. 'Zoro,' 'Z-Roc,' and the pedestrians block out the rubble in their conversation as they have built their life around the shrinking infrastructure. Instead of centering on the South Bronx as an apocalyptic and de-humanized space often seen in the public news media discourse, the ruins become a background and a stage against which the creativity is performed. Compared to the previously discussed filmic examples, the abandoned landscape is not really threatening, but rather ordinary. This idea of the ordinary and 'everyday' in this scene is supported by the use of daylight and the fact that other pedestrians are also walking in the street. The public spaces in *Wild Style* take on a different meaning as background, as stage, and as home (see Monteyne 103), demonstrating that it has an important function for the personal development of its residents and diverse urban community.

Wild Style establishes the South Bronx as a multiracial contact zone in which ethnic boundaries are imaginatively transgressed (Nitzsche, "Hip-Hop Culture"). This is especially evident when art journalist Virginia (Patti Astor) drives from Manhattan to The Bronx to do a report on the emerging graffiti culture with The Union Crew. Her outward appearance bears striking similarities to that of Debbie Harry, lead singer of the New Wave band Blondie. By collaborating with Ahearn on *Wild Style* (see Chang 184-85), this band had an important influence on emerging hip-hop culture. In passing the so-called "hub," a busy intersection of 3rd Avenue and 149th Street in the Melrose neighborhood, the minor female character Virginia initially brings an outside perspective to the area. While the radio plays the Blondie song "Pretty Baby," she shows little reaction to the increasingly degenerating landscape. The car is her safe space, at least until it breaks down. Suddenly, Virginia feels unsafe. When a group of children approach her, the art critic shouts at them: "You can't touch the car! I am calling the police!" The over-the-shoulder shot taken from inside her safe space shows Virginia sitting in her car, raising her hands to her face, and hysterically reacting to the children. She mimics the fear of the inner-city inhabitants which is mostly that of hegemonic white suburban middle-class perspective perpetuated in the dominant news media discourse. However, her outside perspective is immediately resolved when she becomes aware of her own hysteric attitude towards the innocent black kids on the street. The camera changes its position to that of the kids standing and frames her in a close-up shot looking out of the driver's window with a smile on her lips asking them, "Where is the telephone?" The perceived juvenile gang consists of black children who eventually help the stranded driver by bringing her to her interviewees, The Union Crew. This scene plays with the notion of the South Bronx as a fearful place by ironically deconstructing the white hegemonic image of the urban space as infiltrated by black juvenile crime and violence. Instead of fear, this sequence presents cooperation, learning, and an interest in the local culture, which is much stronger than white fear and paranoia (see Macek).

Wild Style's narrative and spatial creativity as a response to urban shrinkage is extended to the level of genre and media. The film is a mixture of live-action, romance, teen, and coming-of-age narrative, animation, documentary, and "folk and show musicals" (Monteyne 96). The movie's minor romance and coming-of-age plot centers on the relationship between Ray and his fellow writer Rose. Their relationship is only vaguely sketched out and taken up sporadically over the course of the film as *Wild Style* begins after they have already broken up. This plot element is frequently interrupted by lengthy sequences of music. Whereas Rose is part of The Union Crew (which paints murals for money), Ray is the lonesome graffiti hero striving for respect. Rose is a stronger and more self-confident character than Ray who appears insecure and rather self-centered. Rose is also the one who reminds him of his position compared to the MCs, DJs, and breakers at the final jam: "They're going to be the stars of this thing, not you!" Her exclamation affirms the community's role in the success of the final performance. Compared to the filmic examples analyzed earlier, Ray's – and the neighborhood's success story – is based on a communal (as opposed to individual) effort where Ray and Rose serve as facilitators. Clearly, the urban space is not exclusively focalized through a romance narrative as compared to the live-action feature films *Fort Apache: The Bronx* or *Gloria*, but through an extensive mosaic of artists, performances, and stories staged against a decaying urban backdrop that is poised for renewal.

While most of the film stock is made up of live-action scenes suggesting a conventional Hollywood movie, it includes several animated sequences, namely the opening sequence and, later, at a hotel to suggest sexual activity (see Monteyne 116). Terms such as "rap" and "pop" in the opening credits, for instance, are animated to the rhythm of a non-diegetic hip-hop beat. The colorful graphic elements together with beats and scratches from the track "Military Cut" by DJ Grandwizzard Theodore further reinforce the idea that graffiti, DJing, and rap are the defining features of *Wild Style*. Those shots demonstrate "media convergence" (H. Jenkins 15-16) where the newer medium of film converges with older forms of visual culture such as graffiti, illustration, and comics. The inclusion of these subcultural aesthetics highlight the participatory nature of postmodern media production as they show new ways of working with established media. This new aesthetic resonates with Marshall Berman who argues for new media as a response to decline (Ch. 1.2). This media and generic mixture supports the idea of The Bronx as a creative place already in the film's opening sequences and attributes the film with a self-reflexive attitude (Monteyne 115).

This self-reflexive attitude is complemented by the documentary genre and mode. The documentary mode is a longstanding device that appears in a variety of media genres, such as photography, film, and television. American film scholar Bill Nichols distinguishes four types of documentary practice in his study *Representing Reality: Issues and Concepts in Documentary* (1991): expository, observational, interactive, and reflexive (23). The documentary mode is claimed to be much more authentic and realistic than the autobiographic and melodramatic modes because it suggests the representation of unfiltered reality. The perhaps best example is the iconic documentary photograph *Migrant Mother* (1936) by Dust Bowl photographer Dorothea Lange. This photograph carefully staged a portrait of an immigrant mother with her children. Like the autobiographic and melodramatic modes, the documentary mode changes in time and across media. It is also expressed in *Wild Style*, for instance, in the film stock: the music scenes appear as live recordings from actual jams (parties) and breakdance battles (dance competitions). Such sequences provide the viewer with a first-hand impression of the immense creativity and unity taking place in hip-hop culture in The Bronx. They, thus blur the boundaries between audience and performer "giv[ing] the film spectator the impression of being part of the diegetic theater audience shown on screen" (Monteyne 98), which is probably one of the main reasons why the film was so successful.

The documentary mode is most evident in the acting and cast of *Wild Style*. The acting appears improvised, amateurish, and unscripted. The films analyzed in the previous chapters included professional actors such as Paul Newman (Murphy in *Fort Apache: The Bronx*), Gena Rowlands (*Gloria*), and Albert Finney (*Wolfen*'s Dewey), all of whom attended acting schools and appeared in many national and international feature films in a variety of settings. In contrast, the Charlie Ahearn movie not only includes cameo appearances of real-life practitioners of all four elements of hip-hop, but also other important figures who influenced emerging hip-hop culture. For example, the main protagonists Raymond 'Lee' George Quiñones (Ray 'Zoro') and Sandra 'Lady Pink' Fabara (Rose) were real-life graffiti artists. The Union Crew's artists include the graffiti pioneers Crash 'Daze' Ellis and John 'Crash' Matos. The famous breakdance group The Rock Steady Crew makes a cameo appearance. MCs, DJs, and crews such as Grandmaster Flash, The Cold Crush Brothers, The Fantastic Five, and Grandmaster Caz (who also appear in the film) were all hip-hop artists who grew up in The Bronx and influenced hip-hop culture with their raps, styles, and performances. Patti Astor, the actress who played art journalist Virginia, was vital in introducing the uptown graffiti culture to the East Village art scene when she co-founded the Fun Gallery in 1981 (Chang 180; Hoban 152-53). The inclusion of notable real-life hip-hop figures, according to Canadian communication scholar Murray Forman, is the source of the movie's cult status: "Not quite a documentary, *Wild Style*'s lasting reputation for authenticity is also based on the inclusion of key personalities who claimed the Bronx and uptown boroughs as their own" (255-56). Hence, by introducing a documentary mode within a semi-fictional narrative, *Wild Style* creates a local, inside perspective of the South Bronx as a creative space where "everyone can be captured as a performer" (Montenye 121).

Rap music is constantly present in the film through diegetic and non-diegetic sound. Frequent musical and breaking performances produce a sense of creative community. The rap crew Double Trouble performs an a capella "Stoop Rap." The Cold Crush Brothers perform a battle rap with the Fantastic Freaks in the "Basketball Throwdown Cold Crush," which was inspired by the musical *West Side Story* (see Monteyne 108). Grandmaster Flash is filmed spinning his records in his kitchen. During a jam at the Dixie Club, Virginia 'steps into the cypher,' joins the dancing crowd, and performs her own moves among the party guests creating a diegetic contact space (see Nitzsche, "Hip-Hop Culture"). The film climaxes in a 15-minute final outdoor concert at an amphitheater "feverish[ly] reimagining [...] a Bronx park jam [shot] at an abandoned amphitheater near the Williamsburg Bridge in [Manhattan's] East River Park" (Chang 186). As background sound, the music is constantly present during dialogue scenes, such as at an art party in Manhattan. The musical experience in the South Bronx is cinematically facilitated through close-up shots of rappers and DJs who show their rhyme and scratch skills, long takes of live scenes at the amphitheater which evoke the feeling of 'being there,' as well as dance scenes conveying fun and unity. The sound and editing functions to suggest the feel of a first-hand experience of the African American and Latinx youth culture that emerges as a communal activity amidst the urban devastation and as "complex strategies of collective empowerment" (Monteyne 97). *Wild Style* draws on the genre conventions of the musical, romance, and coming-of-age narrative without giving in to either of them.

This unconventional treatment of different media, aesthetic, and generic conventions leads to a unique viewing experience. *New York Times* film critic Vincent Canby had mixed feelings about the cinematic realization in his 1983 review after the film had been shown in the framework of the "New Directors/New Films" series in Manhattan:

> Unfortunately for the film, Mr. Ahearn, who is an artist as well as a film maker, never discovers a cinematic rhythm that accurately reflects and then celebrates the rare energy and wit of the artists within the film. Too often *Wild Style* has the effect of dampening the enthusiasm of its amateur actors or of not being able to keep up with their nonstop pace. It always seems to be trailing them, as if it were a little brother who can't run as fast as the others. ("*Wild Style*")

Canby notes that *Wild Style* displays a discrepancy between the plot development and the acting. His criticism of the film's dynamic affirms that it violates cinematic standards and conventional viewing expectations, such as the pace of the narration. Yet, by violating established audio-visual and spatial conventions, it raises questions about their legitimacy and opens up a self-reflexive dialogue about the state of filmmaking. Similarly, this younger generation of artists breaks with established musical (DJing) and visual conventions (graffiti) to articulate their own creative response to urban devastation.

Compared to the success and frontier narratives analyzed in literature and film earlier, *Wild Style* presents a new take on the American Dream (see Ch. 1.4). Unlike the literary heroes Kate, Stevie, and Danny who eventually leave the South Bronx in their pursuit of social upward mobility, Ray's answer to the urban decline is not to escape it, but to stay in the neighborhood and face the urban destruction and low standard of living. Unlike the filmic protagonists Murphy and Gloria who are either hindered from escaping or forced to escape because of the violence in The Bronx, Ray approaches graffiti as an activity that will eventually provide him with the financial support, re-spect among his peers, and a way out of his marginalized lower-class status. Whereas the earlier literary and filmic works proposed an individual solution as a response to decay, the Ahearn production emphasizes local resources, collective unity, and grassroots energy. *Wild Style*'s locally-based narrative and rejection of escape as a solution to devastation is therefore one of the first cin-ematic representations besides *Wolfen* which openly, creatively, and directly challenges the status quo of the neoliberal economic forces leading to down-fall. *Wild Style* builds on the idea that by staying (instead of escaping) and tackling pressing urban issues in a communal, optimistic, forward-looking, and democratic way, and also by working with shrinkage instead of against it, hip-hop culture is the most important creative local grassroots response to the de-industrialization of the 1970s and early 1980s.

The documentary mode as well as the creative grassroots and community-based response to the downfall of the South Bronx packaged as a local suc-cess story is certainly one of the most important reasons as to why *Wild Style* had such a global appeal. It establishes a sense of place by taking up the per-spective of the local youth, using local artists as amateur actors, providing a detailed account of the various dance, music, and writing techniques, and by shooting on location. *Wild Style* thus serves as a "detailed audio-visual hip-hop manual" (Nitzsche, "Hip-Hop Culture" 185) for the founding of further hip-hop cultures inside and outside of the United States. It was aired in Germany in 1983 on ZDF, the second-largest public TV station in Western Germany. It was also distributed and broadcasted in the UK and Japan through mechanisms of "global convergence" (H. Jenkins 113), where it had a substantial impact on youth cultures. In addition to becoming a key document in the development of hip-hop culture worldwide, *Wild Style* influenced subsequent films such as *Beat Street* and *Style Wars*, eventually setting the foundation of an entire film genre that Forman terms "hip-hop cinema" (255). As the success of this low budget hip-hop film lies in the fact that it is so bound to and rooted in the local, it managed to generate a following that transcends space and time and continues to reach generations of teenagers from different gender, sexual, ethnic, and class backgrounds even today. In revising the American Dream as a locally-based collective narrative, *Wild Style*, a film that promoted a new version of self-determined entrepreneurial spirit which is guided by ideas of participation, community-orientation, and a 'do-it-yourself' attitude, has become a key text for a youth culture that has incorporated the mechanisms of global capitalism over the past 30 years. *Wild Style*'s paradoxical success consists of the fact that it revised parameters of the American Dream narrative from a younger multiethnic and multiracial perspective while in a way affirming its very foundations.

In conclusion, *Wild Style* introduces a version of the American Dream narrative in the age of deindustrialization which establishes the South Bronx as a place of urban creativity, entrepreneurship, and its residents as creative agents. While *Fort Apache: The Bronx*, *Gloria*, and *Wolfen* are rather skeptical of the era of decline, *Wild Style* works with it. *Wild Style* convincingly demonstrates that in the midst of decay there is enough freedom to develop a new cultural form which eventually not only reintegrates The Bronx back into earlier urban history but also sets a global example. At the same time the film personalizes the devastation by focusing on the narrative perspective of the Puerto Rican graffiti writer Ray 'Zoro.' It generates empathy for the youth living in this context predominantly through graffiti, DJing, breaking, and MCing. Graffiti constitutes a new type of urban practice that emerged in a landscape that is abandoned by authorities and architects. In turn, it empowered a younger generation from many different cultural backgrounds to speak up against their marginalization.

Wild Style demonstrates that creativity can be executed on the level of genre as well. A mixture of musical, romance, coming of age narrative, documentary, live-action, and animated, extensive writing and performance sequences in *Wild Style* provide a first-hand feel of the vibrancy and spontaneity of early hip-hop, thus making the culture accessible to a large national and international audience. *Wild Style* negotiates the media-generated public image of the South Bronx as a post-apocalyptic and de-humanized area by introducing creativity and community as an answer to urban shrinkage processes. Instead of producing The Bronx as a de-humanizing and post-apocalyptic space, Ahearn shows in his production that The Bronx is an ordinary space, a home (see Berman), and a space of exploration. Creativity in that context means improving the situation of the African American, Caribbean, and Latinx youth, and actively responding to marginalization by creating a new means of expression. The younger generations shown in the movie are neither drug addicts nor criminals as seen in *Fort Apache: The Bronx*, but local artists who question the legitimacy of urban decline and the meaning for the people who live there by introducing a new aesthetic, cultural practices, and ultimately triggering an urban regeneration process. The next chapter will explore how this notion of creativity, artistic, generic, and urban regeneration is taken up in the song and music video for Grandmaster Flash and the Furious Five's "The Message."

4.2 "It's like a jungle sometimes": Afrodiasporic Masculinity, Youth Resilience, and Genre Innovation in "The Message" (1982)

While *Wild Style* affirms an optimistic, creative, and grassroots-based version of the American Dream, the rap song "The Message" updates the Dream's promise of hope, resilience, and optimism by combining it with a greater skepticism about ongoing structural inequalities in The Bronx. "The Message" is the most famous track on the album *The Message* by Grandmaster Flash & the Furious Five. Although Flash is named as an artist, he was not involved in the song and appeared only lip-syncing in the video (Chang 178).[1] Sugar Hill produced the album with Sylvia Robinson and Ed 'Duke Bootee' Fletcher who also produced "Rapper's Delight," the first major rap single released in 1979 (Chang 178).

The "fifth rap single to reach gold-selling status" (Chang 179), "The Message" became a rap hit in early hip-hop culture. It was also released as a music video, a relatively new phenomenon as MTV had only been founded in 1981. At that time, music videos were short four to six-minute clips which visualize the music they are intended to sell in the popular music market. As converging media forms, they incorporate sound, voice, music, rhythm, melody, beats, lyrics, narrative as well as cinematic and visual components in their art (Berland). While MTV started to recognize the commercial potential of rap music videos only in the early to mid-1980s (Forman 128-29), "The Message" is a pioneering example to study the meaning of the American Dream in The Bronx.

As "The Message" is a key song in the early history of hip-hop culture, various scholars such as Murray Forman, Mark Naison ("Rap: Morrisania Roots"),

---

1   The complicated production history of "The Message" is a "Pandora's Box" (Chang 178). As Chang notes, the song "was credited to Grandmaster Flash and the Furious Five" (178), but Melle Mel and Ed 'Duke Bootee' Fletcher provided all of the raps with the group only "lip-syncing" in the music video (Chang 178). When writing about the lyrics and the video, I will refer to the emcee/performer who I think is the most fitting.

Tricia Rose, Roy Shuker, and Joseph Winters have examined its musical style, lyrical poetics, and urban context. This chapter expands their analyses by closely investigating how "The Message" updates the American Dream narrative by playing with conventional assumptions on blackness, masculinity, class, space, and genre in the age of decline. I argue that the music video for "The Message" contains perhaps the biggest skepticism of the American Dream narrative in this cluster of texts while at the same time it reaffirms its core values of resilience, hope, humor, and individualism. I will draw on Winters's reading of "The Message" as a sorrow song and extend more pessimistic claims of scholars who have argued that in "The Message" the American Dream "had been all but exhausted in the midst of a more widespread structural erosion" (Forman 88-89) by showing how there is also hope in despair, creativity in shrinkage, and innovation in deindustrialization. I will show how the music video converges cultural narratives and decay iconographies seen earlier in order to facilitate the poetic resurrection of The Bronx by claiming it as the geographical origin of hip-hop culture and of a new rap music genre: message or conscious rap.

The music video for "The Message" establishes a sense of place by opening with two young African American men walking down a street in the Morrisania section of the South Bronx (Naison, "Rap: Morrisania Roots") in a sunny afternoon setting. Both are moving self-confidently towards the camera on the sidewalk while the performer on the right (Grandmaster Flash) carries a boom box on his shoulders. As a long shot of the two young men walking on the sidewalk, the frame reveals the neighborhood as a dilapidated place in its lower part where grass is overgrowing the streets and the buildings are abandoned. The video takes up the performers' local perspective through the camera eye which is positioned on the same level as the performers. This impression is reinforced by the accompanying lyrics: "Broken glass everywhere / people pissing on the stairs, you know they just don't care / I can't take the smell, I can't take the noise." Melle Mel describes the place as an unbearable area which is marked by piercing smells and sounds invading his personal space. The destruction of the urban landscape is expressed in the synecdoche "broken glass everywhere." The video and the lyrics take up the colonial idea of the South Bronx as a frontier space as seen in *Fort Apache: The Bronx* and *Wolfen*. The depiction of urban decay amidst a sunny afternoon setting is strongly reminiscent of the opening ruin shots of *Wolfen*, but the colonized subjects position themselves prominently in the frame of "The Message." This opening scene powerfully states that the young men reclaim their urban space which has been taken away from them in lieu of deindustrialization.

Similar to all of the films discussed in this study, "The Message" introduces The Bronx as an implicit geographical frame of reference. Instead of introducing streets, corners, or neighborhoods verbally and/or visually by including subtitles or street signs, "The Message" refers to the area as a spatial entity in order to highlight racial and class discrimination. Melle Mel raps: "You grow in the ghetto, living second rate." He draws on the spatial imaginary of the ghetto as a racially and socially homogenous urban space which is strictly confined by its boundaries for the residents. As a negatively connoted "geocultural enclave" (Forman 64), the spatial concept of the ghetto unfolds a white hegemonic power position (Forman 64) and evokes associations of other ethnic enclaves, such as the Warsaw ghetto from which the narrator Kate Simon from the autobiography *Bronx Primitive* escaped (see Ch. 2.1). "The Message" counters the hegemonic gaze by adopting the first-person narrative perspective of a black male subject who speaks out against the grim situation in the area. By referring to their own neighborhood as a "ghetto," rapper Melle Mel constitutes a subaltern speaker (Spivak; see Ch. 2.1) who takes up white colonial language thus subverting existing racial and spatial power relations.

"The Message" presents the first-person perspective of a younger generation of black men. People of African descent have been part of The Bronx since the Colonial Era when they were brought over as slaves (Ultan, *Northern Borough* 27). During the Second Great Migration, African Americans moved from the South to the urban centers of the North including The Bronx in hopes of finding better employment opportunities and greater racial equality (Ultan, *Northern Borough* 267). This tendency intensified in the 1950s when older immigrant groups from Europe left for the suburbs. Black residents found a new home, for instance, in the district of Morrisania in their pursuit of social mobility (Ultan, *Northern Borough* 270, 291). However, this new generation of residents of color was much poorer than their European predecessors. African Americans' need for housing coincided with large-scale urban renewal projects which were built to house mostly lower income residents. As a result, many lower class people of color found themselves living in the iconic high rise projects of The Bronx which were erected in many areas all over the borough, such as in Melrose, Morrisania, Soundview, Castle Hill, to name but a few. Soon these high-rise housing projects would deteriorate without the necessary funds for renovation, which led to crime and violence.

Melle Mel articulates these hardships of living "second rate" in a place dominated by poverty and social immobility: "Got no money to move out, I guess I got no choice [...] I tried to get away, but I couldn't get far / 'cause the man with the tow truck repossessed my car. [...] Can't take the train to the job, there is a strike at the station." Melle Mel is trapped in different ways. First, he lacks the financial resources, for instance, to pay the fine on his towed truck. He struggles to survive and to earn a living in the crime-ridden streets which are filled with "smugglers, scramblers, burglars, gamblers / pickpockets, peddlers and even pan-handlers." Second, although he makes an effort to escape, his endeavor "to get away" is unsuccessful which suggests the immense difficulty of leaving this place. Third, and perhaps most importantly, he sketches the city as an immobile urban fabric. Public transportation is unavailable since MTA workers are on strike for better payment. Perhaps not surprisingly, the young African American speaker refers to himself also as an "outlaw" as his situation is marked by social, spatial, and class immobility. "The Message" thus converges the frontier narrative of the filmic examples discussed in Chapter 3 which also build on the idea of The Bronx as a place from which an escape is hardly possible. "The Message" breaks down the local living conditions to the individual level of a young black resident thereby creating a grim, dystopian vision of The Bronx. As such it introduces a localized 'hood perspective into early rap music which is primarily concerned with the experience of mostly male black youth for whom individual growth and success stories are much harder to achieve than, for instance, people of Eastern European descent.

"The Message" employs the spatial metaphor of the jungle in order to express skepticism of individual progress narratives. This metaphor is especially important in the construction of the declining space as it is part of the chorus: "It's like a jungle sometimes; it makes me wonder / how I keep from going under." A jungle is a wild and uncivilized place that is connected to struggle for survival. Imagining the urban space as a jungle means that it is a dangerous, bewildering, and disorderly territory where one has to fight in order to survive.

By portraying The Bronx as an urban jungle, "The Message" continues a longstanding motif in American literary and cultural history. Many novels, films, and musical pieces employ this image to highlight the difficult circumstances people face within a decaying and discriminatory urban space, starting with Upton Sinclair's ground-breaking naturalist 1906 novel *The Jungle* about the grim conditions in the meatpacking industry in Chicago or the 1955 film adaptation of Evan Hunter's novel *Blackboard Jungle* (1954) based on Hunter's experiences as a teacher in The Bronx. Discussing the jungle metaphor in "The Message," Forman emphasizes that it "mobilizes a perception of the structuring forces influencing social existence" (92). The narrator is bound to his difficult situation because the overarching social structure is more rigid, powerful, and leaves him without possibilities. The jungle imagery strongly resonates with a naturalist sensibility which critiques upward mobility because the individuals are so tightly bound to their class system (Fluck, "Realism" 569).

Despite the widespread skepticism and despair depicted at the beginning of the video, Grandmaster Flash and the Furious Five are far from giving up in this situation. Religious studies scholar Joseph Winters points out that the video "expresses a desire to escape these circumstances [and] to break from these social realities" (14). The artists' resilience and their refusal to surrender to the racial and class fatalism is an important feature of the American Dream (Cullen; Samuel; see Ch. 1.4) and it happens in different ways in the video.

In terms of language, "The Message" subverts the jungle metaphor. By invoking this figure of speech, Melle Mel translates his particular urban experience to a widely known metaphor that makes his situation accessible to a wider American audience (see Forman 92). In articulating poverty and the lack of social mobility in the language of the dominant population group, "The Message" symbolically destabilizes white colonial power positions. Thus, the rap crew creatively appropriates a long-standing cultural trope to critique systemic inequalities in contemporary urban America. It also affirms the artistic creativity in the age of decline since the stylistic device of the urban jungle can be added to the list of earlier spatial re-imaginations of The Bronx as heterotopia, home, and frontier/fort. They all build on a space that is dominated by borders and limitations but that also allow possibilities for empowerment, freedom, and opportunity. As many of the spatial imageries of The Bronx appear in "The Message" in audio-visual contexts, they respond much more strongly to the visual imagery of the South Bronx generated by the hegemonic news media.

"The Message" also shows spatial resilience by extending the notion of social inequality from The Bronx to Manhattan. The music video features scenes from Midtown Manhattan as a place filled with pedestrians and yellow cabs, signifying flow, rupture, and im-/mobility. Street-level shots are accompanied by frames of an elderly white homeless woman sitting on the street as well as short takes of Midtown ambulances and Times Square peep show entrances.

Blurring racial, gender, age, and geographic boundaries, they manifest Manhattan as a space of social inequalities similar to The Bronx. The downtown shots are therefore crosscut with images of The Bronx which consist of abandoned buildings filmed with a computer-enhanced color filter to symbolically unify the seemingly different cityscapes. This dialogue between uptown and downtown, between center and periphery, is established on a technological and medial level by sections that are interchanged, juxtaposed, and converged between empty and full spaces. Thus the music video blends social boundaries similar to *Wild Style*. "The Message" claims that inequality is a city-wide, and perhaps even nation-wide, phenomenon which is caused by global neoliberal forces that affect white and non-white residents alike.

In reversing the colonial gaze from the South Bronx to Manhattan, the music video shifts the focus to Manhattan to demonstrate the universality of the crime, racism, discrimination, poverty, and moral and urban decay. The music video demonstrates that poverty and inequality are not just problems of one particular place, but they are part of a larger system of inclusion and exclusion, domination and subordination. In claiming that the issues are of structural nature, the music video makes a similar point to *Wolfen*. Even the agent is similar: in *Wolfen* a supernatural and abstract wolf creature signifies different versions of cultural Otherness whereas here the Other is a specific demographic who are directly affected by the devastation in their lives. Hence, "The Message" critiques the notion of the shrinking territory as an isolated crisis space and singular historic event by highlighting structural inequalities in Manhattan, which is a symbol of financial power. The video empowers the marginalized subjects who are most affected by it and uses subversion and resilience as aesthetic devices to challenge official stories and spatial imaginations.

In symbolically (re-)claiming the urban space that has been neglected by city officials and planning authorities, "The Message" provides its audiences with hope and empowerment. In his influential study *The Practice of Everyday Life* (1984), French cultural theorist Michel de Certeau proposes a definition of urban space that consists of individual practices and stories which are detached from the official city structure like streets, traffic lights, or road signs (93-95). De Certeau emphasizes walking as an urban practice (97) that undermines existing power structures in a city. For instance, jay walking can be understood as a subversion of traffic rules, as it means crossing the street in a non-designated area. The only means of mobility in the "ghetto" environment of "The Message" is walking. By walking, the performers challenge their own physical, social, geographic, and economic immobilities. Their energetic movement towards the camera can be interpreted as a symbol of regaining the power over their very own streets, sidewalks, and corners in the South Bronx. Here, the group functions as representative for an entire group of younger people of color who strive for visibility and power.

Similar to *Wild Style*, "The Message" humorously subverts racial stereotypes, such as black juvenile crime (see Macek; Ch. 3.1). The last part of the music video features a "streetside arrest skit recalling Stevie Wonder's interlude in 'Living for the City'" (Chang 178). The sequence shows the Grandmaster Flash and the Furious Five gathering at a street corner. Soon after they meet and crack jokes, a NYPD police car arrives at the scene to arrests all of them, even forcing them to put their hands on the car to be frisked. The skit ridicules the police's overreaction when they encounter seemingly dangerous black masculinity. It ironically comments on random police violence by building up on the idea that the posse is a group of offenders in the eyes of the police force. However, the reaction of the white police force is to arrest the entire group without even asking about the reason for their get-together. They swiftly arrest the entire crew, including an 'innocent' bystander friend. In ridiculing the notion of black juvenile crime, the music video harshly criticizes racial profiling and police violence and reinforces the seriousness of the racially motivated incident.

The song and music video also tackle media issues such as black people's misrepresentations in popular culture. The lyrics below, for instance, criticize their invisibility on early 1980s American television: "My brothers doing fast on my mother's TV, / says she watches too much, it's just not healthy / *All My Children* in the daytime, *Dallas* at night / can't even see the game or the Sugar Ray fight." The emcee Ed 'Duke Bootee' Fletcher (Love) accentuates the fact that American television is predominantly white despite popular sitcoms such as *The Jeffersons* (1975-85, CBS), *Stanford and Son* (1972-77, NBC) and the historic miniseries *Roots* (1977, ABC). Soap operas such as *All My Children* (1970-2011, ABC) and the prime-time soap *Dallas* (1978-91, CBS) mentioned in the lyrics are concerned with predominantly middle and upper-class suburban families. Both series are in-/famous for their all-white cast which leave out the experiences of the African American, Latinx, and Afro-Caribbean characters. American television became somewhat more inclusive only in the mid-1980s when the sitcom *The Cosby Show* (1984-92, NBC) emerged which narrated the life of the black Huxtable family (Mittell 326).

"The Message" challenges the media invisibility of black characters with a montage of the performers in front of an empty lot. The artists are inserted one after another via visual overlay onto the ground. The superimposition of the artists serves as a powerful statement against racial invisibility. Here they claim the center of the frame, one by one underlined by their determined body language. Leaving space next to each other, each of the men is positioned as an individual artist marked by stylized costuming while at the same time their spatial composition forms a strong group identity. The montage shot can be interpreted as a participatory act in Henry Jenkin's sense of re-claiming the urban terrain of the South Bronx, of black people's visibility in the media, and of their version of the American Dream.

In order to symbolically reclaim the American Dream narrative, "The Message" draws on the African American oral tradition. The lyrics address the audience using the pronoun "you" especially in the last stanza. The intended audience are the artists' peers in the neighborhood: "You say I'm cool, I'm no fool / but then you wind up dropping out of high school." Melle Mel urges his peers to step out of the vicious circle of poverty, violence, and crime. Similarly, the performers in the video are conscious of their position in the frame as they break down the so-called fourth wall, an imaginary border which separates the audience from the stage, and directly address the camera while rapping and walking. Perhaps more aggressively than the earlier cinematic representations, the performers establish an open and direct dialogue with the audience by breaking down this invisible wall between the viewer and the performer that is usually maintained in feature films or in theater. This practice of looking (back), talking (back), and walking (back) is aimed at a larger white suburban, urban, and rural American audience which is far away from the decline of the inner city.

The performance strategy of directly approaching the audience in "The Message" is part of the documentary mode. As I pointed out earlier, the documentary mode aims at suggesting a feel of 'this is how it is.' In establishing a dialogue with the viewer, the protagonists narrate their stories from a local, inside perspective, thus elevating their experience and their position as witnesses of shrinkage. Their position can be compared to the writers of autobiographies (Simon's BP; Ch. 2.1) and documentary films where eyewitnesses recollect their personal experiences. The documentary mode is also expressed in the local cast and on-location setting, which both serve to justify the credibility of the performance. While the inside perspective of the emcees Melle Mel and Ed 'Duke Bootee' Fletcher resonates with the autobiographical narratives in Chapter 2, the two latter aspects, the local cast and the on-location setting, work in a similar way to the documentary mode in *Wild Style* (Ch. 4.1). "The Message" is therefore a complex media text which appropriates genres and modes from literary as well as audio-visual texts in order to convey resilience, hope, and optimism as a way of coping with the area's devastation.

Likewise, "The Message" converges generic and musical conventions in Henry Jenkin's sense. The music video, for instance, draws on the genre conventions of the performance video (Railton and Watson 47-48). Typically used in rock music videos, artists 'do' the music, that is, they move their lips and pretend to be playing instruments while music is added to the film stock at a later time. Many white rock and hard rock videos in the 1970s show bands performing on a stage or in front of an audience, for instance, Queen's "Bohemian Rhapsody" (1975), or AC/DC's "Highway to Hell" (1979). Elements of rock music are also evident in the mis-en-scène and fashion as some of the crew members wear leather boots, pants, jackets, and hats. Those costumes are also reminiscent of the disco group The Village People which became popular because of its elaborate performances on stage and on screen. "The Message," however, deconstructs performance video conventions by positioning the artists not on a stage, but on the stoops of an abandoned house in the South Bronx. Grandmaster Flash and the Furious Five subvert the idea of the stage by performing their track in the street in front of an abandoned building. Repurposing the shrinking urban landscape as the stage for the music video counters the spatial imaginations in the lyrics, as it is described as a "jungle," place of poverty, and neglect. In reworking the typically white performance video genre and combining it with the South Bronx as the setting of the video, "The Message" creates the archetypical version of the ghetto, which became the blue print for many rap videos in the 1980s and 1990s.

By tightly connecting the rap song with the visual imagery of the inner city, "The Message" marks the emergence of a new musical genre on the American music market (Forman 95): conscious rap, message rap, knowledge rap or reality rap (Forman 83). American hip-hop journalist Jeff Chang observes that the music of the rap song sticks out because at that time it was "the grimmest, most downbeat rap ever heard" (179). As an emerging genre at the time, it is more politically outspoken and much more "radical" (Forman 82) in its musical style than earlier rap music representatives such as The Sugarhill Gang which centered their narratives on "the party, nightclub, or roller rink" (Forman 83). "The Message" therefore echoes Marshall Berman's idea that decline stimulates new modes of expression (see Ch. 1.2). It combines the visual iconography of the declining Bronx with a new protest sound of conscious rap and makes a gritty urban landscape the spatial prerequisite for credible (to its audiences) message rap performances worldwide. This converging and participatory text (H. Jenkins) is probably the best example of how cultural texts on the declining Bronx facilitate its poetic rebirth. "The Message" embodies the American Dream's mantra of resilience, hope, and perpetual poetic renewal.

Globally disseminated through music television, this notion of the 'real' South Bronx ghettoscape inspired many artists to appropriate and subvert this conscious genre in their own dilapidated and run-down urban territories. In Germany, for instance, the new music show *Formel Eins* ("Formula One," 1983-90, ARD) which quickly became a staple for young audience before the advent of music television in Germany, aired an excerpt of the music video on 24 May 1983. Detlef Rick aka DJ Rick Ski who later produced one of the earliest German hip-hop albums *Watch Out for the Third Rail* (LSD, 1991), explains in an interview how he and his peers used to watch *Formel Eins* to learn about rap music. Since the early 1990s, rap artists in Germany, for instance, re-imagine the shrinking space of The Bronx in their musical productions. In the 1990s, the rap crew Fettes Brot perform their party hymn and music video "Nordisch by Nature" (1995) on an abandoned graffiti-covered roof in Hamburg. The Stuttgart-based crew Die Fantastischen Vier use the abandoned industrial landscape in and around the East German city of Leipzig as the setting of their 1992 humorous music video "Die Da!?!" The rap crew use the shrinking setting as a performance stage and symbolically equate the decaying post-socialist industrial architecture with the abandonment in the South Bronx. Since the 2000s, mostly male rappers, such as Sido, Bushido, and Haftbefehl have increasingly situated their stories of poverty, symbolic violence, and survival in urban spaces, streets, blocks, and neighborhoods. They nod to the origins of the culture in the United States and affirm their own realness, toughness, and authenticity. All of these groups present their versions of the shrinking ghettoscape as an artistic response to "The Message" and its successors because the songs and videos managed to construct a narrative of urban decline and cultural rebirth.

The abandonment shown in "The Message" as well as the complex strategies of resilience demonstrates these films' deep commitment to the American Dream narrative. On the one hand, the music video highlights the fate of young black men who experienced the post-Civil Rights Movement disillusion after Dr. Martin Luther King Jr.'s Dream of racial and social equality had not turned into reality. "The Message" shares many similarities with the horror film *Wolfen* as both texts point urgently to the downside of the American Dream. However, the song is much more humorous, optimistic, and playful in its response than *Wolfen*. The music video 'flips the script' and shows a myriad of ways to combat the structural inequalities as they are localized in New York City. As a result, the iconic legacy of the track, albeit skeptical, affirms the American Dream and the mechanisms of the capitalist (music) market as it succeeds in subverting existing linguistic, aesthetic, spatial, generic and visual conventions. The iconic legacy of the track and its artists affirms the possibility of the transformation and perennial rebirth of the American Dream for a new generation of young black performers.

To sum up, "The Message" is one of the most popular and widely recognized texts in the era of decline that I have analyzed in this study of the poetic resurrection of The Bronx. The rap single and music video succeeds in presenting a powerful and, most importantly, credible localized narrative which criticizes social conditions in the South Bronx by relating them to larger structural factors. The track's musical innovation and cultural creativity subverts several existing colonial perceptions of the place as a dangerous territory, young male African Americans as juvenile delinquents, and early rap music as a predominantly party genre. The American Dream's creativity and renewal discourse in "The Message" manifests itself in the new genre of conscious rap which is born out of the local realities which the producers of the music video play with. Although the South Bronx it is never explicitly mentioned as the setting of the track and the video, its iconography serves as the blueprint for many contexts where rap music developed inside and outside the US. "The Message" provides individual agency, participation, and subjectivity to young performers who symbolically re-claim, re-articulate, and re-vision the urban space that had been taken away by politicians, the real estate sector, and city authorities. The text's lasting popular success lies in the fact that the lyrics, music, and performance tell the story of decline, decay, discrimination, marginalization as well as creativity, community, and empowerment. In how far this creative innovative potential of early hip-hop culture in the shrinking South Bronx feeds the spirit of the American Dream in the present day will be of concern in the final analysis of the photo book *Born in The Bronx: A Visual Record of the Early Days of Hip-Hop*.

4.3 "A self-starting culture": Grassroots Agency, Media Diversity, and Coffee Table Gentrification in *Born in The Bronx: A Visual Record of the Early Days of Hip-Hop* (2007)

The final step of this study investigates how the photo book *Born in The Bronx: A Visual Record of the Early Days of Hip-Hop*, published by Swedish "collector, curator, and editor" Jonathan Kugelberg (Cruz-Logo 72), revises the American Dream narrative in the shrinking Bronx. *Born in The Bronx* is particularly relevant for a number of reasons. It features photographs of the emerging hip-hop culture between 1977 and 1982 (Kugelberg, Introduction 31), this study's rough time frame. While the pictures capture the cultural vibrancy and a renewed sense of the American Dream, the book design recollects the achievements of this time period and allows an examination of the changing spatial, generic, economic, and identity discourses surrounding the South Bronx in the late twentieth and early twenty-first centuries. Kugelberg's photo book therefore bridges the gap between the shrinking past and the post-shrinking present when it was published in 2007.

The photo book underlines hip-hop's convergence nature: It tells the story of a popular culture through a mixture of literature, graphic design, illustration, and photography. A photo book is a particularly fascinating medium in the representation of decline because its combination of visual (photographs, illustrations, album covers, flyers) and verbal texts (quotes, essays, criticism) create complex narratives through space and time. In contrast to an exhibition catalogue, a photo book focuses much more on the photographer and their oeuvre, such as Robert Frank's famous *The Americans* (1958). Due to the special material quality of photography which can be reframed, repurposed and repackaged in a variety of contexts (see Ch. 1.2), *Born in The Bronx* therefore constitutes a perfect example of how hip-hop converges the cultural narrative of the American Dream by blurring existing visual, verbal, and aural media boundaries. I argue that *Born in The Bronx* responds to the social, political, and urban challenges of the early 2000s by renewing the promise of a Bronx-based American Dream narrative in the light of hip-hop's global success story.

Born in The Bronx opens by remembering the cultural trauma during the era of decline. The inner book jacket features a powerful double-page black-and-white photograph of the Charlotte Street area in the South Bronx in 1977, which was visited by President Jimmy Carter that year (see Ch. 1.3). The photograph is framed by rubble in the foreground and abandoned windowless tenements in the background where a large Puerto Rican flag hangs across the building. In presenting the South Bronx as a dilapidated neighborhood, the opening photograph establishes devastation as the urban context out of which the youth culture emerged in the 1970s. The Puerto Rican flag on the right-hand side of the photograph signifies the appropriation of the place by Puerto Rican residents and counters hegemonic imaginaries of the Bronx as a de-humanized urban territory and as an 'all-black space.' At the same time, the graphic composition reminds post-9/11 readers of the attacks on the World Trade Center where the American flag was positioned near the rubble as a symbol of strength and hope. Here, the destruction of the neighborhood is symbolically equated with the destruction of the Twin Towers. The opening photograph therefore establishes a semantic link to suggest that if New York City and, on a larger scale the United States, could emerge from the destructive events of 9/11, so too could The Bronx overcome deindustrialization and decline. Alluding to the metaphor of a phoenix rising from the ashes, the photograph encapsulates the indomitable spirit of America and echoes the frontier narrative that violence is necessary for spiritual renewal (see Ch. 3). Against this background, Born in The Bronx shifts the perspective away from the iconography of rubble and debris in the remainder of the book to a detailed portrait of hip-hop culture in its early nascent years.

The photographs in Born in The Bronx portray the South Bronx as a space of peaceful community, harmonic unity, and democratic cooperation. Many photographs display the interaction between young people from different cultural backgrounds, both among themselves and with their respective audiences. The double-page black-and-white photograph on page 40-41, for instance, prominently features the rapper the Almighty KG on stage at a night club in 1982. The photo frames, and thus centers, the relationship between the MC and the euphoric crowd. While handing a poster to his audience, he appears to be shouting at them, which conveys spontaneity and energy. This communal feeling between the artist and his fans is symbolized in the graphic crossing of the hands and posters in the right-hand side of the picture. It is emphasized by the position of the photographer who is in a mediating position between the performer/stage and the audience/pit. The dark background of the interior snapshot further suggests that much of the music and performances took place at night in indoor spaces, such as clubs or high school gymnasiums, but not necessarily in the devastated areas and public spaces as the music video "The Message" claims (Ch. 4.2).

The idea of community is conveyed through a generic mixture of spontaneous portraiture as well as documentary, party, band, and performance photographs. British artist and scholar David Bate defines portraiture in his monograph *Photography: The Key Concepts* (2000) as "more than 'just a picture,' it is a place of work: a semiotic event for social identity" (67). Portrait photography is the photographic performance of a person's identity in front of a camera in a certain public or private, indoor or outdoor, open or enclosed space. As a long-standing genre in American photography (Orvell 13), portraiture tells the viewer how Americans construct themselves in front of and behind a photo camera and how they engage in a relationship with their immediate surroundings.

Born in The Bronx uses the genre of portraiture to provide an inside perspective to the cultural vibrancy of the early days of hip-hop. Pages 186-87, for instance, feature a double-page snapshot of the hip-hop crew The Treacherous Three who were also signed to Sugar Hill Records. The snapshot shows the three young performers Kool Moe Dee, LA Sunshine, and Special K sitting on a bench in the center of the photograph in what looks like the gymnasium of the Norman Thomas High School in Manhattan. Their pose consists of leaning their upper bodies slightly forward while having their arms folded and conveys a self-confident, forward-looking, creative, fun, harmonious, and unified black masculinity. The interlinked bodies suggest the formation of a new relational identity and their stylized posing conforms to the conventions of hip-hop performance culture. Because their pose is exaggerated, the picture also exposes the conventions of portrait photography: The young men convey to the camera that they are fully aware of their crew identity thereby affirming to the viewer a flexible individual and social identity formation which depends on the respective setting or context instead of essentialist criteria such as skin color or social class. Thus, their performance of a relational identity in portrait photography correlates to that of the relational identity formations discussed earlier.

Likewise, the genre of portraiture personalizes the urban experience of young people in early hip-hop. Portrait photography allows the viewer to establish a personal connection with the performers, as their feelings, emotions, and actions become visible. The photographs suggest that early hip-hop culture proved to be a productive and sustainable strategy of resilience, hope, and optimism. Early hip-hop photographs were centered on founder Afrika Bambaataa's mantra of "peace, love, unity, and having fun" (Gosa 64) which appeals to contemporary viewers as well. In using photographic genres which center on the experience of individuals and their respective communities, *Born in The Bronx* visually empowers its creative local agents.

This approach differs from other photographic accounts of that time which highlight the seriousness of the locals' experience in the age of decline (Ch. 1.2). The exhibition *Devastation/Resurrection: The South Bronx* took place roughly around the same time when the photograph of The Treacherous Three was taken. The catalogue features a section called "South Bronx Narratives" (Goodson 55-68) where black and brown locals tell their stories of discrimination and displacement. This section provides a forum for the residents who "were interviewed during the summer of 1979 about their lives today and their memories of the recent past" (Goodson 55). The residents' cut-out portrait photographs are accompanied by their first-person accounts of damaged infrastructure, of the discrimination of the landlords towards the tenants, and of the residents' resilience and self-reliance. While the tenants are represented mainly as residents suffering from urban shrinkage in this section, the performers in Kugelberg's photo book are constructed as actively and much more positively countering the devastation by means of art and creativity.

Born in The Bronx depicts the emerging hip-hop culture in The Bronx (and Manhattan) in the era of decline through a multiplicity of gazes, voices, and stories. Most of the photographs were taken by Joe Conzo, a Puerto Rican Bronxite and "hip-hop's first photographer" (Cruz-Logo 71). Other photographers include Charlie Ahearn (Ch. 4.1) and Henry Chalfant, the director of the iconic hip-hop documentary *Style Wars* and co-author of the cult photo book *Subway Art*, both of which documented the emerging graffiti culture in New York City in the early 1980s. This diversity of photographic angles and perspectives suggests the formation of an alternative, egalitarian, and democratic approach to resurrecting the shrinking Bronx.

The book's graphic design and materiality echoes the egalitarian attitude and cultural diversity as it closes with thirteen first-person essays. They are written by a variety of hip-hop practitioners from The Bronx, such as the aforementioned photographer Joe Conzo, Afrika Bambaataa, founder of the Universal Zulu Nation and founder of hip-hop, the 'Scratch Creator' Grandwizzard Theodore (see Ch. 4.1), graffiti icon Carlos 'MARE139' Rodriguez, and many others. The essays and interviews are separated from the glossy portrait photographs by the use of a different, cardboard-style paper. The different paper imparts the writers' stories an additional dimension of authenticity as their stories are apparently not as polished, staged, and stylized as the glossy photographs.

Born in The Bronx reconstructs the South Bronx as the buzzing epicenter of creativity, innovation, and economic activity in the late 1970s and early 1980s through the media convergence (H. Jenkins 15-16) of materials and media atypical for the photo book genre. The section "The Humble Beginnings of Hip Hop on Wax," for instance, features stickers of records. The vinyl stickers provide an overview of the musical output of the time. Because of the limits of the medium of photography and a photo book, this book only focuses on visual depictions of hip-hop culture as it was emerging at the time. To compensate this 'lack' and still create a sense of musicality, the book builds its way around the music with other media such as stickers. It incorporates a great variety of visual and verbal paratexts ranging from scans of flyers and records to playlists, maps, and a timeline compiled by hip-hop journalist Jeff Chang. This broad notion of text is further indicated in the title of the book which is not called a collection of "portraits" or "photographs," but a "visual record of the early days of hip-hop" pointing to the multifaceted textual variety and claiming the accurateness of the stories presented. Thus, the book reinforces the idea that not only the music but all kinds of everyday and ordinary artifacts and media from the period can tell us about the development of hip-hop in The Bronx.

Born in The Bronx suggests that The Bronx in early hip-hop culture was a hub of self-made economic activity. Besides photographs and label stickers, the photo book features handwritten rap lyrics, newspaper clippings, and flyers among other items. The flyers are especially noteworthy in this context as converging media. They are small leaflets that are produced in large quantities and are distributed all over the city for free to advertise upcoming parties and events. Flyers are promotional 'waste' media, because they are thrown away as soon as the information is spread or when the event is over. The leaflets are inserted throughout the book to demonstrate the great variety of visual creativity and graphic styles that were part of hip-hop's early visual culture. While these flyers complement the performance photographs and personal stories discussed earlier, they also provide key data about the spaces, places, parties, and venues where portraits were made and performances took place. The leaflets rework the urban landscape into a landscape of party and celebration. They contain information about the party locations, such as the Ecstasy Garage Disco on 1476 Jerome Avenue in the Highbridge area which was owned by the former Cold Crush Brother manager ("Hip-Hop Map of The Bronx"). The double-paged flyer on pages 104-05, for instance, announces a party dedicated to one of the most famous artists at that time, Buddy Esquire, whose memories are also included in the back of the book (203). This flyer also contains the names of DJs, MCs, and performers The Brothers Disco DJ Breakout and The Funky 4 Plus One on the lower right-hand side (104-05). Many of the leaflets shown in the book display wrinkles, some contain private notes or lyrics on the background of the notes, and some even show remains of tape (104-05) showcasing the materiality of the medium and providing the reader with a sense of 'this is how it looked like.' The flyers literally map the locations where hip-hop emerged in The Bronx, relating the venues mentioned on the leaflets to the photographs of the parties and creating a culturally as well as economically vital urban space in the era of decline.

As the flyers create a flourishing landscape of entertainment and enjoyment, they succeed in the appropriation of capitalist sales strategies during the economic crisis of the 1970s. The nightclubs advertise specials on the leaflets, such as "1st 100 Girls Free" (72-73) or "[$] 50.00 for best dress" (24), tactics which amount to creative marketing techniques and sales strategies deployed to attract a large (female) audience to the parties. Some of the nightclubs also state the dress code for the night, such as "no sneakers" [sic] (25), "Positively NO Sneakers Admitted!!!" (66), or "DRESS TO IMPRESS" (159). Those dress codes suggest an upscale and upbeat party crowd also seen to a certain extent in *Wild Style* which bears few similarities with the social inequalities presented in "The Message." They also suggest that people dressed in the 'flyest' fashions they could manage to pull together allowed them to visually signal either that they were not suffering from decline or that they were able to resist decline without actually leaving The Bronx.

In the accompanying essays, the writers function as cultural experts, eye witnesses, and self-made storytellers who highlight individual agency in order to survive and be successful. Photographer Joe Conzo, for instance, remembers in his essay "A Lost Time" the people's coping mechanism during the destruction: "Yes, the Bronx was burning at the time. You didn't know if your building was going to be there the next day, because if you lived in an old tenement, your building might be marked for arson. But it was part of the time. You just picked up and moved on" (193). His statement highlights American virtues such as resilience and a pragmatic attitude towards overcoming shrinkage. MC and DJ Grandmaster Caz emphasizes the transformative potential of hip-hop culture when New York City was dominated by gangs: "[H]ip hop seemed to convert even the most negative and violent intentions into healthy and competitive ones" (198). Caz points to the transformative potential of cultural practices as a response to urban decline. He affirms that hip-hop culture facilitated a new version of capitalist competition born out of a context of violence and decay.

The renewal of capitalist mechanisms is tightly interwoven with the re-newed promise of American Dream for this generation. In his first-person story entitled "A Picture is Worth a Thousand Moves," Jorge 'Popmaster Fabel' Pabon, b-boy and member of the Rock Steady Crew who also appeared in *Wild Style* remembers growing up in The Bronx of the 1970s and 1980s: "Extreme intensity molded our personalities and characters" (204). Pabon stresses the formative qualities of the urban frontier space which ultimately form their new American character. By remembering 'what it was like' in the early days, these pioneers claim their knowledge of and part in the development of hip-hop in The Bronx to discursively renew the promise of individualism, the self-made man as well as a community spirit and, ultimately, the American Dream.

The artists' statements emphasize that the difficult situation in the declining Bronx had provided them with unique American character traits enabling them to develop and succeed in coping with decline, all of which eventually fostered the emergence of hip-hop culture. They present the devastated Bronx as a space of challenges, conflicts, and tensions which can nevertheless be overcome by particular American virtues of self-reliance, self-confidence, and optimism put forward by Cullen and Samuel (see Ch. 1.4). The success of this American Dream narrative is underlined by the fact that the artists have worked themselves up the social ladder of hip-hop culture without the support of official institutions, the state, or government. B-boy Pabon, for instance, signed his personal story with his hierarchical position in this sub-culture: "Vice President of the Rock Steady Crew / Member of the Supreme World Council of the Universal Zulu Nation / Honorary Member of the Electric Boogaloos" (205). The personal accounts affirm that shrinkage facilitates new social order, leadership, and a renewal of patriarchic masculinity.

These somewhat romanticized retrospective success narratives in the personal accounts of *Born in The Bronx* bear surprising similarities to the first-person autobiographical narratives examined in the novels at the beginning of this study. They all remember The Bronx as a place which provided challenges and which ultimately constitutes the starting point of their own individual success stories. However, while the literary texts re-create the Jewish American Dream from the narrative perspective of one narrator, here the perspective is not exclusively bound to one narrator: The interview sections combined with the photographs form a collage which incorporates many voices and perspectives in the re-creation of the 'lost' early days of hip-hop, which began at the height of the age of decline. The first-person voices presented in the back of the photo book thus challenge conventional assumptions about authorship, ownership, and agency, and they construct a community-driven founding narrative of hip-hop in the South Bronx. At the same time, they affirm a multiethnic and ultimately mostly male-dominated perspective on the emerging culture in which men tell the stories while women are to be looked at in the photographs. By writing about their past experiences, the narrators re-configure the potential of The Bronx as a location for the American Dream for a younger generation of (male) African Americans and Latinx people in The Bronx of the 1970s. For them today that time is associated with artistic creativity and youthful invention.

All of the aforementioned genre, material, aesthetic, spatial, and media aspects contribute to the documentary mode in *Born in The Bronx*. Firstly, the photo book establishes a localized point of view from a younger generation which is marked by values such as community and creativity. Secondly, the photographs pay close attention to what French photographer Henri Cartier-Bresson once coined the expression "decisive moment" which consists of capturing a unique moment and revealing an intimate glimpse into a person's mind. Thirdly, the materiality of the artifacts suggests an immediate, unfiltered, and airbrushed glance into the past. The documentary mode underlines the discourse of urban creativity as a coping mechanism of decline by focusing on the performers, their audiences, and their memories of the late 1970s and early 1980s. This mode affirms the credibility and bottom-up nature of hip-hop's success story and renewed version of the American Dream and passes on knowledge of this emerging culture, its creative potential, and its economic vibrancy in the past today. Similar to *Wild Style*, the documentary mode in *Born in The Bronx* provides a detailed account of American characteristics which eventually led to a renewed version of the American Dream situated in the borough. The global success of hip-hop culture is the proof that character traits such as self-reliance, pragmatism, optimism, a do-it-yourself attitude, and the democratic principles of each one teach one and strength through community lead to a new success story.

The creativity discourse, the documentary mode, and the American Dream in *Born in The Bronx* speak to a new spatial discourse that emerged in the 2000s, that of legacy. This discourse, which will be the focus of the last part of this chapter, bridges the past and the present as it celebrates the South Bronx as the buzzing epicenter where the promise of the American Dream has been renewed. The convergence of creativity and legacy discourses becomes most apparent when comparing the two maps included in the book. The first map, entitled "The World of Hip-Hop Circa 1979," was drawn by *Wild Style* director Charlie Ahearn. The hand-drawn map centers on the South Bronx by calling it its nickname "Boogie Down Bronx" and shows the many venues and clubs where hip-hop emerged such as the Dixie Club (see Ch. 4.1) and the Ecstasy Garage Disco as well as Harlem World or the Celebrity Club in Harlem. It literally reconfigures the geographic, racial, and class boundaries between domination and marginalization by integrating Manhattan's Harlem into the creative place of hip-hop while simultaneously excluding white affluent Manhattan's Upper West Side. Harlem is incorporated as a place of 'cool' while the white upper middle- and upper-class neighborhoods and power centers in Midtown and Lower Manhattan are cut off from this map in its lower part. The map challenges the origin myth that hip-hop only originated in The Bronx and establishes a link to a tradition of black musical, literary, and artistic creativity which peaked in during the Harlem Renaissance, the intellectual and aesthetic forerunner of hip-hop, in the 1920s. Ahearn's map revises existing socioeconomic boundary formations in New York City as he connects the South Bronx and Harlem subcultures and countervails them with the financially wealthy white Anglo American culture referred to as "Money Making Manhattan" in the left part. This map thus starkly distinguishes between grassroots do-it-yourself creativity and colonial capitalist commodification.

The second, more recent "Hip-Hop Map of the Bronx" represents the idea of the birthplace of hip-hop differently. Compiled by photographer Joe Conzo together with Tony Tone, member of the Bronx crew The Cold Crush Brothers (see Ch. 4.1), it is printed on the inner book jacket and can be unfolded into a poster. Its unusual location speaks to media convergence as the medium of a map is transferred to another medium, the book jacket. Similar to the Ahearn map, the updated version contains various Bronx locations: high schools, venues, clubs, and housing projects in which early hip-hop flourished. In contrast to the 1979 map, the "Hip-Hop Map of the Bronx" focuses solely on the Bronx and leaves out Harlem. The current map therefore self-consciously and proudly claims the entire Bronx as the cradle of hip-hop by excluding northern Manhattan and thereby limiting hip-hop's creative territory only to The Bronx. The colorful map also relates the venues to the subway lines much more intensively. The subway lines highlight not only the importance of public transportation as the main means of mobility in New York City, but also the fact that its cars were an important surface and vehicle for the distribution of early graffiti culture. A comparison of the maps demonstrates that while both maps reinforce the idea of the Bronx as an interconnected network of artists, parties, and venues, the "The Hip-Hop Map of The Bronx" affirms the increasing importance of the legacy discourse of The Bronx as the mythical birthplace of hip-hop for readers in the early twenty-first century.

This success narrative and legacy discourse in *Born in The Bronx* constructs a romanticized version of the shrinking Bronx in the late 1970s and early 1980s seen earlier. In a review of the book, photographer Conzo sums up that "[b]ack then [...] it was more about fun than business" (qtd. in Cruz-Logo 70). His statement resonates with the change of The Bronx in the early 2010s when urban regeneration lead to gentrification, especially in the former South Bronx neighborhoods of Mott Haven, Melrose, and Hunts Point. The photo book glorifies the local grassroots enthusiasm and low-budget mentality of the 1970s and critically nods to today's hip-hop culture as the 'cash cow' of the global multi-billion-dollar music industry. The artists presented in the photo book have taken on the challenges that were presented in The Bronx as an opportunity to grow and, as a result, have also successfully moved upwards and established their own versions of the American Dream in their respective communities. Here, the circle closes as the success and American Dream narratives moved from the early 1980s autobiographical narratives to the mid-2000s, from literature to hip-hop culture, from former to current residents, and from a success narrative which was concerned with individual upward social mobility to a collective American Dream narrative.

The legacy discourse evident in *Born in The Bronx* is also expressed across a wide variety of audio-/visual texts since the 1990s. A new generation of Bronx artists celebrates their pride in the South Bronx, such as Fat Joe on his 1995 album *Jealous One's Envy*, Jennifer Lopez on her record *This is Me ... Then* (2002) with its best-selling single and music video "Jenny from the Block" (2002), and Lord Tariq and Peter Gunz on their release *Make It Reign* (1998). Lord Tariq and Peter Gunz, for instance, challenge the audience in their single "Uptown, Baby (Déjà Vu)": "But if it wasn't for the Bronx / this rap shit probably never would be going on / so tell me where you from? / Uptown baby, uptown baby." In the music video the artists perform inside Yankee Stadium and celebrate The Bronx as the place where rap and hip-hop were born. As noted earlier, Yankee Stadium is home to the New York Yankees, one of the most iconic teams in America's favorite game, baseball. By positioning themselves in that iconic space, they insist upon their validity by aligning themselves with a symbol of America's great pastime. Drawing on the African American call-and-response tradition, they ask the TV viewers "so tell me where are you from?" indicating that The Bronx can easily take up the competition against other places which claim their share in the development of hip-hop culture. Recent rappers coming out of The Bronx such as Cardi B and Princess Nokia continue the legacy discourse and affirm that the success story of The Bronx has become commercially attractive while issues of shrinkage, loss, popular music, and urban creativity have become lucrative in the marketplace.

As such, *Born in The Bronx* is a commodity which appropriates the marketability of the South Bronx in the light of the global popularity of hip-hop. *Born in The Bronx* was published by Rizzoli, a Manhattan company, after an exhibition of the artifacts had toured Europe and Japan (Cruz-Logo 70). The Swedish editor Kugelberg is a symbolic figure for the global fame of the borough as the birthplace of hip-hop. He stands for a new generation of international white male hip-hop aficionados who are fascinated by this myth and "attempt[...] to document the early days of hip-hop [where] artifacts are practically nonexistent" (Introduction 31). Likewise, books by Martha Cooper, Jim Fricke and Charlie Ahearn, Jamel Shabazz (*Back in the Days; A Time Before Crack*), and more recently Joseph C. Ewoodzie Jr.'s *Break Beats in the Bronx: Rediscovering Hip-Hop's Early Years* (2017) also allude to the idea of a golden era of early hip-hop, which all but ensures profit on the book market. Hence, Kugelberg's photo book aims to preserve the memory of early hip-hop culture and the American Dream narrative while at the same time clever marketing and packaging stresses its originality. The American Dream narrative, creativity and legacy discourses, and documentary mode help to establish a sense of authenticity that promises a greater readership inside and outside the United States.

Finally, *Born in The Bronx* reinforces the idea of the South Bronx as a place of growth and locus of an American Dream narrative at the beginning of the new century. The suggested retail price of $45 aims at a rather affluent and diverse audience: "If you are a sixteen-year old looking at this book, or if you remember the confusion of what that was like, you should know all of us are capable of accomplishing our life goals and desires" (Kugelberg, Introduction 31). While the author speaks to an older audience who lived through the early years of hip-hop, he also speaks to a younger audience that does not know much about the origins of hip-hop and wants to learn about its past and future. His statement connects the place's vibrancy during the late 1970s and early 1980s with the personal accomplishment of the artists and activists that helped turn the situation around. In that regard, *Born in The Bronx* finally asserts that hip-hop embodies the accomplishment of the American Dream for disenfranchised teenagers and that The Bronx is indeed a very 'American place' enabling such a success story.

To conclude, the 2007 photo book *Born in The Bronx* engages in a multi-faceted dialogue between the past and the present. In reconstructing the vibrant spirit of the South Bronx in the late 1970s and early 1980s, it reinforces the idea of The Bronx as a mythical starting point for a new version of the American Dream narrative in the early twenty-first century (see Samuel). This narrative highlights the optimistic stories of a younger generation of color who succeeded the challenges presented in their declining neighborhoods. The themes of creativity, community, democracy, innovation, and success also translate into the form of *Born in The Bronx*. A mixture of conventional photo book and two-dimensional hip-hop archive, the publication features portraiture, performance, and party photographs as well as pictures of artifacts, flyers, maps, and first-person narratives of male hip-hop pioneers. Because of the seemingly communal, democratic, and egalitarian design, the book questions established notions of authorship and agency.

Born in The Bronx subverts the prevalent destruction discourse by building on the idea of the South Bronx as a multifaceted and diverse urban community. Similar to *Wild Style* and "The Message," *Born in The Bronx* reimagines the declining urban space of the late 1970s and early 1980s as a creative and democratic space which also reimagines existing geographic, racial, class, and media boundaries. The photo book echoes Marshall Berman's idea that shrinkage needs new media by underscoring the importance of a creative response to devastation in the formation of a new local identity and grassroots-inspired participatory economy (340-41).

In remembering the early days of hip-hop culture in The Bronx as a success story, *Born in The Bronx* strongly believes in the validity and the legacy of the American Dream in the era of post-9/11 political conflict and the Great Recession which started with the collapse of the housing bubble the year the book was published. As such it bears striking similarities in its treatment of decline and the American Dream to the literary texts of the early 1980s examined earlier. *Born in The Bronx* engages in the dialects of individualism and community by focusing on self-reliance and the self-made man trope and by combining it with a community-oriented success story of a younger generation. Their upward mobility narrative consists not of a geographic relocation but of staying in The Bronx and fostering community development through themselves.

Finally, the publication responds to the changing urban context in the 2000s by bringing to the surface a legacy discourse. The photo book takes advantage of gentrification by pointing to shrinkage as a much more original phase in the borough's history. In doing so, it constructs a spatial legacy discourse by romanticizing a creative place and highly vibrant culture of a now bygone era. At a time when a younger generation of more affluent New Yorkers rediscovers The Bronx as a place to live, the photo book claims that it has always been a hub of creativity, vibrancy, and cultural innovation, especially during the age of decay in the 1970s and early 1980s. In that sense, the photo book celebrates the South Bronx as a mythical space when the devastation has mostly disappeared while neglecting the fact that the borough continues to be one of the poorest congressional districts in the United States (García Conde).

4.4 Conclusion

Hip-hop culture examined in this chapter reconfigures the American Dream narrative in the age of urban shrinkage by creating the myth of The Bronx as the birthplace of hip-hop culture. Hip-hop strongly believes in the rubble landscape as a fertile urban ground for a new, more community-oriented, participatory, and democratic version of the American Dream. All of the texts are firmly localized in the South Bronx where rubble is depicted as raw material for a new rags-to-riches narrative. A spatial creativity discourse highlights the area as an epicenter of youthful invention. In doing so, it works *with* shrinkage instead of *against* it by emphasizing the manifold DIY community performances and innovative grassroots-based cultural practices.

The cultural texts analyzed earlier showcase a number of virtues that help jumpstart a revised American Dream narrative such as community spirit, grassroots enthusiasm, material creativity, DIY aesthetics, spatial self-reliance, generic innovation, and medial self-reflexivity. In both texts, the heterotopic space of the South Bronx obtains new functions of performance stage and of breeding ground for a new version of the American Dream.

The texts converge, update, and expand existing genres and modes in order to showcase The Bronx' innovative potential as a result of the American Dream narrative. *Wild Style* presents a generic bricolage of animation, musical, romance, and documentary in order to introduce its audiences to the multidimensional nature of hip-hop culture. In repurposing the shrinking urban space as a stage and combining it with the latest musical and media technologies, "The Message" created the new conscious rap genre which articulates the experience of spatial, racial, and social marginalization and empowerment. Both, *Wild Style* and "The Message" showcase media and technological convergence and artistic innovation as they voice both skepticism of and confidence in a revised American Dream. They combine Berman's and Jenkin's claims that new converging and participatory forms of art emerge from deindustrialization which facilitate a poetic, and later, spatial resurrection of The Bronx.

Wild Style, "The Message," and the photo book *Born in The Bronx* also demonstrate a new mode at work in this study, the documentary mode. The documentary mode aims at presenting the urban experience in seemingly unpolished aesthetics. The documentary mode in *Wild Style* and the music video for "The Message" strongly influence the audience's perception of the inner city to help found the myth of the 'ghetto' as a quasi-geographic prerequisite against which hip-hop culture is successfully created locally, nationally, and globally to this day.

Perhaps most surprisingly, *Wild Style*, "The Message," and *Born in The Bronx* repurpose, appropriate, and update cultural narratives evident in the literary and filmic texts produced in the early 1980s. They reintroduce The Bronx as a heterotopia for renewed success and frontier narratives and believe in the unique qualities of The Bronx to create individual and collective success stories. Because of their converging and convincing ways of storytelling, these hip-hop texts create a lasting myth of The Bronx as the birthplace of a renewed American Dream as well as of hip-hop culture. They thus most prominently facilitate the poetic resurrection of The Bronx in the era of decline.

While *Wild Style* and "The Message" promote the idea of The Bronx as the setting of an updated American Dream narrative, *Born in The Bronx: A Visual Record of the Early Days of Hip-Hop* appropriates this myth against the backdrop of gentrification and illustrates a second spatial discourse, the legacy discourse of the American Dream. Intensifying in the 2000s, the legacy discourse expresses people's pride in The Bronx as the birthplace of hip-hop culture. Kugelberg's photo book strongly buys into and cashes in on the founding myth of hip-hop because it shows that the area has always been a center of creativity. The photo book attracts new affluent audiences who want to learn about the legacy of the former, now gentrifying, South Bronx. It even paves the way for new popular cultural texts on early rap music and hip-hop culture, such as *The Get Down* (2016-17, Netflix) and *Hip-Hop Evolution* (2016-, Netflix). *Born in The Bronx* critiques the increasing commercialization of hip-hop inside and outside the US by recalling its creative and seemingly more grassroots bottom-up spirit and more participatory roots.

This chapter has shown that hip-hop culture has participated in the poetic resurrection of The Bronx by updating the cultural narrative of the American Dream. Its success has contributed to the creation of a new place-based myth which, in turn, has become commercially commodified and exploited. The final chapter of this study will explore the larger effects of this poetic resurrection in a transnational perspective.

Conclusions
Global Dimensions of the Poetic Resurrection

This study examined the era of decline in The Bronx as a distressed, but also an enormously productive, creative, and innovative, phase in contemporary American cultural history. I argued that (pop)cultural representations and signifying practices envisioned the poetic resurrection of The Bronx as a creative response to the era of decline. While the public imagination discursively disconnected the urban space from the American experience in much of the 1970s, the cultural texts reconnect it to the American project by questioning, revising, reconfiguring, reaffirming, expanding, and updating its central cultural narratives. The concluding section attempts to refine the phenomenon of the poetic resurrection more robustly before suggesting its applicability for other urban areas, both in the US and beyond, where decline narratives persist in the age of deindustrialization.

The poetic resurrection analyzed in this book is a collective, converging, and participatory phenomenon because the cultural texts revise progress narratives, such as the success story, the frontier, and the American Dream, on a variety of media, genre, and aesthetic levels. The representations range from more traditional and established forms such as novels and semi-autobiographical fiction to pop- and (sub-)cultural genres such as film, music and the music video, all of which stand to reach wide audiences. Artists, writers, and filmmakers collaborated with smaller publishers and independent media companies such as North Atlantic Books (*GUP*), Orion Pictures (*Wolfen*), and Sugar Hill Records ("The Message"), which allowed the artists to tell unique stories on the perceived margins of the commercially-oriented culture industries of the early 1980s.

The popular cultural representations use specific modes as ways to establish a sense of place, identity, and audience identification. The literary works revisit and remember The Bronx as a place of self-made men and women as

well as their social upward mobilities. The filmic representations reimagine
The Bronx as an urban frontier space while the melodramatic mode zooms in
on the dynamic encounters between colonizers and colonized. Hip-hop culture proposes an egalitarian, community-oriented, and place-based American
Dream to dealing with decline and uses the documentary mode to highlight
individual and collective subjectivities. Although the modes manifest themselves slightly differently across a wide variety of media and genres, they can
be understood as more or less the same converging phenomenon appearing
across media. Together with their respective genres they make the causes
and consequences of shrinkage in the South Bronx accessible to larger audiences by literally providing a face to and a personal story about urban devastation. Modes provoke empathy with an audience outside the borough as
they translate the specific local socioeconomic and urban problems into the
larger American context. As such genres and modes are important tools of
identification and facilitate new layers of meaning and experience in the poetic resurrection of The Bronx.

The literary, visual, and audio-visual texts strongly reject the common perception of The Bronx as a one-dimensional, dangerous, hostile, isolated, de-
humanized, and ultimately 'un-American' disaster zone propagated in much
of American news and journalistic media outlets of its time. Instead, the texts
explore a multiplicity of spaces and places within the imagined hegemonic
news media space of the South Bronx. Almost all of the texts analyzed in this
book are set in the shrinking territory of the South Bronx but some without
explicitly mentioning its name. Rather, the texts zoom in on different streets,
corners, buildings, and neighborhoods such as Nelson Avenue in *Growing Up
Bronx*, Lafontaine Avenue in the Tremont section in *Bronx Primitive*, the Concourse Plaza Hotel near Yankee Stadium in *Gloria*, the Charlotte Street area
in *Wolfen*, the Dixie club in *Wild Style*, and various school gymnasiums in *Born
in The Bronx*. The rejection of the term South Bronx critiques the larger structural forces which lead to its shrinkage in the first place. Hence the symbolic
territory of the South Bronx constitutes the most contested site within the
imagined boundaries of The Bronx where cultural domination and subordination are fought over. It is the site where the poetic regeneration most visibly
reconnects the borough to earlier spatial imaginations, memories, and local
identities.

The cultural representations reinforce the idea that The Bronx in the era
of decline is indeed a home for its residents. The fictional protagonists not
only frequent the streets and neighborhoods on an everyday basis, but most

importantly, the borough is their home, a spatial function which is almost completely silenced in public and journalistic media discourses. The space of home is related to larger identity re-/formation processes such as growing-up and maturing, cooperation and conflict, emancipation and aging. The cultural and media texts in this study stress the fact that The Bronx has served as a home in the past, in the present, and will continue to do so in the future. Thus, they expand Berman's observation that postmodern artists recover primarily homes as the spaces of their past (332-33). Such artists emphasize that The Bronx is a perpetual spatial starting point for individual and collective progress narratives. By introducing The Bronx as a home, artists, writers, and filmmakers thus create a sense of local identity, belonging, memory, and history, important elements of the poetic resurrection of The Bronx.

These cultural representations and signifying practices affirm the borough's remarkable variety in terms of gender, ethnic, racial, class, as well as individual and collective identity formations. They counter the idea that The Bronx is a de-humanized place by showing that it is as diverse as the rest of America. Only white Anglo American political and business elites are entirely missing or, if they appear in minor roles and sub-plots, they are presented as corrupt, such as the Van der Veers in *Wolfen*. The texts suggest that they are to blame for the downfall of The Bronx, but that the borough's regeneration is a localized collective effort outside of established institutions. The texts' cultural diversity also foreshadows the decline of white Anglo American dominance and the rise of more egalitarian, integrative identities and communities who strive to reach for their own spatial and spiritual regenerations. The texts' distrust of established institutions together with the representation's celebration of cultural diversity is a uniquely American approach.

All of the works analyzed in this book affirm the validity of progress narratives, such as the success story, the frontier narrative, and the American Dream, in order to help symbolically re-start the verbal, visual, audio-visual, and cultural regeneration processes of the borough. Some of the representations analyzed are more skeptical of the notion of growth and social upward mobility. While a few audio-visual representations such as *Wolfen*, *Fort Apache: The Bronx*, and "The Message" criticize the larger structural forces behind shrinkage, such as inequality, racism, and corruption, they nevertheless affirm the basic ideology of progress: These works are bound up in the logic of growth, expansion, decline, destruction, and renewal, many of which are simply re-articulations of capitalism. *Wolfen* and, to a lesser extent, *Fort Apache: The Bronx* have reached somewhat of a cult status among film buffs while "The

Message" is today known as the first popular consciousness rap song even beyond hip-hop circles.

Therefore, the shrinking Bronx is by no means an exemplary American nightmare as characterized in the news media of the 1970s. On the contrary, the poetic resurrection reinforces and contributes to an inherently American project: The texts refer back to, create alternative versions, and move forward long-lasting cultural narratives, myths, metaphors, virtues, and values such as resilience, individualism, optimism, pragmatism, equality, and progress. In that sense, the representations are much more than just a mirror of the dystopian post-World War II decaying American city, but they are powerful expressions of the ongoing search for an American urban and post-growth identity at the end of the twentieth and at the beginning of the twenty-first century. Hence, in bringing to the surface many different racial, ethnic, class, and gendered voices, angles, stories, and memories, these texts are inherently postmodern, postcolonial, and transnational.

The poetic resurrection conducts crucial cultural work in the urban regeneration process of The Bronx. The cultural texts analyzed here resonate with Marshall Berman's demand "to accept the process of disintegration as a framework for new kinds of integration, to use the rubble as a medium in which to construct new forms and make new affirmations, without such a framework and such a medium, no real growth can take place" (341). Berman's quote highlights the poetic resurrection's main ideological task in an era of late capitalism (Jameson) because the borough's narrative, discursive, and media regeneration is the first step to its spatial and economic regeneration. The texts – deliberately or not – highlight this space's unique cultural legacy, innovative creativity, and commercial potential. In doing so, they attract the curiosity of new, more affluent population groups and suggest that The Bronx is the perfect setting for a new "spatial fix" (Harvey, "Globalization" 24), new cycle of neoliberal economic exploitation at the end of the late twentieth and the beginning of the twenty-first century.

The poetic resurrection of the shrinking Bronx has created a myth which transcends media, geographical, and temporal boundaries, and this re-imagining continues to be adapted. In the late 1980s and early 1990s, for instance, films like *Five Corners* (dir. Tony Bill, 1987) and *A Bronx Tale* (dir. Robert de Niro, 1993) looked back at a time before the era of decline and its subsequent poetic resurrection. They constructed the 1960s Bronx which nevertheless foreshadowed the political, urban, and social conflicts and opportunities to come. The novels *The Bonfire of the Vanities* and *Underworld* rework the frontier discourse and the jungle metaphors seen in the audio-visual examples. In her autobiography *No Disrespect* (1994) African American rapper, writer, and activist Sister Souljah draws upon the success story (Nitzsche, "'Slavery's Consequences'") when she reflected on her childhood and youth in the housing projects in the 1970s. Ironically, with *Rumble in The Bronx* (dir. Stanley Tong, 1996), the 1990s saw a film starring the Chinese American action hero Jackie Chan that drew on the decline myth but rejected the Bronx setting altogether and was shot in Vancouver, Canada.

In the beginning of the twenty-first century, the poetic resurrection seems to have accomplished the spatial resurrection as The Bronx resumed its place as part of urban America in the public imagination. In 1997, the borough was awarded the "All-America City" award by the National Civic League which recognized the successful renewal process (Smalls). The idea of The Bronx changed from an 'un-American' place, an alleged accident in American urban history, to a place epitomizing growth, progress, and rebirth, rising like a phoenix out of the ashes thus following the main idea of the texts analyzed in this book. At the same time, its artists, writers, and filmmakers continue to produce exciting cultural representations that remember and reimagine the poetic resurrection in new and ever changing textual, discursive, generic, and media formats.

Literature, for instance, continues to be a fruitful medium to reimagine the success story from a variety of angles and perspectives (Alda; Naison and Castillo-Garsow; Rice-Gonzáles; Rice-Gonzáles and Vásquez). However, literary texts increasingly draw on the frontier narrative to flash back to the dark, uncanny, and mysterious characteristics during the era of decline in the 1970s. The Puerto Rican writer Abraham Rodriguez Jr. published a series of crime/detective novels set in the South Bronx of the 1960s and 1970s (*Boy Without a Flag; Buddha Book; Spidertown*). His neo-noir-style detective novel *South by South Bronx* (2008), for instance, highlights the dark side of the South Bronx. Similarly, the 2007 short story collection *Bronx Noir* edited by Bronx writer S. J. Rozan combines the genres crime and mystery. It is part of a *Noir* series on different cities that started in 2004 with *Brooklyn Noir* published by Akashic Books, an independent publisher which advertises their mission as "reverse-gentrification of the literary world" (*akashicbooks.com*). *Bronx Noir* presents a multiplicity of Bronx authors like Abraham Rodriguez Jr. or Jerome Charyn who "have found noir corners, dark moments, and rich places of astonishing variety" (Rozan, "Introduction" 15). The coming-of-age novel *Chulito* presents one of the first-ever queer Puerto Rican success stories (Nitzsche, "Ghetto").

At a time when various New Yorker neighborhoods are threatened by gentrification, literature highlights its flipside by shifting to the shrinking South Bronx of the 1970s in crime, mystery, and noir texts. Gentrification in particular threatens to "eat the Bronx" (as the *M*A*S*H* quote ironically suggests). Characterizing gentrification as a destructive force triggers new questions about the changing function of the city in contemporary American culture.

Film and television, by contrast, increasingly highlight the success story and coming-of-age themes found in literature during the era of decline. Gus van Sant's *Finding Forrester* is a coming-of-age story of African American student Jamal Wallace (Rob Brown) who enters an intellectual exchange with the once well-known Scottish American writer William Forrester (Sean Connery). The semi-autobiographical coming-of-age A&E TV film *Knights of the South Bronx* (dir. Allen Hughes, 2005), centers on how teacher Richard Mason (Ted Danson) teaches elementary school students to play chess. Similarly, the melodrama *Doubt* (dir. John Patrick Shanley, 2008) is situated in an educational setting, the (fictional) Catholic St. Nicholas School. The popular HBO series *The Get Down* narrates the coming-of-age stories of a group of teenagers in the early days of hip-hop. Film and television increasingly shift from gangster and crime to coming-of-age genres while literature re-creates the dystopian imaginations of film during the era of decline.

Some cultural representations continue to deconstruct the mythical South Bronx of the 1970s at the beginning of the twenty-first century. The independent production *Mott Music*, for instance, resurrects the unique neighborhood Mott Haven which virtually vanished under the hegemonic image of the South Bronx. The 2009 coming-of-age comedy *City Island* (dir. Raymond De Felitta) is set "in the tiny fishing community at the northern tip of the Bronx" (Catsoulis) in the Long Island Sound. The film reintroduces a seemingly lost insular and coastal imagination of the borough. Likewise, Wayne Lawrence's photo book *Orchard Beach: The Bronx Rivera* (2013) portrays heavily tattooed swimmers and stylish sunbathers at one of Robert Moses' famous urban renewal projects in The Bronx. *City Island* and *Orchard Beach* both direct the popular gaze to the borough's almost forgotten rivers, waterways, and beaches.

Although the representations of poetic resurrection are very specific, the way they revise and reimagine cultural narratives is not spatially or temporally fixed and continues to wander into different media and genres. The meaning of what constitutes the success story and the American Dream, for instance, is continually changing, a signifying system in flux, where discourses, genres, and modes across media are being constantly transformed, subverted, deconstructed, and appropriated at different periods in time. More research is needed on cultural representations coming out of The Bronx inside and outside established production systems, media markets, and distribution channels, such as the street literature phenomenon (see Graff). The Bronx street literature novels *Street Team* (2003) written by former prison inmate Joe Black, *The Blue Circle* (2006) and *A Boogie Down Story* (2008) by street worker Keisha Seignious, and *Pure Bronx* (2013) by writer Melissa Castillo-Garsow and Mark Naison question existing literary conventions, present new takes on the success story in unconventional narrative structures, and rely on vernacular language to present new character constellations to their readers. They draw on the genres of romance, pulp fiction, and urban literature to represent The Bronx in a way that appeals to a younger audience. Those novels have undergone their own success story because even though they were produced largely outside of the book market, they are now available in major bookstores.

More research is needed on poetic resurrection in other popular and converging media forms such as photography, radio, comics, TV, and the Internet. How does the ABC sitcom *The Goldbergs* (2013-) refer back to the Jewish American success stories of the popular radio program *The Rise of the Goldbergs*? What is the meaning of immigration, the American Dream, and shrinkage in comics and graphic novels such as Will Eisner's *The Contract with God Trilogy* (2005), the graphic novel series *The Cross Bronx* (Oeming and Brandon, 2006-07), or the D.C./Vertigo graphic novel *Bronx Kill* (Milligan and Romberger, 2010)? Another fruitful endeavor would be to analyze how the 2007 ESPN documentary mini-series *The Bronx is Burning* reimagines the era of decline in baseball history based on Jonathan Mahler's *Ladies and Gentlemen, the Bronx is Burning* (2005). The Internet as a relatively young distribution medium compared to traditional forms constitutes a rich resource with various types of social media, blogs, videos, short messaging or photo sites that present a multitude of voices, angles, and perspectives.

While on a theoretical level my study mostly approached the era of decline and the American Dream narrative from a post-structuralist and postmodern cultural studies perspective, different theoretical frameworks, such as phenomenology (Merleau-Ponty), affect theory (Ahmed; Berlant), and critical race theory (Crenshaw et al.; Delgado and Stefancic) would certainly generate other important insights into urban transformation processes. A translation and reception study could scrutinize international translations, dubbings, and audience responses of films and novels such as *Fort Apache: The Bronx*. Research could show how this film, its translations, and adaptations have shaped the imagination of The Bronx in different cultural contexts world-wide until today.

A transnational perspective could shed light on the global appropriation of the borough's devastation image. Around 1955, for instance, The Bronx was a short-lived subject in German post-war (pulp) hard cover literary crime stories, such as *Nachts in der Bronx* ("At Night in The Bronx," published by dime novel author Günter Bajog under the pseudonym of J.H. Wayne), *Der Alte von Bronx* ("The Old Man from The Bronx"), *In der Bronx wohnen keine Engel* ("There are No Angels in The Bronx," both published by Hans-Joachim von Koblinski aka Joe McBrown), and *Bomben in der Bronx* ("Bombs in The Bronx," written by Tim Gracer). Smaller publishers located in the West-German Ruhr Area published those crime novels which, today, are largely out of print and therefore relatively hard to obtain. The novels raise important questions of why there was a fascination with a seemingly unsafe Bronx in Germany at a time when the filmic Bronx in the United States was still largely a place of middle-class stability. More research is also needed on the cultural representations made by the newest immigration groups from Central and South America, Asia, and Africa. What can they tell us about The Bronx as an arrival or sanctuary city?

A material culture approach could investigate how The Bronx has become manifest in a variety of objects in other places. For example, it has been incorporated into the name of an indoor climbing wall (the Bronx Rock Kletterhalle) near Cologne, Germany. The Bronx has also been refigured as the name of a young music and lifestyle magazine in Hamburg simply titled *Bronx*. The Munich-based electronic music collective known as Schlachthof Bronx (Slaughterhouse Bronx) has taken a cue from this iconic New York borough. The Bronx increasingly promises to be a commercially successful label for products such as the Dutch shoe company Bronx Shoes. A nightclub in my former hometown of Chemnitz advertised a "Bronx Night," which promised hip-hop music ("BlackBeats") and a Bronx-inspired drink:

Fig. 1 A Bronx Night: The flyer advertises a hip-hop party in Chemnitz which features a special drink called burning Bronx trash can (mid-2000s).

The flyer draws on the era of decline by incorporating an iconic burning garbage can in the flyer's graphic design. That myth is also taken up in the nightly drink special "A Burning Bronx Trash Can" ("SpecialDrink Brennende BronxTonne"). These examples affirm that the commodification of the once shrinking borough has grown on a global scale as the spatial marker of 'The Bronx' increasingly promises revenue even outside of the United States. Research projects working with transnationalism, translation, reception, and material culture studies as theoretical frameworks could reveal greater insights into the various global (economic) flows of the traveling signifier Bronx.

As this study has shown, we need to consider the role of cultural representations in the larger spatial discourse of urban shrinkage processes. While my study demonstrated how popular culture used the era of decline in The Bronx to symbolically revise and reimagine cultural narratives, I am deeply convinced that such approaches also exist in contemporary shrinking cities in the United States. For instance, Detroit has grown into the iconic shrinking city in the early twenty-first century. In turn, it has enjoyed enormous academic and popular interest (Arnaud; Austin and Doerr; Doucet; Moore; Thompson). While there are certainly differences between the era of the decline in The Bronx and Detroit in terms of duration, intensity, and scope, there are striking similarities in the various official and artistic discourses. Blogger and researcher John Patrick Leary, for instance, termed the concept of Detroitism in order to address the recent fascination with the declining Motor City among audio-visual artists. He laments that contemporary ruin porn photography and ruin film "aestheticize[...] poverty without inquiring of its origins." His observation bears striking resemblance to the public discourse of The Bronx in the 1970s. Leary further observes that

> [d]espite their differences, the common problem with many of the Lamenters and Utopians is that both see Detroit as an exception to the contemporary United States, rather than as one of its exemplary places. Detroit figures as either a nightmare image of the American Dream, where equal opportunity and abundance came to die, or as an updated version of it, where bohemians from expensive coastal cities can have the one-hundred-dollar house and community garden of their dreams.

Leary states that some observers interpret the shrinking and decline of Detroit as an exception to the American experience. Their mental maps resemble a similar strategy of exclusion which was at work in the 1970s news media and journalistic discourse on The Bronx. More than four decades after the devastation of The Bronx, similar, partly polarizing, mechanisms remain at work in American cities in distress. The question arises in how far different cultural groups have utilized different media forms, genres, and narrative patterns in order to articulate their respective racial, class, and gender experiences in America's current great shrinking city. Which modes are at work in cultural representations to help audiences understand the spatial complexities in a city which has been shrinking for a much longer time than The Bronx? Where are the texts which subvert and criticize the hegemonic 'ruin porn' aesthetics à la *Wolfen* and "The Message"?

While my study focuses on the American urban context, it would certainly be interesting to scrutinize how representations of shrinking cities on a global scale contribute to ongoing issues in their respective socio-cultural contexts. Which dominant and subordinate discourses are at work in various media in other shrinking cities, such as Osaka, Japan, Manchester/Liverpool, UK, and in the cities of the former East Germany? For example, Eric C. Erbacher and I argue in our case study on my hometown of Chemnitz that the indie rap group Kraftklub openly articulates the post-socialist double rupture of sociopolitical change and urban-economic decline in their songs and music videos. In voicing the difficulties of this former East German city's socioeconomic and cultural transformation, Kraftklub undermine official city marketing campaigns which tabooed shrinking and deindustrialization in the past (Erbacher and Nitzsche). In a similar vein, the edited volume *Bloom and Bust: Urban Landscapes in the East since German Reunification* (2015) examines cultural phenomena in the heretofore understudied East German cities of Erfurt, Frankfurt (Oder), and Dresden. Here, the poetic resurrection of The Bronx could also serve as an analytic lens for their cultural resurrection processes.

The Bronx continues to be one of the most fascinating, intriguing, and complex boroughs in American culture. Its downfall and resurrection deeply influence how people around the world imagine American urban spaces. Similar to the innovative character of hip-hop culture which emerged out of the era of decline, the lessons learned from the shrinking Bronx lead the way to contemporary shrinking contexts inside and outside the United States. As new challenges and opportunities such as gentrification, new waves of immigration from the Global South, and climate change emerge on the borough's horizon, The Bronx continues to evolve, transform, and grow. How those new challenges inspire new generations of artists, musicians, writers, and filmmakers is worthy of more fruitful investigations – hopefully in the field of Bronx Studies – because answering such questions will help us gain a deeper understanding of the fascinating dynamics of the American city in the twenty-first century.

Works Cited

1990: The Bronx Warriors. Directed by Enzo Castellani, performances by Vic Morrow, Christopher Connelly, and Mark Gregory, Shriek Show, 1982.

"A Bronx Morning." Directed by Jay Leyda. 1931. *Picturing a Metropolis: New York City Unveiled*, Image Entertainment, 2005.

A Bronx Tale. Directed by Robert de Niro, performances by Chazz Palminteri, Robert de Niro, and Francis Capra, Euro Video, 1993.

A Catered Affair. Directed by Richard Brooks, performances by Bette Davis, Ernest Borgnine, and Debbie Reynolds, MGM, 1956.

"A Home for the Zoo." *The New York Times*, 22 May 1896, nytimes.com/1896/05/22/archives/a-home-for-the-zoo.html. Accessed 23 Mar. 2020.

A Raisin in the Sun. Directed by Daniel Petrie, performances by Sidney Poitier, Claudia McNeil, and Ruby Dee, Columbia Pictures, 1961.

Abbott, Berenice, and Bonnie Yochelson. *Changing New York: Photographien aus den 30er Jahren*. Schirmer-Mosel, 1999.

AC/DC. "AC/DC – Highway to Hell (Official Video)." *YouTube*, uploaded by AC/DC, 11 Nov. 2012, youtu.be/l482ToyNkeo.

Ahmed, Sara. *The Cultural Politics of Emotion*. Routledge, 2004.

Albee, Edward. *The American Dream and The Zoo Story: Two Plays*. Plume, 1997.

Alda, Arlene. *Just Kids from The Bronx: Telling it the Way it Was: An Oral History*. Henry Holt, 2015.

Alger, Horatio. *Ragged Dick and Struggling Upwards*. 1867. Penguin, 1985.

All My Children. ABC, 1970-2011.

American Dream. Directed by Barbara Kopple, Prestige Films, 1990.

American Matchmaker. Directed by Edgar G. Ulmer, performances by Leo Fuchs, Judith Abarbanel, and Judel Dubinsky, The Rutenberg & Everett Yiddish Film Library, 1940.

Anderson, Linda. R. *Autobiography*. Routledge, 2011.

Annie Hall. Directed by Woody Allen, performances by Woody Allen, Diane Keaton, and Tony Roberts, MGM, 1977.

Anolik, Ruth Bienstock. "The Missing Mother: The Meanings of Maternal Absence in the Gothic Mode." *Modern Language Studies*, vol. 33, no. 1-2, 2003, pp. 25-43. *JSTOR*, jstor.org/stable/3195306. Accessed 21 Mar. 2020.

Applegate, Tim. "Retrospectives: John Cassavetes." *Film Journal*, vol. 1, no. 7, 2003. *EBSCOhost*, search.ebscohost.com/login.aspx?direct=true&db=mzh&AN=2003652779&site=ehost-live. Accessed 23 Mar. 2020.

Arnaud, Michael. *Detroit: The Dream is Now*. Abrams, 2017.

Austin, Dan, and Sean Doerr. *Lost Detroit: Stories Behind the Motor City's Majestic Ruins*. History Press, 2016.

Bachmann-Medick, Doris. *Cultural Turns: Neuorientierungen in den Kulturwissenschaften*. Rowohlt, 2010.

Ballon, Hillary. "Robert Moses and Urban Renewal." *Robert Moses and the Modern City: The Transformation of New York*, edited by Hillary Ballon and Kenneth T. Jackson, Norton, 2007, pp. 94-115.

—, and Kenneth T. Jackson, editors. *Robert Moses and the Modern City: The Transformation of New York*. Norton, 2007.

Barker, Chris, and Emma A. Jane. *Cultural Studies: Theory and Practice*. 5th ed., Sage, 2016.

Bate, David. *Photography: The Key Concepts*. Berg, 2009.

Beat Street. Directed by Stan Lathan, performances by Rae Dawn Chong, Guy Davis, and John Chardiet, Orion, 1984.

Beauregard, Robert A. *Voices of Decline: The Post-War Fate of US Cities*. Routledge, 2003.

Berland, Judy. "Sound, Image and Social Space: Music Video and Media Reconstruction." *Sound and Vision: The Music Video Reader*, edited by Simon Frith, Andrew Goodwin, and Lawrence Grossberg, Routledge, 1993, pp. 20-36.

Berlant, Lauren. *Cruel Optimism*. Duke UP, 2011.

Berman, Marshall. *All That is Solid Melts into Air: The Experience of Modernity*. Verso, 1983.

Bessa, Sergio A., editor. *Three Photographers from The Bronx: Jules Aarons, Morton Broffman, Joe Conzo*. Bronx Museum of the Arts, 2015.

Betsworth, Roger G. *Social Ethics: An Examination of American Moral Traditions*. Westminster/Knox P, 1990.

Black, Joe. *Street Team*. Hampstead Publishing, 2003.

Blondie. "Pretty Baby." *Parallel Lines*, Capitol, 1979.

Bluestone, Barry, and Harrison Bennett. *The Deindustrialization of America: Plant Closings, Community Abandonment, and the Dismantling of Basic Industry*. Basic Books, 1982.

Bolter, David Jay, and Richard Grusin. *Remediation: Understanding New Media*. MIT Press, 2000.

Bordwell, David, and Kristin Thompson. *Film Art: An Introduction*. 8th ed., McGraw-Hill, 2008.

Boskin, Joseph. "American Dream/American Laugh." *Rebellious Laughter: People's Humor in American Culture*, Syracuse UP, 1997, pp. 15-24.

Boulevardier from The Bronx. Directed by Fritz Freleng, 1936. *Dailymotion*, uploaded by InternetAnimationDatabase, 31 Aug. 2015, dailymotion.com/video/x33v1nc.

Bracklow, Robert L. *Bronx Park, on Rocking Stone*. 1895. *Museum of the City New York*, collections.mcny.org/Collection/Bronx%20Park,%20on%20Rocking%20Stone-2F3XC5YZCNM.html.

Brady Hill, Emita, and Janet Butler Munch, editors. *Bronx Faces and Voices: Sixteen Stories of Courage and Community*. Texas Tech UP, 2014.

Breakfast at Tiffany's. Directed by Blake Edwards, performances by Audrey Hepburn, George Peppard, and Patricia Neal, Paramount, 1961.

Bromley, Ray. "Cross-Bronx Expressway." *Robert Moses and the Modern City: The Transformation of New York*, edited by Hillary Ballon and Kenneth T. Jackson, Norton, 2007, pp. 217-20.

"Bronx Dwellers Demand Subways." *The New York Times*, 31 July 1910, nytimes.com/1910/07/31/archives/bronx-dwellers-demand-subways-residents-indignant-over-long.html. Accessed 23 Mar. 2020.

"Bronx Park for the Animals." *The New York Times*, 4 June 1896, nytimes.com/1896/06/04/archives/bronx-park-for-the-animals.html. Accessed 23 Mar. 2020.

Brooks, Peter. *The Melodramatic Imagination: Balzac, Henry James, Melodrama, and the Mode of Excess*. Yale UP, 1995.

Byron Company. *Skating, Van Cortlandt Park*. 1898. *Museum of the City New York*, collections.mcny.org/Collection/Skating,-Van-Cortlandt-Park.-2F3XC54WES2.html.

Canby, Vincent. "Cassavetes's *Gloria*, Moll, and a Boy." *The New York Times*, 1 Oct. 1980, nytimes.com/1980/10/01/arts/cassavetess-gloria-moll-and-a-boy.html. Accessed 23 Mar. 2020.

—. *"Fort Apache, The Bronx*, With Paul Newman." *The New York Times*, 6 Febr. 1981, nytimes.com/1981/02/06/movies/fort-apache-the-bronx-with-paul-newman.html. Accessed 23 Mar. 2020.

—. *"Wild Style*, Rapping and Painting Graffiti." *The New York Times*, 18 Mar. 1983, nytimes.com/1983/03/18/movies/wild-style-rapping-and-painting-graffiti.html. Accessed 23 Mar. 2020.

—. *"Wolfen* with Finney." *The New York Times*, 24 July 1981, nytimes.com/1981/07/24/movies/wolfen-with-finney.html. Accessed 23 Mar. 2020.

Carney, Raymond. *American Dreaming: The Films of John Cassavetes and the American Experience*. U of Berkeley P, 1985.

—. "The Adventure of Insecurity: The Films of John Cassavetes." *The Kenyon Review*, vol. 13, no. 2, 1991, pp. 102-21. *JSTOR*, jstor.org/stable/4336423. Accessed 21 Mar. 2020.

—. *The Films of John Cassavetes: Pragmatism, Modernism, and the Movies*. Cambridge UP, 1994.

Cartier-Bresson. *The Decisive Moment*. Steidl, 2015.

Castells, Manuel. *The Rise of the Network Society*. Blackwell, 2000.

Catsoulis, Jeannette. "A Bronx Tale, With Bait." *The New York Times*, 19 Mar. 2010, nytimes.com/2010/03/19/movies/19cityisland.html. Accessed 23 Mar. 2020.

Caz, Grandmaster. "Casanova Fly." *Born in The Bronx: A Visual Record of the Early Days of Hip-Hop*, edited by Johan Kugelberg, Rizzoli, 2007, pp. 198-200.

Chametzky, Jules, et al. "Wandering and Return: Literature since 1973." *Jewish American Literature: A Norton Anthology*, edited by Jules Chametzky et al., Norton, 2001, pp. 979-86.

Chang, Jeff. *Can't Stop, Won't Stop: A History of the Hip-Hop Generation*. St. Martin's Press, 2005.

Charry, Eric S., editor. *Hip-Hop Africa: New African Music in a Globalizing World*. Indiana UP, 2012.

Citron, Michelle, et al. "The Audience Strikes Back." *Jump Cut: A Review of Contemporary Media*, vol. 22, May 1980, pp. 37-39. *EBSCOhost*, search.ebscohost.com/login.aspx?direct=true&db=mzh&AN=2009130072&site=ehost-live. Accessed 23 Mar. 2020.

City Island. Directed by Raymond De Felitta, performances by Andy Garcia, Julianna Margulies, and Steven Strait, Anchor Bay Films, 2009.

Condry, Ian. *Hip-Hop Japan: Rap and the Paths of Cultural Globalization*. Duke UP, 2006.

Conway, Jim. *Men in Midlife Crisis*. David C. Cook, 1997.

Conzo, Joe. "A Lost Time." *Born in The Bronx: A Visual Record of the Early Days of Hip-Hop*, edited by Johan Kugelberg, Rizzoli, 2007, p. 193.

Cook, Harry T. *The Borough of the Bronx 1639-1913: Its Marvelous Development and Historical Surroundings*. Self-Published, 1913. *Internet Archive*, archive.org/details/boroughofbronx1600cook_0/page/n6/mode/2up. Accessed 25 Mar. 2020.

Cooper, Martha. *Hip-Hop Files: Photographs 1979-1984*. From Here to Fame Publishing, 2004.

—, and Henry Chalfant. *Subway Art*. Thames and Hudson, 1984.

Corman, Avery. *Kramer vs. Kramer*. Grafton, 1992.

—. *My Old Neighborhood Remembered: A Memoir*. Barricade Books, 2014.

—. *The Old Neighborhood*. Bantam, 1981.

—. *The Old Neighborhood*. Double Day, 1985.

—. *The Old Neighborhood*. Linden P, 1980.

Corry, John. "Paul Newman Shoots *Fort Apache* in The Bronx." *The New York Times*, 13 Mar. 1980, p. C17.

Crenshaw, Kimberlé, et al., editors. *Critical Race Theory: The Key Writings that Formed the Movement*. New P, 1995.

Cruz-Logo, Victor. "Gonzo Historiography." *Hispanic*, Febr. 2008, pp. 70-75.

Cullen, Jim. *The American Dream: A Short History of an Idea that Shaped a Nation*. Oxford UP, 2003.

Cunningham-Sabot, Emmanuèle, et al. "Theoretical Approaches of 'Shrinking Cities.'" *Shrinking Cities: International Perspectives and Policy Implications*, edited by Karina Pallagst et al. Routledge, 2014, pp. 14-31.

Dallas. CBS, 1978-91.

De Certeau, Michel. *The Practice of Everyday Life*. U of California P, 1984.

DeLillo, Don. *Underworld*. Picador, 1998.

Delgado, Richard, and Jean Stefancic. *Critical Race Theory: An Introduction*. 3rd ed., NYUP, 2017.

Diamond, George. "I Remember Tremont: 1911-1918." *The Bronx in the Innocent Years, 1890-1925*, edited by Lloyd Ultan and Gary Hermalyn. Harper and Row, 1985, pp. 46-54.

Die Fantastischen Vier. "Die Fantastischen Vier – Die Da?! (Original HQ)." *YouTube*, uploaded by Die Fantastischen Vier, 17 Feb. 2014, youtu.be/VU-osAGDM8Sg.

Dirty Harry. Directed by Don Siegel, performances by Clint Eastwood, Harry Guardino, and Reni Satoni, Warner Bros., 1971.

DJ Grandwizzard Theodore. "Subway Theme." *Wild Style: 25th Anniversary Edition*, Mr. Bongo, 2007.

Doctorow, E. L. *World's Fair*. Random House, 2003.

Döring, Jörg, and Tristan Thielmann, editors. *Spatial Turn: Das Raumparadigma in den Kultur- und Sozialwissenschaften*. Transcript, 2008.

Double Trouble. "Stoop Rap." *Wild Style: 25th Anniversary Edition*, Mr. Bongo, 2007.

Doubt. Directed by John Patrick Shanley, performances by Meryl Streep, Philip Seymour Hoffman, and Amy Adams, Walt Disney Studios, 2008.

Doucet, Brian, editor. *Why Detroit Matters: Decline, Renewal, and Hope in a Divided City*. Policy Press, 2017.

Dreiser, Theodore. *Sister Carrie*. 1900. Penguin, 1994.

—. "The Loneliness of the City." *Tom Watson's Magazine*, vol. 2, no. 4, 1905, pp. 474-75. babel.hathitrust.org/cgi/pt?id=nc01.ark:/13960/t8v98hj9m&view=1up&seq=3. Accessed 23 Mar. 2020.

Eisner, Will. *A Contract with God Trilogy: Life on Dropsie Avenue*. Norton, 2005.

Elsaesser, Thomas. "Tales of Sound and Fury." *Film Genre Reader IV*, edited by Barry Keith Grant, U of Texas P, 2012, pp. 433-62.

Erbacher, Eric C., and Sina A. Nitzsche. "Performing the Double Rupture: Kraftklub, Popular Music and Post-Socialist Urban Identity in Chemnitz, Germany." *International Journal of Cultural Studies*, vol. 20, no. 4, 2017, pp. 437-55, doi:10.1177/1367877916638730.

Esposito, Dawn. "Gloria, Maerose, Irene, and Me: Mafia Women and Abject Spectatorship." *MELUS*, vol. 28, no. 3, 2003, pp. 91-109, doi:10.2307/3595262.

Esquire, Buddy. "Buddy Esquire." *Born in The Bronx: A Visual Record of the Early Days of Hip-Hop*, edited by Johan Kugelberg, Rizzoli, 2007, p. 203.

Estrada, Willie 'M.B.' *The Dancing Gangsters of the South Bronx: Rise of the Latin Hustle*. Latin Empire, 2016.

Ewoodzie Jr., Joseph C. *Break Beats in The Bronx: Rediscovering Hip-Hop's Early Years*. U of North California P, 2017.

Fagan, Kevin. "Gerald Rosen Dies: Novelist, English Professor." *San Francisco Chronicle*, 25 Aug. 2010, sfgate.com/bayarea/article/Gerald-Rosen-dies-novelist-English-professor-3177227.php. Accessed 23 Mar. 2020.

Fat Joe. *Jealous One's Envy*, Relativity, 1995.

Fernandez, Manny. "In the Bronx, Blight Gave Way to Renewal." *The New York Times*, 5 Oct. 2007, nytimes.com/2007/10/05/nyregion/05charlotte.html. Accessed 23 Mar. 2020.

Fettes Brot. "Nordisch by Nature (Official)." *YouTube*, uploaded by Fettes Brot, 23 Jan. 2013, youtu.be/KfWyo2mqXnw.

Finding Forrester. Directed by Gus van Sant, performances by Sean Connery, Rob Brown, and Anna Paquin, Columbia Pictures, 2000.

Fisher, Ian. "Pulling Out of Fort Apache, The Bronx; New 41st Precinct Station House Leaves Behind Symbol of Community's Past Troubles." *The New York Times*, 23 June 1993, nytimes.com/1993/06/23/nyregion/pulling-fort-apache-bronx-new-41st-precinct-station-house-leaves-behind-symbol.html. Accessed 23 Mar. 2020.

Five Corners. Directed by Tony Bill, performances by Jodie Forster, Tim Robbins, and John Torturro, Sunfilm, 1987.

Flash, Grandmaster & The Furious Five. "Grandmaster Flash & The Furious Five – The Message (Official Video)." *YouTube*, uploaded by Sugarhill Records, youtu.be/PobrSpMwKk4.

—. *The Message*, Sugar Hill Records, 1982.

Flint, Peter B. "Kate Simon, Acclaimed Memoirist and Travel Writer, is Dead at 77." *The New York Times*, 5 Febr. 1990, nytimes.com/1990/02/05/obituaries/kate-simon-acclaimed-memoirist-and-travel-writer-is-dead-at-77.html. Accessed 23 Mar. 2020.

Fluck, Winfried. "Funktionsgeschichte und ästhetische Erfahrung." *Funktionen von Literatur: Theoretische Grundlagen und Modellinterpretationen*, edited by Marion Gymnich and Ansgar Nünning, WVT, 2005, pp. 29-53.

—. "Realism in Art and Literature." *American Cultural and Intellectual History*, vol. 1, edited by Mary Kupiec and Peter W. Williams, Scribner's, 2001, pp. 565-72.

Forman, Murray. *The 'Hood Comes First: Race, Space and Place in Rap and Hip-Hop*. Wesleyan UP, 2002.

—, and Mark Anthony Neal, editors. *That's the Joint!: The Hip-Hop Studies Reader*. Routledge, 2004.

Formel Eins. ARD, 1983-1990.

Fort Apache. Directed by John Ford, performances by John Wayne, Henry Fonda, and Shirley Temple, RKO, 1948.

Fort Apache: The Bronx. Directed by Daniel Petrie, performances by Paul Newman, Edward Asner, and Rachel Ticotin, Twentieth Century Fox, 1981.

"Fort Apache, The Bronx." *The Numbers*, the-numbers.com/movie/Fort-Apache-The-Bronx#tab=summary. Accessed 23 Mar. 2020.

"Fort Apache: The Bronx." *Variety Movie Reviews*, no. 1, Jan. 1981, p. 32. *EBSCO-host*, search.ebscohost.com/login.aspx?direct=true&db=f3h&AN=2538051 7&site=ehost-live. Accessed 20 Mar. 2020.

Foucault, Michel. "Of Other Spaces." *Diacritics*, vol. 16, no. 1, 1986, pp. 22-27. *JSTOR*, jstor.org/stable/464648. Accessed 21 Mar. 2020.

Frank, Robert. *The Americans*. 1958. Cornerhouse Publications, 1993.

Franklin, Benjamin. *Autobiography*. 1791. Dent, 1960.

Fricke, Jim, and Charlie Ahearn. *Yes Yes Y'all: The Experience Music Project Oral History of Hip-Hop's First Decade*. Da Capo P, 2002.

Gagnier, Regenia. "Feminist Autobiography in the 1980s." *Feminist Studies*, vol. 17, no. 1, 1991, pp. 135-48. *JSTOR*, jstor.org/stable/3178175. Accessed 21 Mar. 2020.

García Conde, Ed. "Over 50% of Bronx Neighborhoods Experiencing High or Extreme Poverty." *Welcome2TheBronx*, welcome2the-bronx.com/2017/06/08/over-50-of-bronx-neighborhoods-experiencing-h igh-or-extreme-poverty. Accessed 23 Mar. 2020.

Gloria. Directed by John Cassavetes, performances by Gena Rowlands, Julie Carmen, and John Adames, Columbia Pictures, 1980.

—. Directed by Sidney Lumet, performances by Sharon Stone, Jean-Luke Figueroa, and Jeremy Northam, Columbia Pictures, 1999.

Gold, Michael. *Jews Without Money*. 1930. Caroll & Graf, 1984.

Gonzales, Evelyn. *The Bronx*. Columbia UP, 2004.

Goodson, Martia. "South Bronx Narratives." *Devastation/Resurrection: The South Bronx*, edited by Robert Jensen, Bronx Museum of the Arts, 1979, pp. 55-68.

Gosa, Travis L. "The Fifth Element: Knowledge." *The Cambridge Companion to Hip-Hop*, edited by Justin A. Williams, Cambridge UP, 2015, pp. 56-70.

Gould, Heywood. *Die Bronx: Der Roman zum Film*. Translated by Bodo Baumann, Gustav Lübbe, 1988.

Grabel, Richard. "The South Bronx is Up." *Village Voice*, 28 Nov. 1983, p. 86.

Gracer, Tim. *Bomben in der Bronx*. Imma-Verlag, ca. 1955.

Graff, Kristina. *Street Literature: Black Popular Fiction in the Era of US Mass Incarceration*. Winter, 2015.

Haley, Alex. *The Autobiography of Malcolm X*. Grove P, 1965.

Hall, Stuart. "Encoding, Decoding." *Cultural Studies: An Anthology*, edited by Michael Ryan. Blackwell, 2008, pp. 907-16.

—. *Representation: Cultural Representations and Signifying Practices*. Sage, 1997.

Hand, Kenneth M. *"You Can't Take The Bronx Out Of My Dad": The Life and Times of a Young Boy Growing Up in the Bronx of the 1970's....* Hand Written Productions, 2011.

Hansberry, Lorraine. *A Raisin in the Sun.* 1959. Vintage, 2011.

Hanson, Sandra L. and John K. White, editors. *The American Dream in the Twenty-First Century.* Temple UP, 2011.

Hatt, Harold. "The Border as Barrier: Cinematic Images of Hope in Texas and the Southwest: A Theological Reflection of the Movement from Marginalization to Participation in The Border, and *Fort Apache, The Bronx.*" *Journal of American Culture,* vol. 14, no. 2, 1991, pp. 107-11. *EBSCOhost,* doi:10.1111/j.1542-734x.1991.00107.x. Accessed 21 Mar. 2020.

Harvey, David. "Globalization and the 'Spatial Fix.'" *Geographische Revue: Zeitschrift für Literatur und Diskussion,* vol. 3, no. 2, 2001, pp. 23-30.

—. *The Condition of Postmodernity: An Enquiry into the Origins of Cultural Change.* Blackwell, 2015.

Heap, Chad. *Slumming: Sexual and Racial Encounters in American Nightlife, 1885-1940.* U of Chicago P, 2009.

Hip-Hop Evolution. Netflix, 2016-.

Hoban, Phoebe. *Basquiat: A Quick Killing in Art.* Viking Press, 1998.

Hoberman, J., and Jeffrey Shandler. *Entertaining America: Jews, Movies, and Broadcasting.* Princeton UP, 2003.

Hollander, John B. *Sunburnt Cities: The Great Recession, Depopulation, and Urban Planning in the American Sunbelt.* Routledge, 2011.

Hunter, Evan. *Blackboard Jungle.* 1954. New English Library, 1977.

Jaehne, Karen. "Charles Ahearn: *Wild Style.*" *Film Quarterly,* vol. 37, no. 4, 1984, pp. 2-5. *JSTOR,* jstor.org/stable/3697022. Accessed 21 Mar. 2020.

Jakob, Doreen. "The Eventification of Place: Urban Development and Experience Consumption in Berlin and New York City." *European Urban & Regional Studies,* vol. 20, no. 4, 2013, pp. 447-59. *EBSCOhost,* doi:10.1177/0969776412459860. Accessed 21 Mar. 2020.

James, Henry. *Portrait of a Lady.* 1881. Marshall Cavendish, 1987.

Jameson, Fredric. *Postmodernism, or, the Cultural Logic of Late Capitalism.* 2nd ed., Verso, 1993.

Jaws. Directed by Steven Spielberg, performances by Roy Schneider, Richard Dreyfuss, and Lorraine Gary, Universal, 1976.

Jenkins, Henry. *Convergence Culture: Where Old and New Media Collide.* New York UP, 2006.

Jenkins, Stephen. *The Story of The Bronx from the Purchase Made by the Dutch from the Indians in 1639 to the Present Day*. G. P. Putnam's Sons, 1912. *Internet Archive*, archive.org/details/storyofbronxfrom1912jenk/page/n10/mode/2u p. Accessed 25 Mar. 2020.

Jensen, Robert, editor. *Devastation/Resurrection: The South Bronx*. Bronx Museum of the Arts, 1979.

"John Cassavetes." *Columbia Electronic Encyclopedia*, 6th ed., Feb. 2020, p. 1. *EB-SCOhost*, search.ebscohost.com/login.aspx?direct=true&db=aph&AN=134 507591&site=ehost-live. Accessed 21 Mar. 2020.

Jones, Allen. *The Rat that Got Away: A Bronx Memoir*. Fordham UP, 2009.

Jonnes, Jill. *South Bronx Rising: The Rise, Fall, and Resurrection of an American City*. 2nd ed., Fordham UP, 2007.

Joyce, James. "Portrait of the Artist as a Young Man." *The Essential James Joyce*, edited by Harry Levin, Panther, 1977, pp. 177-365.

King Jr., Martin Luther. "Martin Luther King | 'I Have A Dream' Speech." *YouTube*, uploaded by LogistiKHD, 28 Aug. 2013, youtu.be/I47Y6VHc3Ms.

King, Neal. *Heroes in Hard Times: Cop Action Movies in the US*. Temple UP, 1999.

Kinkle, Jeff. "Neoliberalism as Horror: *Wolfen* and the Political Unconscious of Real Estate." *Cartographies of the Absolute*, 14 May 2010, cartographiesoftheabsolute.wordpress.com/2010/05/14/neoliberalism-as-horror-wolfen-and-the-political-unconscious-of-real-estate. Accessed 23 Mar. 2020.

Klepper, Martin. "'From Rags to Riches' and the Self-Made Man." *Approaches to American Cultural Studies*, edited by Martin Klepper, Antje Dallmann, and Eva Boesenberg, Routledge, 2016, pp. 123-31.

Klimmage, Michael C. "The Politics of the American Dream, 1980-2008." *The American Dream in the Twenty-First Century*, edited by Sandra L. Hanson and John K. White, Temple UP, 2011, pp. 27-39.

Klinkowitz, Jerome. *Structuring the Void: The Struggle for Subject in Contemporary American Fiction*. Duke UP, 1992.

Knights of the South Bronx. Directed by Allen Hughes, performances by Ted Danson, Malcolm David Kelley, and Yves Michel-Beneche, Allumination, 2005. *YouTube*, uploaded by Antra DeHub, 23 May 2013, https://youtu.be/PBCLUTCRM9w.

Kramer vs. Kramer. Directed by Robert Benton, performances by Dustin Hoffman, Meryl Streep, and Jane Alexander, Columbia Pictures, 1979.

Kugelberg, Johan, editor. *Born in The Bronx: A Visual Record of the Early Days of Hip-Hop*. Rizzoli, 2007.

—. Introduction. *Born in The Bronx: A Visual Record of the Early Days of Hip-Hop*, edited by Johan Kugelberg, Rizzoli, 2007, p. 31.

Kuhre, Bruce. "The American Dream in Crisis." *Constructing the Eighties: Versions of a Decade*, edited by Walter Grünzweig, Roberta Maierhofer, and Adi Wimmer, Gunter Narr, 1992, pp. 33-49.

Lacan, Jaques. "The Mirror Stage as Formative of the *I* Function as Revealed in Psychoanalytic Experience." *Jaques Lacan – Ècrits: The First Complete Edition in English*, transl. by Bruce Fink, Norton, 2006, pp. 93-101.

Lange, Dorothea. *Migrant Mother*. 1936. *Library of Congress*, https://guides.loc.gov/migrant-mother/images.

Lawrence, Elizabeth A. "Werewolves in Psyche and Cinema: Man-Beast Transformation and Paradox." *Journal of American Culture*, vol. 19, no. 3, 1996, pp. 103-12. *EBSCOhost*, search.ebscohost.com/login.aspx?direct=true&db=mzh&AN=1997060860&site=ehost-live. Accessed 21 Mar. 2020.

Lawrence, Wayne. *Orchard Beach: The Bronx Rivera*. Prestel, 2013.

Leary, John Patrick. "Detroitism." *Guernica: A Magazine of Art and Politics*, 15 Jan. 2011, guernicamag.com/leary_1_15_11. Accessed 21 Mar. 2020.

LeBlanc, Adrian N. *Random Family: Love, Drugs, Trouble, and Coming of Age in the Bronx*. Scribner, 2014.

Lefebvre, Henri. *The Production of Space*. Translated by Donald Nicholson-Smith. 1974. Blackwell, 1991.

Lehan, Richard D. *The City in Literature: An Intellectual and Cultural History*. U of California P, 1998.

Lehmann-Haupt, Christopher. "Books of *The Times*; Return to the Roots Restoring a Continuity." *The New York Times*, 26 Sept. 1980, p. C30.

Lodge, David. "Roman, Theaterstück, Drehbuch: Drei Arten, eine Geschichte zu erzählen." *Intermedialität: Theorie und Praxis eines interdisziplinären Forschungsgebiets*, edited by Jörg Helbig and Erich Schmidt, 1998, pp. 68-80.

Longhurst, Brian, et al. *Introducing Cultural Studies*. 3rd ed., Routledge, 2016.

Lopez, Jennifer. "Jennifer Lopez – Jenny from the Block (Video)." *YouTube*, uploaded by Jennifer Lopez, 3 Oct. 2009, youtu.be/dly6p4Fu5TE.

—. *This Is Me ... Then*, Sony, 2002.

Lord Tariq and Peter Gunz. "Lord Tariq & Peter Gunz – Déjà Vu (Uptown Baby) [Official Video]." *YouTube*, uploaded by LrdTariqPeterGnzVEVO, 21 June 2013, youtu.be/mVnoNpncfho.

—. *Make It Reign*, Sony, 1998.

Love, Damien. "Rap Moves On: The Making of 'The Message' by Grand-master Flash and the Furious Five (An Oral History)." *Damienlove*, damienlove.com/writing/rap-moves-on-the-making-of-the-message-by-grandmaster-flash-and-the-furious-five-an-oral-history. Accessed 23 Mar. 2020.

LSD. *Watch Out for the Third Rail*, Rhythm Attack Productions, 1991.

M*A*S*H – Martinis and Medicine: Complete Collection, created by Larry Gelbart, Gene Reynolds, and Burt Metcalfe, Twentieth Century Fox, 2006.

Macek, Steve. *Urban Nightmares: The Media, the Right, and the Moral Panic over the City*. U of Minnesota P, 2006.

Mackenthun, Gesa. "Haunted Real Estate: The Occlusion of Colonial Dispossession and Signatures of Cultural Survival in US Horror Fiction." *Amerikastudien/American Studies*, vol. 43, no. 1, 1998, pp. 93-108. JSTOR, jstor.org/stable/41157353. Accessed 21 Mar. 2020.

Mahler, Jonathan. *Ladies and Gentlemen, The Bronx is Burning: 1977, Baseball, Politics, and the Battle for the Soul of a City*. Farrar, Straus and Giroux, 2005.

—, creator. *The Bronx is Burning*. Directed by Jeremiah Chechick, ESPN, 2007.

"Manhatta." Directed by Charles Sheeler and Paul Strand. 1921. *Picturing a Metropolis: New York City Unveiled*, Image Entertainment, 2005.

Manhattan. Directed by Woody Allen, performances by Woody Allen, Diane Keaton, and Mariel Hemingway, United Artists, 1979.

Manon, Michelle. *Finding My Way: A Memoir of Abuse, Neglect, Failure, Resilience, Inner Strength and Powering Through Life in The Bronx*. Independently published, 2019.

Margulies, Ivone. "John Cassavetes: Amateur Director." *The New American Cinema*, edited by John Lewis, Duke UP, 1998, pp. 275-306.

Mariani, Robert, and John Mariani. *Almost Golden*. Infinity, 2006.

Matuschewski, Anke. "Revitalisierung Innerstädtischer Slums und Ghettos in New York City?: Das Beispiel Harlem und South Bronx." *Geographische Rundschau*, vol. 57, no. 1, 2005, pp. 14-21.

Marty. Directed by Delbert Mann, performances by Ernest Borgnine, Betsy Blair, and Esther Minciotti, United Artists, 1955.

Massey, Doreen. *For Space*. Sage, 2005.

McBrown, Joe [Joachim von Koblinski]. *Der Alte von Bronx*. Paul-Feldmann-Verlag, ca. 1955.

—. *In der Bronx wohnen keine Engel*. Paul-Feldmann-Verlag, ca. 1955.

McCormick, Ruth. "Wolfen." *Cinéaste*, vol. 11, no. 4, June 1982, p. 60. *EBSCO-host*, search.ebscohost.com/login.aspx?direct=true&db=f3h&AN=3010690 3&site=ehost-live. Accessed 23 Mar. 2020.

Meehan, Paul. *Horror Noir: Where Cinema's Dark Sisters Meet*. McFarland, 2011.

Merleau-Ponty, Maurice. *Phenomenology of Perception*. Routledge, 2012.

Milligan, Peter, and James Romberger. *Bronx Kill*. DC Comics, 2009.

Miner, Robert. "Return to The Bronx, *The Old Neighborhood*." *The New York Times Book Review*, 5 Oct. 1980, p. 15.

Mitchell, Don. *Cultural Geography: A Critical Introduction*. Blackwell, 2000.

Mitchell, Edward. "Apes and Essences: Some Sources of Significance in the American Gangster Film." *Film Genre Reader IV*, edited by Barry Keith Grant, U of Texas P, 2012, pp. 255-64.

Mittell, Jason. *Television and American Culture*. Oxford UP, 2010.

Mogen, David, Sanders, Scott Patrick, and Joanne B. Karpinksi, editors. *Frontier Gothic: Terror and Wonder at the Frontier in American Literature*. Fairleigh Dickinson UP, 1993.

Monteyne, Kimberly. *Hip-Hop on Film: Performance, Culture, Urban Space and Genre Transformation in the 1980s*. U of Mississippi P, 2013.

Moore, Andrew. *Detroit Disassembled*. Damiani, 2010.

Mott Music. Directed by Jarred Alterman, performances by Carl Demmler and Mark Wienert, Fly Away Films, 2005.

Naison, Mark. "From Eviction Resistance to Rent Control: Tenant Activism in the Great Depression." *The Tenant Movement in New York City, 1904-1984*, edited by Ronald Lawson and Mark Naison, 13 Feb. 2013, libcom.org/history/chapter-3-eviction-resistance-rent-control-tenant-activism-great-depression. Accessed 20 Mar. 2020.

—. "Rap: Morrisania Roots of Hip-Hop Culture." *Hip-Hop Area*, hiphoparea.com/rap/morrisania-roots-of-hip-hop-culture.html. Accessed 23 Mar. 2020.

—. *White Boy: A Memoir*. Temple UP, 2002.

—, and Bob Gumbs. *Before the Fires: An Oral History of African American Life in The Bronx from the 1930s to the 1960s*. Fordham UP, 2016.

—, and Melissa Castillo-Garsow. *Pure Bronx*. Augustus Publishing, 2013.

Neale, Steve, and Christine Gledhill. "Melodrama." *The Cinema Book*, edited by Pam Cook and Mieke Bernink, BFI, 1999, 157-72.

Newell, Jimmy. *A Bronx Boy's Tale*. CreateSpace Independent Publishing, 2013.

Nichols, Bill. *Representing Reality: Issues and Concepts in Documentary*. Indiana UP, 1991.

Nieves, Marysol. Foreword. *Urban Mythologies: The Bronx Represented Since the 1960s*, edited by John Alan Farmer, Bronx Museum of the Arts, 1999, pp. 6-8.

Nitzsche, Sina A. "Hip-Hop Culture as a Medial Contact Space: Local Encounters and Global Appropriations of *Wild Style* (1983)." *Contact Spaces of American Culture: Globalizing Local Phenomena*, edited by Klaus Rieser, Silvia Schultermandl, and Petra Eckhart, Lit, 2012, pp. 173-88.

—. "'Slavery's Consequences Still Affect Us': Sister Souljah's *No Disrespect*, Black Women's Literary Traditions and Contemporary Hip-Hop Activism." *Hip-Hop Activism*, special issue of *Journal of World Popular Music*, edited by Adam Haupt and Samy Alim, vol. 5, no. 1, 2018, pp. 108-21, doi:10.1558/jwpm.36676. Accessed 20 Mar. 2020.

—. "'The Ghetto is Coming Out': Charles Rice-Gonzáles' *Chulito* and the Emergence of Queer Puerto Rican Fiction in The Bronx." *Space Oddities: Difference and Identity in the American City*, edited by Stefan L. Brandt and Michael Fuchs, Lit, 2018, pp. 127-45.

—. "The Rural Jostling the Urban: Photographing Spuyten Duyvil in Berenice Abbott's *Changing New York*." *Rural America*, edited by Antje Kley and Heike Paul, Winter, 2015, pp. 425-45.

—, and Walter Grünzweig, editors. *Hip-Hop in Europe: Cultural Identities and Transnational Flows*. Lit, 2013.

Nosferatu: Eine Symphonie des Grauens. Directed by Friedrich Wilhelm Murnau, performances by Max Schreck, Gustav von Wangenheim, and Greta Schröder-Wegener, Film Arts Guild, 1922.

O'Brien, Patrick. "Irish Americans." *The Social History of Crime and Punishment in America: An Encyclopedia*, edited by Wilbur R. Miller, Sage, 2012, pp. 861-64.

Oeming, Michael Avon, and Ivan Brandon. *The Cross Bronx*. Image, 2007.

Oswalt, Philipp, editor. *Shrinking Cities: International Research*. Hantje Canz, 2005.

Pabon, Jorge 'Popmaster Fabel.' "A Picture is Worth a Thousand Moves." *Born in The Bronx: A Visual Record of the Early Days of Hip-Hop*, edited by Johan Kugelberg, Rizzoli, 2007, pp. 204-05.

Pallagst, Karina, Wiechmann, Thorsten, and Cristina Martinez-Fernandez, editors. *Shrinking Cities: International Perspectives and Policy Implications*. Routledge, 2014.

Palmer, Robert. "The Pop Life: Rap and Hip-Hop Music in *Wild Style*." *The New York Times*, 22 Feb. 1984, p. C18.

Pennycook, Alastair. "Linguistic Landscapes and the Transgressive Semiotics of Graffiti." *Linguistic Landscape: Expanding the Scenery*, edited by Elana Shohamy and Durk Gorter, Routledge, 2009, pp. 302-13.

Perez, Richie. "Committee Against *Fort Apache: The Bronx* Mobilizes Against Multinational Media." *Media Justice History Project*, 1985, mediajusticehistoryproject.org/archives/82. Accessed 23 Mar. 2020.

Poe, Edgar Allan. "The Fall of the House of Usher." *Tales of Mystery and Imagination*. Woodsworth, 2000, pp. 148-63.

Powell, Anna, and Andrew Smith. "Introduction: Gothic Pedagogies." *Teaching the Gothic*, edited by Anna Powell and Andrew Smith, Palgrave Macmillan, 2006, pp. 1-9.

Pratt, Mary Louise. "Arts of the Contact Zone." *Conversations in Context: Identity, Knowledge and College Writing*, edited by Kathryn R. Fitzgerald et al., Harcourt Brace, 1998, pp. 74-87.

Price, Richard. *The Wanderers*. 1974. Mariner, 1999.

Queen. "Queen – Bohemian Rhapsody (Official Video Remastered)." *YouTube*, uploaded by Queen Official, 1 Aug. 2008, youtu.be/fJ9rUzIMcZQ.

"Quick Facts: Bronx County (Bronx Borough), New York." *US Census*, census.gov/quickfacts/bronxcountybronxboroughnewyork. Accessed 23 Mar. 2020.

"Quick Facts: New York County (Manhattan Borough), New York." *US Census*, census.gov/quickfacts/fact/table/newyorkcountymanhattanborough-newyork/BZA115217. Accessed 23 Mar. 2020.

Rafferty, Terrence. "The Paradoxes of Home: Three Films by Walter Hill." *Film Quarterly*, vol. 36, no. 1, 1982, pp. 20-27. *JSTOR*, jstor.org/stable/3697181. Accessed 21 Mar. 2020.

Rafter, Nicole. *Shots in the Mirror: Crime Films and Society*. 2nd ed., Oxford UP, 2006.

Raging Bull. Directed by Martin Scorsese, performances by Robert De Niro, Cathy Moriarty, and Joe Pesci, United Artists, 1980.

Railton, Diane, and Paul Watson. *Music Video and the Politics of Representation*. Edinburgh UP, 2011.

Rank, Robert, Hirschl, Thomas A., and Kirk A. Foster. *Chasing the American Dream: Understanding What Shapes our Fortunes*. Oxford UP, 2014.

Ratner, Rochelle. "*Growing Up Bronx* (Book)." *Library Journal*, vol. 110, no. 1, 1985, p. 89. *EBSCOhost*, search.ebscohost.com/login.aspx?direct=true&db=eue&AN=7580670&site=ehost-live. Accessed 20 Mar. 2020.

Reaves, Gerri. *Mapping the Private Geography: Autobiography, Identity, and America*. McFarland, 2001.

Riis, Jacob A. *How the Other Half Lives: Studies Among the Tenements of New York*. 1890. Penguin, 1997.

Rice-González, Charles. *Chulito*. Magnus Press, 2011.

—, and Charlie Vásquez, editors. *From Macho to Mariposa: New Gay Latino Fiction*. Tincture, 2011.

Rishoi, Christy. *From Girl to Woman: American Women's Coming-of-Age Narratives*. SUNY Press, 2003.

Rick, Detlef. "Wie Hip-Hop nach Deutschland kam: Der Durchbruch nach dem Hype." *Spiegel Online*, 8 Aug. 2008, spiegel.de/einestages/wie-hiphop-nach-deutschland-kam-a-949537.html. Accessed 20 Mar. 2020.

Robertson, Roland. *Globalization: Social Theory and Global Culture*. Sage, 1996.

Rodriguez Jr., Abraham. *South by South Bronx*. Akashic, 2008.

—. *Spidertown: A Novel*. Hyperion, 1994.

—. *The Boy Without a Flag: Tales of the South Bronx*. Milkweed, 1999.

—. *The Buddha Book: A Novel*. Picador, 2001.

Roots. ABC, 1977.

Rose, Joel. "On Location: *Fort Apache*, A War Zone in the Bronx." *NPR*, 24 Aug. 2011, npr.org/2011/08/24/139916927/on-location-fort-apache-a-war-zone-in-the-bronx. Accessed 23 Mar. 2020.

Rose, Tricia. *Black Noise: Rap Music and Black Culture in Contemporary America*. Wesleyan UP, 1994.

Rosemary's Baby. Directed by Roman Polanski, performances by John Cassavetes, Mia Farrow, and Ruth Gordon, Paramount, 1968.

Rosen, Gerald. *Blues for a Dying Nation*. Dial P, 1972.

—. *Growing Up Bronx*. North Atlantic Books, 1984.

—. *The Carmen Miranda Memorial Flagpole: A Novel*. Avon, 1979.

Roth, Paul A. "The Virtue of Violence: Dimensions of Development in Walter Hill's *The Warriors*." *Journal of Popular Culture*, vol. 24, no. 3, 1990, pp. 131-45. *EBSCOhost*, doi:10.1111/j.0022-3840.1990.2403-131.x. Accessed 20 March 2020.

Rozan, S. J., editor. *Bronx Noir*. Akashic, 2007.

—. "Introduction: Welcome to da Bronx." *Bronx Noir*, edited by S. J. Rozan, Akashic, 2007, pp. 13-15.

Rudin, Seymour. "The Urban Gothic: From Transylvania to the South Bronx." *Extrapolation*, vol. 25, no. 2, 1984, pp. 115-26.

Rumble in The Bronx. Directed by Stanley Tong, performances by Jackie Chan, Françoise Yip, and Anita Mui, New Line Cinema, 1996.

Samuel, Lawrence R. *The American Dream: A Cultural History*. Syracuse UP, 2012.

Sassen, Saskia. *The Global City: New York, London, Tokyo*. Princeton UP, 1992.

Schatz, Thomas. *Hollywood Genres: Formulas, Filmmaking, and the Studio System*. Temple University, 1981.

Seignious, Keisha. *A Boogie Down Story*. Augustus Publishing, 2008.

—. *The Blue Circle*. Augustus Publishing, 2006.

Sex and the City. HBO, 1998-2004.

Shabazz, Jamel. *A Time Before Crack*. Powerhouse Books, 2005.

—. *Back in the Days*. Powerhouse Books, 2001.

Shadoian, Jack. *Dreams and Dead Ends: The American Gangster Film*. Oxford UP, 2003.

Shepard, Richard F. "Newman Rebuts *Apache* Bias Charge." *The New York Times*, 8 Apr. 1980, p. C5.

Shiel, Mark, and Tony Fitzmaurice, editors. *Cinema and the City: Film and Urban Societies in a Global Context*. Blackwell, 2001.

—, editors. *Screening the City*. Verso, 2003.

Shuker, Roy. *Understanding Popular Music*. 2nd ed. Routledge, 2001.

Simon, Kate. *A Wider World: Portraits in an Adolescence*. Harper and Row, 1986.

—. *Bronx Primitive: Portraits in a Childhood*. Viking P, 1982.

—. *Bronx Primitive: Portraits in a Childhood*. 1982. Penguin, 1997.

Simpson, Katherine. "Media Images of the Urban Landscape: The South Bronx in Film." *Centro Journal*, vol. 14, no. 2, 2002, p. 98-113. *EBSCOhost*, search.ebscohost.com/login.aspx?direct=true&db=aph&AN=8713273&site=ehost-live. Accessed 20 March 2020.

Sinclair, Upton. *The Jungle*. 1906. Penguin 1974.

Singer, Isaac Bashevis. *Enemies, A Love Story*. Farrar, Straus and Giroux, 1972.

Slotkin, Richard. *Gunfighter Nation: The Myth of the Frontier in Twentieth-Century America*. Harper Perennial, 1993.

Smalls, F. Romall. "The Bronx Is Named an 'All-America' City." *The New York Times*, 20 July 1997, nytimes.com/1997/07/20/nyregion/the-bronx-is-named-an-all-america-city.html. Accessed 23 Mar. 2020.

Smit, Alexia. "On the 'Scalpel's Edge': Gory Excess, Melodrama and Irony in *Nip/Tuck*." *Melodrama in Contemporary Film and Television*, edited by Michael Stewart, Palgrave, 2014, pp. 81-95.

Smith, Dinitia. "Following Up on *Kramer vs. Kramer*." *The New York Times*, 18 Oct. 2004, nytimes.com/2004/10/18/books/following-up-on-kramer-vs-kramer.html. Accessed 23 Mar. 2020.

Smith, Neil. *The New Urban Frontier: Gentrification and the Revanchist City*. Routledge, 1996.

Smith, Sidonie, and Julia Watson. "Introduction: Situating Subjectivity in Women's Autobiographical Practices." *Women, Autobiography, Theory: A Reader*, edited by Sidonie Smith and Julia Watson, U of Wisconsin P, 1998, pp. 3-52.

Soja, Edward W. *Postmetropolis: Critical Studies of Cities and Regions*. Blackwell, 2000.

Sontag, Susan. *On Photography*. Penguin Classics, 2002.

Souljah, Sister. *No Disrespect*. Vintage, 1996.

South Bronx Heroes. Directed by William Szarka, performances by Brendan Ward, Melissa Esposito, and Mario Van Peebles, Continental Film, 1985.

Spivak, Gayatri Chakravorty. "Can the Subaltern Speak?" *Marxism and the Interpretation of Culture*, edited by Lawrence Grossberg and Cary Nelson. U of Illinois P, 1988, pp. 271-313.

Stacy, Paul H., and Virginia Hale. "*Fort Apache: The Bronx*: Saint, Sinners, and Symbols." *Literature/Film Quarterly*, vol. 14, no. 1, 1986, pp. 53-57. JSTOR, jstor.org/stable/43797468. Accessed 21 Mar. 2020.

Stanford and Son. NBC, 1972-77.

Star Wars – The Original Trilogy. Directed by George Lucas, performances by Mark Hamill, Harrison Ford, and Carrie Fisher, Twentieth Century Fox, 1977.

Stein, Ellin. "*Wild Style*; Sick of Valley Girls? Meet the Break Boys, Rappers, and Graffiti Guerillias of Charlie Ahean's New Film." *American Film*, vol. 9, no. 2, 1983, pp. 48-50.

Strieber, Whitley. *The Wolfen*. Hodder and Stoughton, 1978.

Strinati, Dominic. *An Introduction to Studying Popular Culture*. Routledge, 2000.

Style Wars. Directed by Henry Chalfant and Tony Silver, PBS, 1983.

Sullivan, Jack. "Behind the Bestsellers: Avery Corman." *The New York Times Book Review*, 21 Dec. 1980, p. BR6.

Sunset Boulevard. Directed by Billy Wilder, performances by William Holden, Gloria Swanson, and Erich von Stroheim, Paramount, 1950.

Tack, Martha B. "*Growing Up Bronx*. By Gerald Rosen." *The New York Times*, 13 Jan. 1985, nytimes.com/1985/01/13/books/in-short-210058.html. Accessed 23 Mar. 2020.

"The 52nd Academy Awards: 1980." *Oscars*, oscars.org/oscars/ceremonies/1980. Accessed 23 Mar. 2020.

The Bonfire of the Vanities. Directed by Brian De Palma, performances by Tom Hanks, Bruce Willis, and Melanie Griffith, Warner Bros., 1990.

The Cold Crush Brothers vs. Fantastic Freaks. "Basketball Throwdown Cold Crush." *Wild Style: 25th Anniversary Edition*, Mr. Bongo, 2007.

The Cosby Show. NBC, 1984-92.

The French Connection. Directed by William Friedkin, performances by Gene Hackman, Roy Scheider, and Fernando Rey, Twentieth Century Fox, 1971.

The Gambler. Directed by Karel Reisz, performances by James Caan, Lauren Hutton, and Paul Sorvino, Paramount, 1974.

The Get Down. Netflix, 2016-17.

The Goldbergs. ABC, 2013-.

—. CBS, 1949-54.

The Jazz Singer. Directed by Alan Crosland, performances by Al Jolson, May McAvoy, and Warner Oland, Warner Bros., 1927.

The Jeffersons. CBS, 1975-85.

The Public Enemy. Directed by William A. Wellmann, performances by James Cagney, Jean Harlow, and Joan Blondell, Warner Bros., 1931.

The Rise of the Goldbergs. NBC, 1929-45.

The Sugarhill Gang. "Rapper's Delight." *Sugarhill Gang*, Sugar Hill Records, 1979.

The Texas Chain Saw Massacre. Directed by Tobe Hopper, performances by Marilyn Burns, Edwin Neal, and Allen Danziger, Bryanston Distributing, 1974.

The Wanderers. Directed by Philip Kaufmann, performances by Ken Wahl, John Friedrich, and Karen Allen, Warner Bros., 1979.

The Warriors. Directed by Walter Hill, performances by Michael Beck, James Remar, and Dorsey Wright, Paramount, 1979.

Thompson, Heather Ann. *Whose Detroit?: Politics, Labor, and Race in a Modern American City*. Cornell UP, 2015.

Tobier, Emanuel. "The Bronx in the Twentieth Century: Dynamics of Population and Economic Change." *The Centennial of the Bronx 1898-1998*, special issue of *The Bronx County Historical Society Journal*, vol. 35, no. 2, 1998, pp. 69-102.

Tudor, Andrew. "Genre." *Film Genre Reader IV*, edited by Barry Keith Grant, U of Texas P, 2012, pp. 3-11.

Turner, Frederick Jackson. *The Frontier in American History*. Henry Holt & Company, 1920. *Internet Archive*, archive.org/stream/frontierinameric1920turn. Accessed 23 Mar. 2020.

Ultan, Lloyd. *The Beautiful Bronx: 1920-1950*. Harmony Books, 1979.

—. *The Bronx in the Frontier Era: From the Beginning to 1696*. Kendall-Hunt Publishing, 1993.

—. *The Bronx in the Innocent Years, 1890-1925*. Harper and Row, 1985.

—. *The Bronx: It Was Only Yesterday, 1935-1965*. The Bronx County Historical Society, 1992.

—. *The Northern Borough: A History of the Bronx*. Bronx County Historical Society, 2009.

—, and Barbara Unger. *Bronx Accent: A Literary and Pictorial History of the Borough*. Rivergate Books, 2006.

—, and Gary Hermalyn. *The Birth of the Bronx: 1609-1898*. The Bronx County Historical Society, 2000.

Vásquez, Charlie, and Kim Vaquedano. *Bronx Memoir Project, Volume 1*. Bronx Council on the Arts, 2014.

—, and Kim Vaquedano-Rose. *Bronx Memoir Project, Volume 2*. Bronx Council on the Arts, 2018.

Vergara, Camilo José. *American Ruins*. Monacelli P, 1999.

—. *The New American Ghetto*. Ruttgers UP, 1997.

Wall Street. Directed by Oliver Stone, performances by Michael Douglas, Daryl Hannah, and Charlie Sheen, Twentieth Century Fox, 1987.

Walpole, Horace. *The Castle of Otranto: A Gothic Story*. 1794. Oxford UP, 1978.

Wayne, J. H. *Nachts in der Bronx*. Georg Wiesemann KG, 1955.

Weidman, Jerome. *I Can Get it for You Wholesale*. 1937. Bodley Head, 1985.

Welsch, Wolfgang. "Transculturality: The Puzzling Form of Cultures Today." *Spaces of Culture: City, Nation, World: Theory, Culture & Society*, edited by Mike Featherstone and Scott Lash, Sage, 1999, pp. 194-213.

West Side Story. Directed by Jerome Robbins and Robert Wise, performances by Nathalie Wood, George Chakiris, and Richard Beymer, United Artists, 1961.

Wharf, Barney, and Santa Arias. *The Spatial Turn: Interdisciplinary Perspectives*. Routledge, 2014.

White, John K., and Sarah L. Hanson. "Introduction: The Making and Persistence of the American Dream." *The American Dream in the Twenty-First Century*, edited by Sandra L. Hanson and John K. White. Temple UP, 2011, pp. 1-16.

Wild Style. Directed by Charlie Ahearn, performances by Patti Astor, Sandra 'Lady Pink' Fabara, and 'Lee' George Quiñones, Submarine, 1983.

Williams, Justin A., editor. *The Cambridge Companion to Hip-Hop*. Cambridge UP, 2015.

Williams, Linda. "Melodrama Revised." *Refiguring American Film Genres: History and Theory*, edited by Nick Browne, U of California P, 1998, pp. 42-88.

Williams, Raymond. *Marxism and Literature*. Oxford UP, 1977.

Winters, Joseph Richard. "Contemporary Sorrow Songs: Traces of Mourning, Lament, and Vulnerability in Hip-Hop." *African American Review*, vol. 46, no. 1, 2013, pp. 9-20. *EBSCOhost*, search.ebscohost.com/login.aspx?direct=true&db=mzh&AN=2014382912&site=ehost-live. Accessed 21 Mar. 2020.

Wolfe, Tom. *The Bonfire of the Vanities*. Farrar Straus Giroux, 1987.

Wolfen. Directed by Michael Wadleigh, performances by Albert Finney, Diane Venora, and Edward James Olmos, Warner Bros., 1981.

Woodstock. Directed by Michael Wadleigh. With Joan Baez, Richie Havens, and Roger Daltrey, Warner Bros., 1970.

Yglesias, Helen. "Also Known as Kaila." *The New York Times*, 23 May 1982, nytimes.com/1982/05/23/books/also-known-as-kaila.html. Accessed 23 Mar. 2020.

Zarzosa, Agustín. *Refiguring Melodrama in Film and Television: Captive Affects, Elastic Sufferings, Vicarious Objects*. Lexington, 2013.

Zorro. ABC, 1957-59.

Cultural Studies

Elisa Ganivet
Border Wall Aesthetics
Artworks in Border Spaces

2019, 250 p., hardcover, ill.
79,99 € (DE), 978-3-8376-4777-8
E-Book: 79,99 € (DE), ISBN 978-3-8394-4777-2

Andreas Sudmann (ed.)
The Democratization of Artificial Intelligence
Net Politics in the Era of Learning Algorithms

2019, 334 p., pb., col. ill.
49,99 € (DE), 978-3-8376-4719-8
E-Book: free available, ISBN 978-3-8394-4719-2

Jocelyne Porcher, Jean Estebanez (eds.)
Animal Labor
A New Perspective on Human-Animal Relations

2019, 182 p., hardcover
99,99 € (DE), 978-3-8376-4364-0
E-Book: 99,99 € (DE), ISBN 978-3-8394-4364-4

Cultural Studies

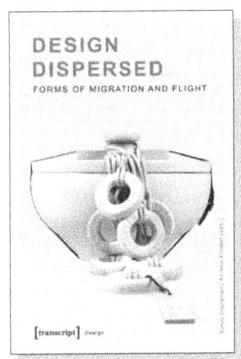

Burcu Dogramaci, Kerstin Pinther (eds.)
Design Dispersed
Forms of Migration and Flight

2019, 274 p., pb., col. ill.
34,99 € (DE), 978-3-8376-4705-1
E-Book: 34,99 € (DE), ISBN 978-3-8394-4705-5

Pál Kelemen, Nicolas Pethes (eds.)
Philology in the Making
Analog/Digital Cultures of Scholarly Writing and Reading

2019, 316 p., pb., ill.
34,99 € (DE), 978-3-8376-4770-9
E-Book: 34,99 € (DE), ISBN 978-3-8394-4770-3

Pablo Abend, Annika Richterich,
Mathias Fuchs, Ramón Reichert, Karin Wenz (eds.)
Digital Culture & Society (DCS)
Vol. 5, Issue 1/2019 –
Inequalities and Divides in Digital Cultures

2019, 212 p., pb., ill.
29,99 € (DE), 978-3-8376-4478-4
E-Book: 29,99 € (DE), ISBN 978-3-8394-4478-8

**All print, e-book and open access versions of the titles in our list
are available in our online shop www.transcript-verlag.de/en!**

GPSR Authorized Representative: Easy Access System Europe, Mustamäe tee
50, 10621 Tallinn, Estonia, gpsr.requests@easproject.com